The Uniform Commercial Code Made Easy

The Story of Stephen's Boats

Robert M. LeVine, J.D.

The Uniform Commercial Code Made Easy is designed to educate the reader regarding the general meaning and structure of the text of the Uniform Commercial Code. The Uniform Commercial Code has been enacted by the legislature of each state, and will often contain some changes, as enacted, within each state. Further, the facts of each case are different, and various courts may interpret the same provision in a different manner. It is explicitly understood that this book is not intended to provide legal advice related to the interpretation and application of the Uniform Commercial Code to any particular situation. The reader is advised to consult with a competent legal professional for legal advice regarding matters pertaining to the Uniform Commercial Code. The author specifically disclaims any liability from the application of the information contained in this book.

For information about the author, please visit
www.uccmadeeasybook.com

Printed in the United States of America.

ISBN-978-0-615-308-35-7

Dedication

This book is dedicated to all children at risk, everywhere.

Acknowledgements

I have lived long enough to understand that nothing of significance is accomplished without the help of others. To the extent this book is meaningful, there are many who made it possible. Teachers, colleagues, friends and family, played an integral part in the writing, publication, and distribution of this book. It is a great privilege to formally recognize and thank them.

First, I would like to acknowledge and thank my family—my wife Mary and my son Jesse—for their unwavering encouragement through the long and challenging process of updating the original version of the book to its current state. Their help and faith were invaluable. I would also like to thank Mike and Rita LeVine for many years of encouragement and support during the rewrite of this book, and for their encouragement and support generally.

Second, I would like to acknowledge and thank Dean Soia Mentschikoff for her tremendous contributions to this book, initially as my commercial law professor at the University of Chicago School of Law, and ultimately as Dean of the University of Miami School of Law. This book is a radical departure in the teaching of law, and Dean Mentschikoff embraced and supported the concept from the beginning.

Lee and Nicola Peterson were extremely instrumental in the whole process, Lee with his relentless encouragement to undertake the rewrite and his ongoing efforts to insure the distribution of the book, and Nicola for creating the business model used for publication and to bring the book to the market; Helen Krug for her great word processing efforts and encouragement in the early drafts of the book; Sharon Gisclair who, with limitless enthusiasm, skill, and patience, took the raw manuscript and painstakingly transformed it into the finished product

Acknowledgements
(Continued)

that it has become; Susi Kilgore who used her great artistic skills and insight to design the cover of the book; Mark Browning who published the first edition of the book, and who has served as a knowledgeable advisor throughout the process; and Jackie and Scott Fried for their support of my work generally.

I would also like to thank the Honorable Gilbert A. Smith Jr. for reviewing the book and sharing his valuable insight on its content; the faculty at the Stetson University College of law for providing me the opportunity to return to the classroom after a twenty-one year absence from that setting; and Nina Amster of The American Law Institute for her kindness and encouragement during the licensing and publishing process. I would also like to acknowledge and thank Kathy Durfee for her commitment and expertise on our website, and for her support of my work with children at risk.

Finally, I would also like to thank my students at the Stetson University College of Law for their integrity, hard work, and inspiration.

The Uniform Commercial Code Made Easy
Suggested Approach

The Uniform Commercial Code Made Easy is designed to create a medium through which the reader can gain a thorough understanding of the meaning of the text of the Uniform Commercial Code, as well as the ability to apply it in any setting to which it is applicable. In order to facilitate this result, an explanation of the structure as well as how to approach the book will be presented. As the most comprehensive commercial statute in history, the UCC governs and regulates billions of commercial transactions occurring simultaneously throughout the United States every working day. The text itself is a reflection of the reality of the business world, and is predicated upon factual assumptions which, in many cases, have evolved over hundreds of years. Conceptually, the UCC can be thought of as a distillation of hundreds of thousands of fact patterns with accompanying rules of law.

The Uniform Commercial Code Made Easy is designed to compress these fact patterns and underlying assumptions into a 'mirror image' through the facts of the story. Moreover, the book uses singular fact patterns to address a multitude of UCC provisions at any one time. As the reader works through the text of the book, an overall understanding of the UCC will emerge.

Each reader has his or her style of learning, and to attempt to direct people to a particular approach of learning would be out of place. However, having studied the text of the Code for thousands of hours as a student, author, and law professor, I believe that I can offer some suggestions which will aid the reader in approaching *The Uniform Commercial Code Made Easy* and gaining a working knowledge of the text of the UCC.

First, the initial read of the book should be approached with a goal of getting a general understanding of the Uniform Commercial Code, and not to gain a comprehensive knowledge of the meaning of every provision. A meaningful number of the provisions of the Uniform Commercial Code lend themselves to a relatively easy understanding which can be obtained on the first read. Other provisions are considerably more difficult, not only in terms of the wording of the statute, but also because of the commercial context in which they take place.

Once the initial read is complete, the reader will be able to approach the second pass through with a foundation of sorts, which will create a basis for further understanding of more detailed and complex provisions. It is much like building a house. The first read creates a basic foundation, and each future read places more bricks on the structure.

Second, the style of the book periodically requires editing of the Code sections under discussion, so that it can be read smoothly within the context in which it is being presented. Thus, while every contingency of the section involved is not presented in the discussion, the overall meaning of the provision involved is conveyed. By way of explanation, a given Code section might have anywhere from five to eight contingencies within the text, each of which is important and activated as facts of a case impact the statute. One of the difficulties in learning the text as a new reader is the reality that the text often pulls you in many directions at the same time. Of course, this is merely a reality of the subject matter, but it creates difficulties when trying to understand the text. Therefore, in order to facilitate learning, I have, in some situations, edited various portions of the text so that it can be applied cleanly to the facts involved in the discussion. Once the reader understands the text as presented in the book, he or she is encouraged to look at the full text of the section under discussion to be fully aware of language which was omitted.

Third, the text has been structured so that once the book is fully understood, the reader will have a very solid working knowledge of the overall content, structure and application of the UCC. Discussions and explanations have been structured to give the reader a large amount of information in a small amount of space while at the same time, not overloading the reader's brain. Hence, while each discussion or explanation is designed to be comprehensive, they are not put together in such a manner that every possible provision of some applicability is discussed. All major provisions however, are dealt with in each discussion. Once the reader has learned the content of the book, he or she will have a thorough understanding of all relevant provisions of the Articles involved, and will see other sections of applicability in each setting.

Finally, while I have titled the book *The Uniform Commercial Code Made Easy*, gaining a solid understanding the Uniform Commercial Code requires effort by the reader. I have done my best to create a format and setting which dramatically facilitates this, but at the end of the day, there is a direct correlation between the level of knowledge obtained and the amount of work put forth. The good news is that with such effort, anyone can learn the UCC and learn it at a very high level.

Special Note on the
Extended Table of Contents

I have prepared a very detailed Extended Table of Contents which follows the standard Table of Contents. The Extended Table of Contents will provide the reader with an overview of the UCC sections to be covered in any given section of the book. These are listed sequentially and provide the reader with the flow the UCC sections as they unfold. This will facilitate learning and should be consulted prior to reading the text. It will also be useful to return to the Extended Table of Contents as the text is being read to maintain an overall continuity of the law being discussed, as well as the commercial setting involved.

PART TWO

Extended Table of Contents

Part One

Section 6

Part Two

Section 1

Section 6

Section 7

Section 8

Section 10

Appendix II

Introduction

Prior to the enactment of the Uniform Commercial Code, the law governing commercial transactions presently within the purview of the UCC varied significantly among jurisdictions throughout the United States. The resulting lack of consistency created unease and uncertainty among individuals and entities seeking to engage in such transactions across state lines.

The Uniform Commercial Code was designed, in large part, to make the law 'uniform' for those areas within its coverage. By creating certainty among all the states, parties could conduct commercial transactions throughout the United States with relative assurance that the law of their jurisdiction was the same as that of the jurisdiction with which they were contracting. In actuality, the Official Text is reviewed by the legislature of each state before enactment, while making any changes [within reason] for their jurisdiction. Therefore, the text of the Code is not precisely the same in all jurisdictions, although it is substantially the same. Similarly, courts interpreting various provision of the Uniform Commercial Code do not always agree on the meaning of the text of the Code as it may apply to the case before the court.

It is easy for today's student of the Uniform Commercial Code to overlook the enormity of the task of creating this magnificent legislation. Getting agreement among the diverse parties impacted by the UCC was, in and of itself, an enormous challenge. The steps required to reduce the relevant concepts to legislation that parties could agree on was equally daunting. It took twenty years and a unique collaborative effort by hundreds of lawyers, bankers, and men and women from business to bring the Uniform Commercial Code to fruition. The drafting involved some of the greatest legal minds in history. The result is a comprehensive commercial statute unlike any other, which is filled with information within its statutory provisions, and contains the essence of commercial transactions, generally.

I was extremely fortunate to have Dean Soia Mentschikoff, the Associate Chief Reporter to the Uniform Commercial Code, as my Professor of commercial law at the University of Chicago School of Law, and equally fortunate, and grateful, to have been selected by her to teach the Uniform Commercial Code at the University of Miami School of Law where she became Dean. I owe an incredible debt to Dean Mentschikoff for teaching me the underlying policies which permeate the UCC and which bring the statute to life. As the Associate Chief Reporter, Dean Mentschikoff spent twenty years involved in the oversight, along with her husband, Karl Llewelyn, of the drafting of the whole UCC. The creation of the Uniform Commercial Code was described by Dean Mentschikoff as follows:

> *The Uniform Commercial Code, a joint product of the American Law Institute and the Conference of Commissioners on Uniform State Laws...is the most ambitious codification ever undertaken in the Anglo-American legal world and is the result of twenty years of effort by literally hundreds of American lawyers and businessmen.*
>
> *--The Modern Law Review, March 1964*

With the passage of time, it has became necessary, and prudent, to review the text of the Code and make various changes which better fit current commercial needs. Dean Mentschikoff was a part of this amendment process in her role as a consultant to the Permanent Editorial Board of the UCC. Changes to the Official Text of the Uniform Commercial Code have been accomplished through the oversight of the same entities that produced the original text: The American Law Institute and the National Conference of Commissioners on Uniform State Laws. For most of the history of the UCC, these changes occurred relatively infrequently and were generally adopted as the Official Text and ultimately by the state legislatures. In recent years, the frequency of proposed changes has dramatically increased, as has disagreement about the need and wisdom of some of those changes.

In writing *The Uniform Commercial Code Made Easy*, a decision had to be made as to what version of the Official Text was going to be incorporated into the book. When I first started to do the update, revised Article 1 had been enacted in a minority of the states, and revised Article 7 had not been incorporated into the Official Text. Since that time, Article 1 has been enacted in nearly 40 states, and Article 7 has been enacted in a growing number of states. The new revisions to Article 2A have not been adopted among the states, but have been incorporated into the Official Text. In addition, there are proposed changes of certain Articles which have not been incorporated into the Official Text.

At the time I received the amendments to Article 7 and Article 2A, I was ready for publication; however, I made the decision to revise the book to include these changes since they were incorporated into the Official Text. I did this for several reasons. As for Article 7, states are beginning to enact the amended version. The new text explicitly provides for electronic documents as well as the negotiation and transfer of those documents. Reissue in an alternate medium is also a part of the amended version. While all of these changes could have been brought into the Code via the commercial policies embodied in Section 1-103—for example— '*modernization of the law governing commercial transactions*' under Section 1-103(a)(1) or '*expansion of commercial practices*' under 1-103(a)(2)—the specific inclusion of electronic documents and related provisions under amended Article 7 makes this clear and explicit.

For these reasons, and the fact that states have begun to enact revised Article 7, it has been included in the text of this book.

The revisions to Article 2A, like those in Article 7, are not sweeping; however, once again, many changes to Article 2A reflect the reality of the electronic medium in commercial transactions. Thus, there is explicit recognition of electronic signatures, electronic agents, and the validity of electronic transactions generally. There are other changes of significance, for example, an explicit recognition of the right to cure in a revocation of acceptance situation in a non consumer lease transaction under Section 2A-513(1). It is also my personal and professional opinion, that the changes in the Official Text improve the clarity and content of the earlier version. This is not to criticize the earlier version, but simply to state my thoughts on the matter.

Rather than wait for the changes to be enacted, I decided to undertake the updates of Article 2A and to include them in this book. Many law professors will teach the Official Text and hence will use this amended version. Moreover, advocates will use the amended version as persuasive before courts when it lines up with their cases. Furthermore, as noted, the overall changes of Article 2A are not of such a magnitude as to change the major structure or laws contained in Article 2A. The majority of the actual text is identical to the earlier version, and often the only change is a renumbering of the section.

All of these reasons aside, I wanted this book to reflect the up-to-date Official Text of the Uniform Commercial Code as it is currently written, and will probably ultimately be enacted. This approach remains consistent with the major two goals of the book: first, to create a vehicle for understanding the meaning of the text and that statutory interactions within the text of the Uniform Commercial Code; and second, to create a structural framework through which Uniform Commercial Code fact patterns can be processed and analytically understood.

I began writing _The Uniform Commercial Code Made Easy_ [originally entitled _An Operational Translation of the Uniform Commercial Code_] in the summer of 1977 when I was an assistant professor of law at the University of Miami School of Law, in Coral Gables, Florida. I predicted that the book would be completed within six months. It ended up taking three-and-a-half years and twenty-five drafts. The word 'translation', used in the original title, seemed most appropriate, inasmuch as the UCC is like a foreign language for most of us when we start the process of reading and learning it.

As a student, I found the UCC brutally difficult to understand, but fascinating to study once a working knowledge was accomplished. Accomplishing that objective requires understanding the basic meaning of the text, as well as the policies and statutory connections that permeate the whole Code. Having a working knowledge of the text is extremely valuable, for not only does it create a formidable intellectual power, it opens many new avenues for learning.

Once the meaning of the text is understood, the student can go on an incredible intellectual journey through the many levels at which the Uniform Commercial Code can be interpreted and applied. The text of each Article has interactive clusters of sections and policies. Multiple Articles apply in every transaction, each with their own interactive sections and policies. When the unique facts of each case are processed through these statutory and policy frameworks, the activation of UCC sections, and accompanying policies, is enormous. _The creativity available is unlimited._

Within this backdrop, _The Uniform Commercial Code Made Easy_ is designed to create a story which distills and mirrors the underlying factual assumptions upon which the UCC was drafted. In so doing, an extremely efficient medium for understanding and applying the Code is created. Information is presented using communication and teaching techniques which are unavailable in traditional methods, among them: dialogue, opinion letters, online learning, legal memoranda, instant messaging, email communications, and conference calls. Logical questions of the reader regarding particular provisions are anticipated and accommodated in a sequential manner through these and other communication devices.

The anticipation of questions, and the communication devices for sharing information, are two of many advantages to delivering information through these diverse channels. As learning occurs through different channels, the brain is stimulated in different ways, increasing the efficiency of learning while limiting overload. Moreover, the communication devices utilized are regularly used in everyday life, and which are therefore familiar to the reader. The continuity of characters, combined with real life commercial settings going out 'live', in an evolving story, create a very learning-friendly environment. Of particular importance to the students regarding the text of the Uniform Commercial Code are the clearly stated fact patterns in this book which allow the reader to focus full attention on understanding the statute.

The Uniform Commercial Code Made Easy does not discuss and analyze every section of the Uniform Commercial Code. I am confident, however, that the reader will be able to understand and apply any omitted sections (there are few) to fact patterns and discussions in the book, once the content of the book is understood.

PART ONE

Section 1

On June 17, 2005, Stephen Seller received news that he had inherited $1.25 million from his grandfather, Stephen Seller I. His grandfather had been in the garment business in New York City and had moved to south Florida in December, 1988. Stephen Seller I, being a believer that hard work was the best way to succeed, attached one condition to the inheritance of young Stephen: namely, Stephen was required to invest all the money from the inheritance in a business venture within one year from the time the inheritance became his.

His grandfather wanted him to appreciate the true value of money. The will specifically prohibited Stephen from getting any help from his father, Stephen Seller II, other than what Stephen's grandfather called "directional guidance." This stipulation posed some problems for Stephen who, although probably bright enough to succeed in the "real" world, had no experience in business. In fact, Stephen, who had graduated from the University of Miami in June 2001, had done hardly anything since graduation except to go the beach or work on one of his three boats. If he wasn't working on one of the boats or at the beach, then he was out fishing or sailing. In short, Stephen was leading the "good life."

As a matter of choice, Stephen would have preferred not to work at anything; however, the money which his grandmother had left him when she died in 1997, some $300,000, was almost gone. If he was going to maintain his high lifestyle, which he found getting higher all the time, he knew that the money would have to start coming in from somewhere soon. He also knew that if he handled $1.25 million wisely, he might be able to set himself up for the rest of his life. *That* idea appealed to him. So he went to the beach to decide what he wanted to do with the inheritance.

Sitting under his favorite thatched hut on the beach at Key Biscayne, Florida, Stephen soberly sipped on a piña colada and gazed out at the ocean liners on the horizon, interrupted by the smaller boats closer to the shore. It saddened him to think he couldn't be with his boats everyday after he went into business—for more than anything else, he loved those boats. Then it dawned on him, he was going to enter the boat business.

Entering the boat business made good sense for a number of reasons, not the least important of which was his love for boats; however, it made good sense for other reasons as well. First of all, Stephen was a gifted boat mechanic; several times in fact, he had been able to correct difficulties with people's boats that dealers couldn't correct. Second, Stephen had a working knowledge of how the sales operations of a retail boat outlet worked. He had, after all, spent much time shopping for his own three boats and would often go out and look at boats and price them just for the fun of it. Finally, Stephen was very friendly with Ted Cummings, a salesman for Marina Boats. Ted was always willing to answer Stephen's endless questions about the business, and Stephen had learned a lot from him. With all of this going for him, Stephen was confident that he could be successful in this business. He even became a little excited, especially as he thought of becoming successful! He finished his piña colada and left for his parents' home to tell them the good news.

Stephen's father was a quiet man who had been very successful in the liquor business. He never pushed Stephen to work because he had to listen to "Pops," as he called Stephen's grandfather, about the virtues of working for 23 years. Not only did he vow never to hassle his kids about working, but many mornings as he prepared to go to work, he questioned whether his father had been right. He often wished he was out on the boat with Stephen.

Mr. Seller listened attentively as Stephen presented his idea. He was somewhat impressed with the idea and was surprised at Stephen's enthusiasm. He tried not to show this to Stephen.

"Stephen," said Mr. Seller, "I think you might have a good idea here. You ought to know a few things, though. First, it's extremely doubtful that you can get started for $1.25 million. Your initial inventory of boats will probably cost you almost that much. The big ones wholesale in the $90,000 - $135,000 range, and the smaller ones will run you $10,000 - $20,000. You're going to need a place of business, and of course, there will be legal expenses."

"What do you suggest Dad?" Stephen asked.

"I would suggest talking to Alan Lawyer or any attorney who is knowledgeable about getting something like this going," said Mr. Seller.

"If you would like, I'll call Alan and try to set up an appointment for you next week to discuss all of this with him. He will probably be able to give you a lot of help. By the way, have you decided where you want to locate yet?" Stephen's father asked.

"Yes I have," Stephen said. "I would like to buy some land in west Dade County."

"West Dade County," said his father. "Isn't that a little bit out of the way?"

"That's exactly why I want to buy it there," Stephen said. "I figure that I can buy the land for much less than I would be able to purchase similar property near the water. By doing so, my costs will be lower and I believe that I can offer a much better price than the competition. One thing Stephen had learned from Ted, and from his own shopping experience, was that the consumer would be willing to travel the extra distance if he thought he could save enough money.

"It sounds like a good idea," said Mr. Seller. "Would you like to see Alan next Thursday afternoon?"

"That will be fine," Stephen said.

"Okay," said his father, "Unless you hear otherwise from me, I will set up an appointment for you to meet with Alan, say, at about 2:00 p.m. next Thursday."

Section 2

Stephen's father was able to arrange the meeting for the following Thursday, and accordingly, Stephen went to Alan's office at 2:00 p.m. Thursday June 23rd, 2005. He approached the receptionist and stated that he was there to see Alan Lawyer.

"Your name please?" she asked.

"Stephen Seller," he said. "The appointment was made by my father last Friday."

"Just a moment Mr. Seller, I will telephone Mr. Lawyer. Please have a seat in our waiting room."

The law firm was of modest size by south Florida standards. There were twenty lawyers in the firm, eight partners and twelve associates. Stephen had heard that a friend of his who had just recently graduated from the University of Miami School of Law had gotten a job there. Stephen meant to ask Alan about it later on. Just then, Alan's secretary came out.

"Mr. Seller?" she asked. After Stephen nodded, she said, "Come with me, please."

Stephen went into Alan's office. "Hi Alan," Stephen said.

"Hi Stephen, it sounds like you have a pretty good idea from what your father said. I'd like to hear more about it."

Alan had known Stephen since he was just a young child and was as surprised as anybody at Stephen's desire to go into business for *any* reason. Alan knew Stephen because Alan was a friend of Stephen's older brother and in fact had done a lot of legal work for Stephen's father. He was pleased to be able to do something for the family once again.

Stephen proceeded to tell Alan about his idea for the boat business. He told Alan he planned to locate in the western part of Dade County and he had seen a nice piece of property out there earlier in the week with a good building on it. The asking price was $875,000. He told

Alan about his idea to cut costs initially by purchasing this piece of property as opposed to one closer to the water. Furthermore, Stephen revealed a part of his plan that he hadn't even told his father. Namely, he told Alan that it was his hope not to become a franchise dealer of one particular manufacturer; rather, he hoped to purchase boats from three manufacturers, Royal, Marina, and Crown Boats, and sell all three types of boats from his premises at the same time. He felt that by offering this wide selection of boats, he would be able to further lure the consumer to visit his showroom. He figured that for those consumers who might be reluctant to drive all the way out to his place to see just one boat, the facility and ease of having three types of boats to view at the same time would definitely bring customers who might not come otherwise.

"Have you suggested this to the manufacturers?" Alan asked.

"I did make some phone calls to people I know at these outfits," Stephen said. "They all indicated a willingness to sit down and talk it over with me." Stephen knew from his own personal experience how anxious these dealers were to move their large boats and had therefore tried to make the idea very appealing to them by indicating that he would purchase primarily large boats.

"How much extra money do you think you are going to need Stephen?" Alan asked.

Stephen had done some research since he had spoken to his father initially. "At least $800,000," Stephen said. He based his estimate on the cost of land and building which was set at $875,000, certain equipment that he felt he would need that was valued at approximately $150,000, and his desire to have enough cash on hand to purchase a good start-up inventory. He even included some back up funds in case the market looked really good and he wanted to make some quick purchases. Stephen had learned from his discussions with Ted Cummings that periodically manufacturers will drastically reduce their wholesale prices in order to move their inventory. Sometimes this was due to new models coming out; at other times it was done simply to increase sales to distributors. When prices dipped during one of these periods, the manufacturers wanted cash. Stephen knew that. He did not want to be short of cash in such a situation and thus be unable to capitalize on a good business opportunity should it arise. He therefore felt he would like to have this additional cash on hand to make a good purchase at the right time.

Alan suggested to Stephen that perhaps he should simply wait and gain additional funds at a time when he would need them. Stephen was quick to point out, however, that in many situations where he would need additional funds, so would everybody else. If at that time the economic situation in the country were one of tight money, Stephen might be placed in a situation where he would be forced to pay very high interest rates, or even worse, not be able to get the financing he needed. He was therefore very insistent, at least from a business standpoint, that it would be to his advantage to secure the funds now as opposed to later.

At the conclusion of the meeting, Stephen asked Alan if he was interested in representing him in the purchase of the property, as well as in helping him set up his operation. If things worked well, Stephen hoped Alan would continue to represent him after the business was operative.

Alan was pretty impressed with the whole package that Stephen had presented. He said he would be delighted to represent Stephen, and in addition, had a proposition for him. "I'll tell you what," Alan said, "Since your initial cash position is not very good, how would you like it if I came in the business with you as a ten percent partner and performed all legal services for ten percent of the profits of the business?"

This seemed a very reasonable arrangement to Stephen and he agreed to take Alan in as ten percent partner. It was understood that if the business failed, Alan would not charge an hourly rate against Stephen for the time involved.

"Where do we go from here?" Stephen asked.

Alan said, "The first thing we do is incorporate. Next, we have to enter into negotiations for the purchase of the property. I will contact some institutional lenders to see if we can find someone interested in loaning us the $800,000." "In the meantime," Alan continued, "why don't you see what you can do in securing contracts from Royal, Crown and Marina?"

Stephen agreed to contact the manufacturers, and that the corporation would be known as *Stephen's Boats, Inc.*

Another meeting was set up for the following month.

Section 3

As soon as Stephen left, Alan got right to work. He went through the appropriate procedures with the Secretary of State in Tallahassee and incorporated Stephen's Boats, Inc., a corporation organized under the laws of the state of Florida. Furthermore, for $10,000 he got an option to purchase the piece of land Stephen wanted, to be exercised when Stephen got the additional funding. The terms of that sale were that Stephen would pay 20% down, the balance to be paid over a 25 year mortgage. In addition, Alan contacted three banks in Miami in order to discuss with them the possibility of funding the loan in the amount of $800,000.

During the same time period, Stephen was able to get a commitment from one of the manufacturers, Royal Boats, Inc., who would sell Stephen the type of large boats he hoped to sell as well as some of the reasonably priced speed boats. The smaller reasonably priced boats would help get buyers into the showroom. The other two manufacturers, Crown Boats, Inc., and Marina Boats Inc. were hesitant to make a decision as to whether or not they would be interested in the type of agreement Stephen was talking about. It was, after all, highly unusual for someone in the business to be selling three different types of boats for different manufacturers on the same lot at the same time. Nevertheless, they told Stephen to get in touch with them after his operation got going and they would definitely consider entering into an arrangement at some future date. Stephen, while somewhat disappointed that he couldn't secure the Crown and Marina contracts as he had hoped initially, was confident that he would move Royal's boats well enough that Crown and Marina would quickly want to get into the business. Accordingly, Stephen was set to proceed with the business solely on the basis of his future agreement with Royal.

With the land that Stephen wanted set to be purchased, and with one franchise guaranteed, Stephen and Alan were ready to discuss their plans with a potential lender. Meetings were then scheduled with the three lenders that Alan had contacted. The first two lenders were eliminated, since, due to Stephen's youth and lack of actual experience in the business world, both of them required a guarantee from Stephen's father before they would close the loan. Stephen knew it would be impossible for his father to guarantee the loan inasmuch as his grandfather's will have precluded the possibility of just that type of assistance. Only South Dade Bank had expressed a willingness to proceed without a guarantee from Stephen's father. After initial discussions between Alan and South Dade looked promising, a meeting was set up between Stephen's Boats Inc. and the South Dade Bank for July 15, 2005.

Section 4

Present at the meeting were Stephen Seller, Alan Lawyer and Fred Luvick, the vice president in charge of loans up to $2 million. Stephen presented his plans for his business in much the same fashion as he had done for Alan; however, the important difference was that Stephen was not in position to state to the bank, as Alan had, that three boat dealers would sell boats to Stephen for his independent sales operation.

Stephen tried to minimize this; however, Fred had come into the meeting with a certain set of expectations and told Stephen he would not be able to speak for the rest of the committee who had reviewed the proposed loan based on the facts given to them by Alan. Fred indicated however, that in his opinion the other features of the plan seemed good enough that he felt the loan committee would still approve the loan, but perhaps not in the amount of $800,000. Before any loan could be approved, however, Fred had some questions for Stephen which he wanted to clarify.

"How do you plan to operate on a daily basis?" Fred asked.

"What do you mean?" Stephen said.

"Do you plan to sell your boats on some sort of credit terms or are you going to insist upon cash payment?"

"Well, it's very doubtful that very many people are going to come in and pay cash for some of the boats that I am going to have in stock," Stephen said, "so, of course, I plan to sell under some form of credit arrangement. I haven't exactly decided what I'm going to use; I do, however, intend to insist on a rather substantial down payment by the buyer before I will go into any form of credit arrangement."

"Well, our committee will have something to say about how you operate if we fund the loan, but I suggest," Fred said, "that you will probably be selling by way of conditional sales contract. Of course you know," Fred continued, "that the bank will require security for the loan before the loan can be made."

Stephen had briefly discussed this with Alan and knew that the bank would require security before it would give the loan. Stephen, of course, was willing to give the bank whatever security it needed, exclusive of a guarantee or any other involvement from his father.

"What type of security did you have in mind?" Stephen asked. Fred indicated it was his opinion that before the bank would agree to a loan in any amount they would need security in the form of all boats which Stephen would have on his property for sale or lease, all equipment which Stephen would have on his property to be used in connection with the business, anything Stephen received upon the sale of a boat (for example, cash) and, in addition, any property which Stephen might thereafter receive which was located on the business premises. The bank would also want a second mortgage on the real estate.

This was basically what Alan had told Stephen that the bank would want, and, accordingly, Stephen expressed no surprise or concern at the requests made by Fred. He told Fred he realized that the bank would seek the security he was requesting.

"Whatever you need." Stephen said.

The meeting was adjourned with the understanding that Fred would go to the loan committee and would call Alan the next week if he didn't hear from him first.

After the meeting, Fred took the new plan to the loan committee. He explained to them that Stephen was unable to get the three distributorships that he had hoped for in his independent sales operation. Fred, however, indicated to the committee that Stephen's idea, even without the additional dealerships, was sound. Fred had financed other boat dealers and realized the tremendous savings which Stephen could expect simply from the location he had thought of. Furthermore, Fred was impressed with Stephen and had known Alan for a long time. He made a recommendation that the committee approve the loan in the original form in which it had been discussed. Several members of the committee, however, were not as optimistic as Fred was. Some of the committee wanted to scrap the whole project; others, however, convinced by Fred's urging and the general desire of the bank to break out of its conservative format, wanted to go through with the loan in some form. Accordingly, they proposed that the bank make a commitment to loan Stephen the $800,000 upon certain performance criteria.

Ultimately, the committee decided to loan Stephen $800,000 in two installments. The first $400,000 could be drawn down as soon as Stephen officially secured the Royal distributorship; the second $400,000 could be drawn upon as soon as Stephen secured one of the two remaining boat dealerships. The latter plan was approved. Fred was pleased with the action taken by the committee and telephoned Alan of the committee's decision.

Alan discussed the matter with Stephen, and although Stephen was somewhat disappointed that he didn't get the full $800,000, he was realistic enough to know that it was the best deal he could get. Furthermore, he figured that if the business did what he expected it to, he would have no trouble securing either the Crown or the Marina distributorships and hence the additional $400,000. He was set to proceed. Accordingly, Stephen and Alan authorized the bank to prepare any and all appropriate documents in connection with the loan. A tentative closing date was set for September 7, 2005, with the documents in their proposed form to be delivered to Alan no later than August 15, 2005.

Section 5

As per the agreement with the bank, the documents arrived on August 15, 2005. Upon their arrival, Alan reviewed them primarily to ascertain whether or not they conformed to the terms discussed in his meetings with the bank. Upon receipt of the documents and their initial review, Alan called Stephen, who came down to the office to discuss the documents. As an attorney, Alan wanted his client to understand, as completely as possible, every provision that was contained in the documents so that Stephen would know what his obligations were under the agreements before he signed them. Not only did he find it offensive that so many attorneys didn't take the time to fully explain documents to their clients, he also realized the potential for a malpractice action against him and the firm if he failed to adequately carry out this duty. Furthermore, all of the discussions with the bank had made Stephen somewhat uneasy, inasmuch as he did not understand the actual mechanics of setting up one of these transactions. He therefore was quite eager to understand what was being done as well as the reason it was being done.

The bank sent three documents to Alan: a security agreement, a financing statement and a proposed loan agreement. The security agreement[1] read as follows:

---

[1] In drafting this Security Agreement, the primary emphasis has been to create a vehicle for explaining the legal concepts contained in the appropriate provisions of the Uniform Commercial Code, rather than pointing out various transactional alternatives to the ones chosen. In this connection however, it must be noted that in drafting the Code, input from the business as well as the legal community was sought, received and considered. The statute thus incorporates, in its operational text, the more prevalent business practices in the various commercial areas involved. Furthermore, through provisions noted later in this book, the Code provides a vehicle whereby changes in business practices can be incorporated into the Code.

SECURITY AGREEMENT

WHEREAS, Stephen's Boats, Inc., hereinafter referred to as Debtor, is desirous of entering into the retail boat business, said business to include the sale and lease of boats at retail as well as the service thereof; and

WHEREAS, Debtor needs capital to enter into said business; and

WHEREAS, Debtor has made an application to South Dade Bank, hereinafter referred to as the Secured Party, for a loan of up to $800,000; and

WHEREAS, the Secured Party has agreed to loan Debtor an amount up to $800,000, under the terms and provisions of this Security Agreement and the loan agreement executed on even date herewith;

NOW, THEREFORE, in consideration of the money to be loaned to Debtor under the loan agreement referred to above, the Debtor hereby grants to the Secured Party a security interest in the following collateral:

1. All inventory now or hereinafter acquired by Debtor in connection with Stephen's Boats, Inc.;

2. All equipment now or hereinafter acquired by Debtor in connection with Stephen's Boats, Inc.;

3. All proceeds received by Debtor from the sale or lease of inventory or equipment

which is subject to the security interest in Paragraphs 1 and 2 noted above, including but not limited to any cash, instruments or chattel paper;

4. A security interest in all chattel paper received by Debtor in connection with the sale of any inventory, with the Secured Party purchasing said paper in the face amount of the principal reflected therein;

5. All deposit accounts maintained by the debtor in connection with the operation of Stephen's Boats, Inc.

Debtor further agrees:

1. To make a daily accounting to the Secured Party for all proceeds received in connection with Stephen's Boats, Inc.;

2. That the lien created by said security interest in favor of the Secured Party shall constitute a first lien at all times that this agreement is in effect;

3. That Debtor cannot further encumber any property which is the subject of the Secured Party's security interest without the express written consent of the Secured Party.

The Secured Party agrees to abide by the terms and conditions of the loan agreement executed on even date herewith; specifically, the Secured Party agrees that upon execution of this security agreement, the financing statement and the loan agreement referred to above it will commit to lending the Debtor $800,000 in two $400,000 installments, the first installment due upon execution of a distributorship agreement with Royal Boats.

The Secured Party further agrees, in accordance with the terms of the loan agreement referred to above, that in the event that the Debtor secures either the Crown or Marina account, the Secured Party will lend an additional $400,000 within sixty days after said account is obtained by Debtor.

Any failure of Debtor to pay any of its obligations in the ordinary course of business, and any failure of Debtor to fulfill any of its obligations to the Secured Party or to perform any of its promises under this Agreement or the loan agreement executed of even date herewith shall be a default under this Security Agreement.

If Debtor is in default, the Secured Party shall have the right to declare all obligations of Debtor immediately due and payable.

Upon Default by Debtor, and such declaration by the Secured Party, the Secured Party shall have all of the rights and privileges of a Secured Party as provided in the Uniform Commercial Code.

Signed, Sealed and Delivered in the presence of:

_____

South Dade Bank

_____

Stephen's Boats, Inc.

Stephen read the Security Agreement, looked up at Alan and said, "What does it mean, Alan?"

Alan explained to Stephen that the agreement was covered by Article 9 of the Uniform Commercial Code.[2] "In order for you to really understand the agreement," Alan said, "it is going to be necessary for us to get into a rather detailed discussion involving both business and law."

"That's OK with me," said Stephen. "I don't want to go to anymore of these meetings without understanding what people are talking about. Furthermore, I don't think I should sign any documents unless I really understand what is being said."

Alan had every intention, and felt quite capable of giving Stephen a thorough explanation of the documents. Although Alan had very little practical experience with UCC transactions, he had been to numerous seminars on secured transactions under Article 9 of the Uniform Commercial Code. In this area of the code, he felt competent. He also fancied himself to be very good at explaining Article 9 concepts, and had even spoken to a law class recently. Of course, all these considerations

---

[2] Except as otherwise provided in subsections (c) and (d), this article [Article 9] applies to:

(1) *a transaction, regardless of its form, that creates a security interest in personal property or fixtures by contract;*

(2) *an agricultural lien;*

(3) *a sale of accounts, chattel paper, payment intangibles, or promissory notes;*

(4) *a consignment.* Section 9-109(1)(2)(3)(4).

Many of the terms noted above in the quoted portion of Section 9-109 probably will have no meaning to the reader at this point; however, as the reader works through the materials, most of the types of personal property listed there will be discussed and defined.

aside, Alan did not want any client of his to sign any agreement which the client did not understand to the best of his or her ability. Accordingly, Alan was only too pleased to explain the security agreement to Stephen, although, for such an explanation he wished he were charging an hourly rate.

"Well, it is pretty clear what the *'Whereas'* clauses are about, right?"

Stephen nodded.

"Okay, let's get down to the *'Now Therefore'* clause."

Stephen looked at his xeroxed copy of the agreement and waited for Alan to continue. "As you can see, you will be granting the bank a 'security interest' in the property listed in the paragraphs 1, 2, 3, 4 and 5 below the *'Now Therefore'* clause."

"What is a 'security interest'?" asked Stephen.

"Remember," responded Alan, "when we were at the bank and Fred Luvick told you that the bank would need security of some sort before it would fund the loan?"

Stephen nodded.

"Well," continued Alan, "the legal vehicle by which it will get the security in the property listed in paragraphs 1, 2, 3 and 4 is called a **security interest.** It is defined in the Uniform Commercial Code in part as: "...*an interest in personal property...which secures payment...of an obligation...*"[3]

"What interest in the property will the bank have?" Stephen asked.

"Its interest will be comprised of certain legal rights it will have in the listed property," responded Alan, "which it can exercise in the event you fail to perform your obligations to it under the terms of the Security Agreement or Loan Agreement."

---

[3] Section 1-201(b)(35).

"If for example, you failed to meet your obligations to the bank under the Loan Agreement by not meeting your payment schedule, the bank could, under certain circumstances, take possession of your inventory and sell it to recover the money you owe."

"By the way," Alan said, "this property is called *collateral* under the Code."[4]

Alan could see that Stephen was having some trouble grasping the concept. "Stephen," he said, "Let me give you an example which can help clear this up for you. Let's assume that instead of borrowing money from the bank for the boat business, you are borrowing $750 from a pawnbroker. As you know, he won't give you the money unless you give him some property. And of course the property must be worth at least as much as the loan or he probably won't lend to you. Anyway, let's assume that he takes your watch worth $1200 and you agree that if you don't pay him back within 60 days, he can keep the watch. In Article 9 language, he would have a *security interest* in the watch."

"That is, the pawnbroker would have '*an interest in personal property*' i.e. the rights you and he agree that he shall have in the watch, which '*secures payment of an obligation,*' i.e., your obligation to repay the money you borrow from him."

Alan continued, "Your situation with the bank is basically the same, except, of course, that bank won't have physical possession of the boats. First, the bank, like the pawnbroker, won't lend money without security. In the pawnbroker situation, the security is the watch, in the bank situation it will primarily be the boats. Failure to make your payments to the bank will give the bank similar rights with the boats and other property listed that

---

[4] *"Collateral" means the property subject to a security interest....* Section 9-102(a)(12).

the pawnbroker would have with the watch. For example, subject to certain rules, the bank can sell the boats to recover money you owe if you don't meet your obligations to them. Thus, the interest which the bank has in the collateral, i.e., the security interest, like the pawnbrokers interest in the watch, *secures payment* of your obligation to it to repay the money borrowed."

"The Uniform Commercial Code gives special names to the parties in such a transaction. Since the bank would be a lender in whose favor you would be creating the security interest, the bank would be called the **secured party**.[5] Since you have an interest in the collateral, you will be called the **debtor**.[6] As you can see, this agreement is titled **Security Agreement**. The reason is because it is an agreement which creates a security interest."[7]

---

[5] *"Secured party" means a person in whose favor a security interest is created or provided for under a security agreement....* Section 9-102(a)(72)(A).

[6] *"Debtor" means a person having an interest, other than a security interest or other lien, in the collateral, whether or not the person is an obligor.* Section 9-102(a)(28)(A).

[7] *"Security agreement" means an agreement which creates or provides for a security interest.* Section 9-102(a)(73).

The general validity of a security agreement is set forth in Section 9-201: *"Except as otherwise provided in [the Uniform Commercial Code] a security agreement is effective according to its terms between the parties, against purchasers of the collateral, and against creditors."* Section 9-201(a).

There are exceptions to the basic rule noted above which are contained in subsections (b), (c) and (d). Most notable among these exceptions is subsection (b) which deals with *"...any applicable rule of law which establishes a different rule for consumers...."*

The distinction between merchants [professionals in business] and non merchants permeates the Uniform Commercial Code.

"Let me see if I have it right," Stephen said. "The obligation secured is my obligation to repay the bank, right?"

Alan nodded.

"Since I have rights in the collateral, I am a debtor. The bank is the secured party since it is the lender in whose favor I am granting a security interest. And, the agreement we're going over is a security agreement since it creates a security interest. Is that correct?"

Alan nodded again.

"Okay," said Stephen, "let's go on."

Alan continued with the agreement and began discussing with Stephen the different types of property in which the bank was seeking a security interest. Alan noted that the primary security of the bank would be the boats themselves. He then told Stephen that inasmuch as the boats are going to be held for sale or lease, the boats are called *inventory* under the Code.[8] Alan contrasted this to the equipment referred to in subparagraph two. Alan explained that *equipment*, as opposed to inventory, is not held for sale, and will generally be goods used in the business.[9] Alan noted, for example, that if Stephen purchased certain machines to polish the boats or to sand the boats, those items would be equipment.

"May I ask a question?" Stephen said.

"Certainly." replied Alan.

"Well, really I have two questions. First of all, the bank is looking to my inventory for protection, so how is the bank protected when I sell a boat or other inventory? It

---

[8] *"Inventory" means goods, other than farm products, which: "are held by a person for sale or lease or to be furnished under a contract of service..."* Section 9-102(a)(48)(B).

[9] *"Equipment" means goods other than inventory, farm products, or consumer goods.* Section 9-102(a)(33).

seems to me," Stephen said, "that the bank's security would be gone as soon as I sell the boat. Second, what is the language concerning inventory *'now or hereinafter acquired'* in clause 1 of the Security Agreement?"

"Let me answer your second question first, if you don't mind," Alan said. "As a general proposition, a security interest in inventory is considered a **floating lien.** Alan continued, "that is, as one piece of inventory is sold, you will replace it with the purchase of a new piece of inventory, i.e. you will purchase a new boat to replace the one you sell. Or, you may sell motor accessories such as propellers, ignition switches, or the like. When you do, you will similarly replace the piece of inventory sold with a new piece of inventory. The bank has a security interest in *inventory*. When you purchase a piece of inventory, small or large, the bank's security interest extends to that piece of inventory. Hence, the lien 'floats.'

"Why then," interrupted Stephen, "does the bank need an interest in inventory 'now or hereinafter acquired'?" Stephen asked. "If it extends to inventory as it comes in, it seems to include the hereinafter acquired."

Alan responded, "Earlier in the evolution of commercial law, some courts reached decisions that a security interest in inventory did not extend to new inventory as it replaced old inventory, but only applied to the inventory on hand when the security interest was created. In order to protect against such a result, the bank takes an interest in your inventory 'now or hereinafter acquired' i.e. inventory you have when the agreement is executed [the now] as well as inventory you acquire in the future [the hereinafter acquired]. This clause is called an **after acquired property clause**, and was looked upon with judicial disfavor prior to the enactment of the Uniform Commercial Code.[10] Many

---

[10] Comment 2 to Section 9-204 of the prior text of Section 9-204 explained this as follows:

courts refused to enforce these provisions," Alan continued. "With the enactment of the Code, however, the legislature has validated the 'after acquired property clause.'"[11]

"I see," said Stephen. "But how is the bank protected from the time the boat is sold until I purchase new inventory? You know, some of those boats sell for $70,000 or $80,000 or $100,000 or more. If I sold one or two on one day, the bank would have anywhere from $70,000 to $170,000 unaccounted for and a dishonest person in my situation might leave town."

"You're starting to sound like a law student," Alan said, half jokingly. "First of all, Stephen, let me say one thing. It is impossible to draft around fraud. The Uniform Commercial Code assumes honesty in commercial transactions. Of course, this is generally the rule. So dishonesty aside, how does the bank protect itself? Well, one way it protects itself is by taking a security interest in 'proceeds.' As you can see, this is set forth in the third numbered paragraph of the 'Now Therefore' clause."

"What are proceeds?" Stephen asked.

The widespread 19th Century prejudice against the floating charge was based on a feeling, often inarticulate in the opinions, that a commercial borrower should not be allowed to encumber all his assets, present and future, and that for the protection not only of the borrower but of his other creditors, a cushion of free assets should be preserved.

[11] *Except as otherwise provided in subsection (b), a security agreement may create or provide for a security interest in after-acquired collateral.* Section 9-204(a).

Comment 2 to current Section 9-204 states:

This section adopts the principle of a "continuing general lien" or "floating lien." It validates a security interest in the debtors existing and (upon acquisition) future assets, even though the debtor has liberty to use or dispose of collateral without being required to account for proceeds or substitute new collateral.

Alan said, "Basically **proceeds** will be what you receive upon the sale of a boat."[12] The conditional sales contract your purchaser signs, and any down payment the purchaser may give you are examples of proceeds. The security interest that the bank has in the boat automatically attaches [becomes enforceable] with regard to the proceeds.[13] There are two major classifications of proceeds: **cash proceeds** such as legal tender or checks, and **non cash proceeds** such as the conditional sales contracts generated when Stephen's Boats makes a sale."[14]

Stephen was familiar with conditional sales contracts since he had purchased all of his boats under a conditional sales method. Thus, when Stephen purchased his last boat, he remembered entering into an agreement which called for 36 monthly payments of $550 each. Furthermore, Stephen remembered a provision in the agreement which basically stated that in the event he failed to make payment as called for under the

---

[12] *"Proceeds ... means the following property: (A) whatever is acquired upon the sale, lease, license, exchange or other disposition of collateral."* Section 9-102(a)(64)(A).

[13] A security interest in proceeds is automatic under Section 9-315(a)(2) which states that:

Except as otherwise provided in this article and in Section 2-403(2):

. . .

(2) a security interest attaches to any identifiable proceeds of collateral.

[14] *"Cash proceeds" means proceeds that are money, checks, deposit accounts, or the like.* Section 9-102(a)(9).

"Noncash proceeds" means proceeds other than cash proceeds. Section 9-102(a)(58).

conditional sales contract, the seller would be entitled to retake the boat. Thus, Stephen was able to appreciate the conditional sales concept from the standpoint of the consumer or a seller, but did not understand how it worked from the standpoint of a lender, such as South Dade Bank.

Alan explained that the typical conditional sales contract did two things. First, payments are made over an agreed term, typically on a monthly basis. The ultimate sale to the buyer is 'conditioned' upon the buyer making payments called for under the contract; hence the denomination 'conditional sales contract.' Second, Alan explained how the businessman-seller was protected.

"As you indicate Stephen, if you fail to make the payments under the conditional sales contract the seller can, subject to certain rules, retake the merchandise since the conditional sales contract will create a security interest in the seller's favor. He is thus protected in the sense that if he doesn't get paid, he *can* get his boat back."

"So, when I sell boats under this type of method, I will be able to take the boats back when a buyer fails to make a payment?" Stephen asked.

"Yes, if the contract makes that an event of default. Of course, you will want this and the bank will insist on it. In such a situation," Alan continued, "*you* would have a security interest in the boat."

Alan explained that when Stephen sold boats in his business under a conditional sales contract, he, Stephen, would have two things. First, his purchaser would be obligated to make monthly payments to Stephen for the duration of the conditional sales contract. Second, if his purchaser failed to pay Stephen, Stephen would be entitled, with some limited exceptions, to retake possession of the boat for purposes of realizing the money owed to him under the terms of the agreement, as a result of his security interest in the boat.

"Here," Alan said, "let me draw this for you. It will probably make this easier for you, plus it will give me a chance to show how the bank is also protected in this transaction." Alan took out a piece of paper and a pen and said, "Okay, Stephen, here you are, the seller, and here is buyer. Buyer comes in to you and wants to buy a boat for, let's say, $20,000. Here is the boat. Buyer does not have adequate money to pay cash for the boat, so he wants to sign a conditional sales contract. That is, he wants to pay you a certain amount of money over 36 months for example. Let's say he wants a $20,000 boat so he puts down $5,000 leaving a balance of $15,000. With interest included in that amount he would have to pay you say, $500 a month for 36 months. You make the sale and buyer gives you $5,000 cash, and in addition, signs a conditional sales contract. This contract does a few things.

First, it contains buyer's obligation to pay you $500 a month for 36 months.

Second, it gives you, as seller, a security interest in the boat so that if buyer defaults on his obligations to you on any of the $500 payments, subject to certain rules and limitations, you will be entitled to repossess the boat.[15] Since this paper contains a monetary obligation on the part of the buyer to pay you for the boat and it also creates a security interest in the boat purchased, the writing is called **chattel paper**.[16]

---

[15] After default, nonpayment by the debtor is, obviously, that of greatest concern to the Secured Party. However, it is by no means the only one. Failure to properly take care of collateral, or failure to pay various taxes or insurance are other examples of what might constitute a default.

[16] *"Chattel paper" means a record or records that evidence both a monetary obligation and a security interest in specific goods....* Section 9-102(a)(11).

"In this transaction," Alan continued, "you would be the secured party and your buyer would be an *account debtor*."[17]

"How is the bank protected?" Stephen asked.

"One of the ways the bank is protected is because it has an interest in *'proceeds'*. Here, the bank would have a security interest in the $5,000 as *cash proceeds* and in the chattel paper as *non cash proceeds*. That is, the

---

"Record"... means information that is inscribed on a tangible medium [the conditional sales contract] or which is stored in an electronic or other medium and is retrievable in percelvable form. Section 9-102(a)(69).

[17] *"Account debtor" means a person who is obligated on ... chattel paper ... Section 9-102(a)(3).*

Stephen's security interest in such a transaction is called a *purchase money security interest* by reason of Sections 9-103(a)(1)(2)(b). A purchase money security interest has special significance throughout Article 9 which will be discussed throughout this book.

The definition of a purchase-money security interest is found under Section 9-103(b)(1):

A security interest in goods is a purchase-money security interest:

(1) to the extent that the goods are purchase-money collateral with respect to that security interest; . . .

"[P]urchase-money collateral" means goods or software that secures a purchase-money obligation with respect to that collateral... Section 9-103(a)(1).

"[P]urchase-money obligation" means the obligation of an obligor [the boat purchaser] incurred as all or part of the price of collateral [the boat]... Section 9-103(a)(2).

A typical conditional sales transaction at Stephen's Boats would be a purchase-money security interest, since the obligation of the boat purchaser to pay is incurred as part of the price of the boat [purchase money obligation], and the obligation is secured by the boat [purchase money collateral].

bank has a security interest in your buyer's obligation to make 36 monthly payments."

"So, by taking an interest in my chattel paper as proceeds, the bank is protected, right?"

"Sort of," Alan said. "However, if you go on to the next numbered paragraph, you can see that the bank has also taken a security interest in your chattel paper. Thus, it has an interest in your chattel paper not only as proceeds, but also as direct collateral which it has contracted to purchase from you under paragraph 4 of the Security Agreement."

This really confused Stephen. It seemed to him that if the bank had an interest in the chattel paper as proceeds; it didn't make sense that it would also want another security interest in the same piece of paper. "I don't understand," Stephen said. "They have a security interest in the chattel paper as proceeds, right?"

"Yes," Alan said.

"Then why is it necessary for them to take *another* security interest in the same piece of paper?"

"Okay, I hope this isn't too complicated for you, but I am going to try to explain this the best way I can," Alan said. "If it doesn't make sense to you now, it will make more sense to you after we finish our discussion of these documents."

"Let me go back to the drawing for a second. As you can see, the seller at this point in time, that is, at the point right after the sale, is in physical possession of this piece of chattel paper. Now obviously, this paper is worth something. It is worth $500 times 36 which is $18,000 less some amount of inflation as it stretches over time."

"You, as a seller, are probably going to want to sell this paper to a third party. The reason is obvious. You can't take this piece of paper and buy inventory with it or pay employees with it. You need cash. Thus, you will sell this chattel paper."

"To whom?" Stephen asked.

"Although you are obligated to sell the chattel paper to South Dade Bank, in reality you could sell it to anyone." said Alan, "But in all likelihood you would sell it to someone like Diablo Finance Company, who is in the business of purchasing such paper. If Diablo purchased the chattel paper *'in the ordinary course'* of its business, and for *'new value'* (as opposed e.g. to a pre-existing debt Stephen owed the Diablo), and the chattel paper does not indicate that it has been assigned to an identified assignee [e.g. South Dade Bank] then the proceeds interest of the bank in that paper would be defeated."[18]

"That doesn't make much sense to me," Stephen said. "Why would the law allow for a third party to come in and cut off a proceeds interest? I thought you said that by taking a security interest in proceeds, the bank would be protecting its security interest. And why would I want to sell my chattel paper to Diablo if South Dade and I already have a deal?"

"Perhaps Diablo was offering a much better price for the chattel paper than South Dade. Obviously, you would be in breach, but in business, sometimes these things happen. Aside from that possibility, the fact that someone would be cutting off the bank's proceeds interest does not mean that the bank is unprotected. It still has a security

---

[18] *A purchaser of chattel paper has priority over a security interest in the chattel paper which is claimed merely as proceeds of inventory subject to a security interest if:*

(1) in good faith and in the ordinary course of the purchasers' business, the purchaser gives new value and takes possession of the chattel paper or obtains control of the chattel paper under Section 9-105 [control of electronic chattel paper]; and

(2) the chattel paper does not indicate that it has been assigned to an identified assignee other than the purchaser. Section 9-330(a)(1)(2).

interest in its primary collateral, the boats. Furthermore, the money received from the sale of the chattel paper will presumably be used in the business, further protecting the bank."[19]

"And of course, you must realize," Alan continued, "the first lender can do exactly what South Dade is doing here, i.e. it can purchase the chattel paper itself.[20] Of course, this paper is a good investment for the bank to

---

[19] It should also be noted that if such a subsequent purchase of chattel paper were not so protected, sales of such paper would dramatically decrease, or become more expensive to reflect the increased risk of the original lender claiming a superior interest.

[20] The bank's interest even as the direct purchaser of the chattel paper [as opposed to merely a proceeds interest] might be defeated if Stephen chose to sell the paper to someone other than South Dade. In order for the subsequent purchaser to prevail over South Dade in such a situation, however, the subsequent purchaser would have to take the paper without knowledge that the purchase violates the rights of South Dade:

> A purchaser of chattel paper has priority over a security interest in the chattel paper which is claimed other than merely as proceeds of inventory subject to a security interest if the purchaser gives new value and takes possession of the chattel paper or obtains control of the chattel paper under Section 9-105 [electronic chattel paper] in good faith, in the ordinary course of the purchaser's business, and without knowledge that the purchase violates the rights of the secured party. Section 9-330(b).

A legend on the chattel paper indicating the assignment will protect the original lender from having its interest defeated:

> For purposes of subsections (b) and (d), if chattel paper or an instrument indicates that it has been assigned to an identified secured party other than the purchaser, a purchaser of the chattel paper...has knowledge that the purchase violates the rights of the secured party. Section 9-330(f).

[This is elaborated on in a subsequent discussion between Alan and Stephen].

make. It is relatively safe since the boat purchaser is checked out from a credit standpoint prior to the purchase, and the high interest yield on chattel paper makes the investment a good one for the bank to make."[21]

"Another way the bank is protecting itself", continued Alan, "is to require you to make a daily accounting to the bank for all proceeds received in connection with the boat business.[22] Thus, at the end of every day or early the following morning, you will be required to turn over anything you receive in connection with the sale of a boat: for example, checks or cash which would, in all probability, be deposited in your account with South Dade Bank. Since the bank has a security interest in any deposit accounts you have with South Dade, they would have further protection as to these assets." [Deposit accounts will be discussed shortly.]

"You will give the bank any chattel paper as well, not only as proceeds, but as original collateral for which the bank would give Stephen's Boat's a direct credit to your deposit account."

"The daily accounting," Alan explained, "is a business decision made by the lender as opposed to a legal requirement under the Uniform Commercial Code. Prior to the enactment of the Code, the United States Supreme

---

[21] The agreement between Stephen and the bank would probably provide for direct payment by the account debtor [the purchaser of the boat who is obligated on the chattel paper] to the bank. Since the bank per the security agreement is purchasing the paper for the principal amount of the paper, the interest reflected in the payments would be profit to the bank.

[22] In this connection, the bank from time to time will probably send somebody to "spot check" Stephen's inventory, in order to make certain that the amount of daily proceeds which Stephen is turning over to the bank corresponds to the amount of boats which have been sold off the lot.

Court had held in a New York case that if a lender allowed a debtor complete control over the collateral and the proceeds, the security interest was void as being a fraud on other creditors. Section 9-205 of the Code changed that." Alan said.[23]

"A third way the bank protects itself," continued Alan "is to keep possession of the title until the boat is fully paid for."

"Do you think you understand everything so far?" Alan asked.

"I think so," Stephen said. "Could you excuse me for a moment? I would like to make a phone call."

"Certainly," Alan said.

Whereupon Stephen left to make a phone call and Alan had his secretary get Doug Hawkins, a young associate with the firm whose specialty was the Uniform Commercial Code.

"Hi Doug, how are you doing?" Alan said. "I just wanted to get you in here because I think we are going to be getting some really good Code business for you to do," Alan said. "Do you know Stephen Seller?" he asked.

---

[23] *A security interest is not invalid or fraudulent against creditors solely because:*

   (1) the debtor has the right or ability to:

    (A) use, commingle, or dispose of all or part of the collateral, including returned or repossessed goods;

    (B) collect, compromise, enforce, or otherwise deal with collateral;

    (C) accept the return of collateral or make repossessions; or

    (D) use, commingle, or dispose of proceeds, or

(2) the secured party fails to require the debtor to account for proceeds or replace collateral. Section 9-05(a)(1)(A)(B)(C)(D) (2).

"Sure I do," said Doug, "We went to school together at the University of Miami."

"Well, why don't you stick around for a minute and say hello to him because I think this matter I'm working on may be getting into some other Articles of the Code that you are more familiar with than I am."

Stephen walked in and saw his friend Doug. "I heard you were working here and I had hoped to see you today. How are you doing?"

Doug and Stephen exchanged a few minutes of conversation and agreed to meet for lunch sometime in the near future, but for now, Stephen wanted to hurry up and finish reviewing this agreement so that he could get to the beach as soon as possible. After all, until he was really in business, he had no intention of giving up his hut on the beach for anybody. As a matter of fact, Stephen was ready to go to the beach then and asked Alan if he would simply prepare a short letter to him explaining the rest of the agreement and Stephen would review it at home.

Alan agreed to do so, and Stephen left. Just after Stephen left, Alan buzzed his secretary and asked her to come in for some dictation. Alan was anxious to keep on top of this business venture as he viewed it as an excellent opportunity to make some money. After all, ten percent of a boat business could be very lucrative.

"Judy, please address this letter to Stephen Seller and reference it proposed financing with South Dade Bank."

August 17, 2005

Stephen Seller
4554 Boat Lane
Miami Florida, 33421

Dear Stephen:

Pursuant to your request of today, I am writing this letter to continue our discussion with reference to the Security Agreement proposed by South Dade Bank. A copy of this Agreement is enclosed herewith for your convenience.

We had finished discussing, when you left, all of those paragraphs numbered 1, 2, 3, 4 under the "Now Therefore" clause. In addition, we discussed the daily accounting requirement of the Bank with respect to proceeds. We left off on paragraph 2 under where it states "debtor further agrees". That paragraph requires that the security interest which the bank gets from you will be a "first lien" at all times that the agreement is in effect. When South Dade gets its security interest in the collateral described, it will have "lien" on your property, which can be thought of as a claim on that property. In requesting a "first lien" it is requesting a lien entitled to first priority with respect to the property involved.[24]

If for example, you don't pay your state or federal taxes in the state of Florida or if the United States government gets a tax lien on your property, in certain circumstances, that tax lien would take priority over the interest of South Dade bank. Hence, South Dade Bank would not have a first lien on that property, which would place you in violation of the terms of the agreement until the tax lien was removed, which would occur upon payment of the taxes.

-----

[24] When more than one party has a security interest in the same collateral, the question of priority comes into play. The creditor which has first priority with respect to the collateral will be entitled to exercise its rights in the collateral prior to the other parties claiming an interest in the property. Some of these rights are discussed shortly in the letter from Alan to Stephen.

The next paragraph states that you cannot further encumber any of the collateral which is the subject of the security interest without the express written consent of the bank. If you need additional funds that the bank either doesn't want to lend you or which you can get cheaper elsewhere, the bank wants to know ahead of time who you are going to get the funds from and under what arrangements. To the extent that for some reason the bank doesn't want you to borrow these monies, it can refuse under the terms of the agreement to give written permission. It is important to note, however, that although this provision can constitute an event of default under the terms of the agreement upon your violation of it, it does not prevent a subsequent transfer of your interest in collateral from being an effective transfer of that interest.[25]

That is, you still have the right to borrow money and put up any of the collateral as security whenever you want. By doing so, however, you will have violated the terms of your agreement with South Dade who can, if it chooses to, declare you in default.

As you can see, the loan agreement is specifically referred to in the Security Agreement in the last paragraph before the default provisions. As you notice, the bank is under an obligation to lend you additional money in the amount of $400,000 upon your securing either the Crown or Marina account. This obligation on the part of the

---

[25] *An agreement between the debtor and secured party which prohibits a transfer of the debtor's rights in collateral or makes the transfer a default does not prevent the transfer from taking effect.* Section 9-401(b).

bank is sort of like the after acquired property clause we discussed this morning. This particular clause is called a *future advance clause.* It, like the after acquired property clause, was looked upon with disfavor in earlier case law. It has now been validated by Section 9-204 of the Uniform Commercial Code.[26]

The remaining provisions of the agreement deal with default. Obviously, if you fail to make payment under the terms Security Agreement or Loan Agreement, you will have defaulted in your obligations to the bank. Furthermore, as the Security Agreement indicates, should any of the conditions of the Security Agreement or the Loan Agreement be breached, you will have breached your contractual obligations under those agreements, similarly resulting in a default. For example, upon signing the Security Agreement, you will have promised the bank that the bank will have a first lien on the property. Failure to abide by this would constitute default. Similarly, although the clause prohibiting future encumbrances does not prevent you from creating another security interest in the collateral, it is still valid as between you and the secured party to constitute a default. Thus, to the extent you go out and borrow money using the inventory or any of the other collateral as collateral for this second borrowing or third borrowing without prior written consent of the bank, you will have breached an obligation to the bank, for which it can declare you in default.

As you can see, upon your default the bank claims the rights provided to a secured creditor

---

[26] *A security agreement may provide that collateral secures ... future advances or other value ...* Section 9-204(c).

under the Uniform Commercial Code. Part 6 of Article 9 deals with default. This is a fairly extensive part of Article 9 and I am not going to give a whole lot of detail with respect to it. I will just try to set out the basic rights being referred to.

If you do default under the terms of the Security Agreement, the bank will have the right to exercise any of the powers contained under the agreement, and in addition, those provided in part 6 of Article 9.[27]

The bank could, for example, take possession of the collateral on default without judicial process. The bank, however, will not be allowed to do this unless it can be done without breach of peace.[28] Of course, we don't expect to use any of the provisions of part 6 of Article 9 anyway!

---

[27] *After default, a secured party has the rights provided in this part and, except as otherwise provided in Section 9-602, those provided by agreement of the parties. A secured party:*

(1) may reduce a claim to judgment, foreclose, or otherwise enforce the claim, security interest, or agricultural lien by any available procedure; and

(2) if the collateral is documents, may proceed as to the documents or the goods they cover. Section 9-601(a)(1)(2).

[28] *(a) After default, a secured party:*

(1) may take possession of the collateral; and

(2) without removal, may render equipment unusable and dispose of collateral on a debtor's premises under Section 9-610.

(b) A secured party may proceed under subsection (a): pursuant to judicial process; or
without judicial process, if it proceeds without breach of the peace. Section 9-609(a)(1)(2).

If the bank takes possession of the boats upon default, it may sell, lease, or dispose of the boats to recover the amounts it has advanced.[29] If it does sell, lease or dispose of the boats, it must do so in a commercially reasonable manner.[30]

Furthermore, should an event of default occur and the bank takes possession, there are specific notice provisions which must be followed in connection with the disposition of collateral.[31] Before the bank [the secured party], disposes of the collateral or enters into a binding commitment for its disposition, you would have the right to redeem the collateral by tendering fulfillment of all the obligations secured by the collateral. If you pay

---

[29] *After default, a secured party may sell, lease, license, or otherwise dispose of any or all of the collateral in its present condition following any commercially reasonable preparation or processing.* Section 9-610(a).

[30] *Every aspect of the disposition of collateral, including the method, manner, time, place, and other terms, must be commercially reasonable. If commercially reasonable, a secured party may dispose of collateral by public or private proceedings, by one or more contracts, as a unit or in parcels, and at any time and place and on any terms.* Section 9-610(b).

Section 9-627 states the law with regard to what is considered commercially reasonable. It is a very straightforward section and has been reproduced in the statutory supplement.

[31] *Except as otherwise provided in subsection (d), a secured party that disposes of collateral under Section 9-610 shall send to the persons specified in subsection (c) a reasonable authenticated notification of disposition.* Section 9-611(b). The debtor is one of those to be notified under 9-611(c)(1).

Subsection (d) to 9-611 goes on to state:

Subsection (b) does not apply if the collateral is perishable or threatens to decline speedily in value or is of a type customarily sold on a recognized market. Section 9-611(d).

all obligations due to the bank you would have the right to get the boats back.[32] Finally, the bank is under an obligation to proceed in accordance with provisions of part 6 of Article 9. As indicated, for example, the bank is required to give proper notification and sell in a commercially reasonable manner. It will be liable for damages caused by its failure to do so.[33] If the bank proceeds according the terms of part 6 of Article 9 and does not receive enough money from the sale of the boats and other collateral to cover the amount you owe it, you will be liable for any deficiency.[34]

---

[32] *A debtor, any secondary obligor, or any other secured party or lienholder may redeem collateral.* Section 9-623(a).

To redeem collateral, a person shall tender:

    (1) fulfillment of all obligations secured by collateral; and

    (2) the reasonable expenses and attorney's fees described in Section 9-615(a)(1). Section 9-623(b)(1)(2).

A redemption may occur at any time before a secured party:

    (1) has collected collateral under Section 9-607;

    (2) has disposed of collateral or entered into a contract for its disposition under Section 9-610; or

    (3) has accepted collateral in full or partial satisfaction of the obligation it secured under Section 9-622.

Section 9-623(c)(1)(2)(3).

[33] *Subject to subsection (c), (d), and (f), a person is liable for damages in the amount of any loss caused by a failure to comply with this article. Loss caused by a failure to comply may include loss resulting from the debtor's inability to obtain, or increased costs of, alternative financing.* Section 9-625(b).

[34] *If the security interest under which a disposition is made secures payment or performance of an obligation, after making the payments and applications required by subsection (a) [application of*

It is important to note, Stephen, that your obligation with respect to the deficiency judgment or with respect to the deficiency owed would only go to the amount advanced under the terms of the Loan Agreement and would not include any amounts involved in the sale of chattel paper to the Bank.[35]

I look forward to seeing you soon.

Alan

Just as Alan was getting ready to discuss the financing statement which was also contained in the documents sent over, Stephen telephoned him. It seemed that Stephen had feelings of guilt while on the

---

cash proceeds] and permitted by subsection (c) [application of noncash proceeds];

(2) the obligor is liable for any deficiency. Section 9-615(d)(2).

[35] If the underlying transaction is a sale of accounts, chattel paper, payment intangibles, or promissory notes:

. . .

(2) the obligor is not liable for any deficiency.

Section 9-615(e)(2). [This will be discussed in the next few pages].

"Account"... means a right to payment of a monetary obligation whether or not earned by performance, (i) for property that has been or is to be sold, leased, licensed, assigned, or otherwise disposed of, (ii) for services rendered or to be rendered.... Section 9-102(a)(2).

beach and he couldn't even relax knowing that he hadn't fully reviewed the terms of the Agreement. It was becoming apparent that Stephen was finally starting to mature and see that the truly important things of life could not wait until later. Accordingly, a meeting was set up between Alan and Stephen for Friday afternoon. Stephen told Alan to go ahead and send the letter and that he would get it in the morning so that part of that discussion would be unnecessary. Stephen said that if he had any questions about it, he would bring them up at his meeting with Alan.

The next afternoon Stephen showed up ready to go. The change in Stephen was beginning to worry his father, although his mother was delighted with the new Stephen, and his friends didn't know what to do with him. Lately, it seemed all he could talk about was business. That didn't bother his friends too much, but when he started telling them that what they were doing was wrong, they really didn't know what to do. In any event, Stephen was deriving much satisfaction from knowing that he was finally getting on the right track.

"I understood most of the letter you sent me yesterday," said Stephen. "I only have two questions with respect to what you said. First is this part at the end where you talk about my not being liable for a deficiency judgment to the Bank for any amounts owing from sales of chattel paper to the Bank. My question is: How could I be? I mean, if I sell the paper to the bank, am I not out of the transaction in regard to the chattel paper?"

"You may or may not be," responded Alan. "In the first place, even though you sold the paper to the Bank, you might be making the collections for the bank. As a matter of fact, until the account debtor receives notification of the assignment, he is authorized to pay you.[36] In a situation

---

[36] *[A]n account debtor on . . .chattel paper. . . may discharge its obligation by paying the assignor until, but not after, the account*

such as this, however, the Bank will probably make the collections."[37]

"Anyway," Alan continued, "regardless of how the collections are made, some account debtors may stop making payments for some reason. For example, a boat may be defective and the account debtor may refuse to make further payments."

"Can they do that?" Stephen interrupted. "When I bought my second boat I had all sorts of trouble with it and threatened to stop making payments, but I was told that I had to keep making them."

"To whom?" Alan asked.

"Cosmopolitan Finance Company," said Stephen. "You know, the one where you dial 'Pleasure' in Dade County. You've seen the commercial, haven't you?"

"Yes," responded Alan.

"Well, did I have to pay them?"

"That depends," said Alan, "on whether you signed an agreement when you purchased the boat in which you agreed not to assert claims or defenses' against an assignee of the paper, and whether or not the boat was purchased as a consumer item or for business purposes.[38] If you did purchase the boat as equipment

---

debtor receives notification, authenticated by the assignor or assignee, that the amount due or to become due has been assigned and that the payment is to be made to the assignee… Section 9-406(a).

[37] Even if the Bank had not been making collections under the arrangement with Stephen, if Stephen defaulted his obligations to the Bank, the Bank would thereafter be entitled to notify the account debtors to make payment to it.

If so agreed, and in any event after default, a secured party:

(1) may notify an account debtor or other person obligated on collateral to make payment or otherwise render performance to or for the benefit of the secured party. Section 9-607(a)(1).

[38] See footnote 38 in Appendix I on page 346.

[which many would do for legitimate business use and resulting favorable tax implications] then you would not be entitled to stop payment. You would, however, still be able to sue the seller if the goods were defective."

"Wouldn't South Dade structure the transaction in such a manner?" asked Stephen.

"Probably," said Alan, "But some account debtors might be unable to pay the installments or simply refuse to, despite their legal obligation to do so. One good thing here is that since you will be selling the chattel paper to South Dade, South Dade will not be able to hold you liable for the deficiency owed to it by an account debtor.[39] Actually," continued Alan, "it is irregular for the Bank not to have made you assume this burden."

"Now what's your other question?" Alan asked.

"What is the importance of this other little piece of paper? This thing called the UCC-1 *Financing Statement.*" Stephen continued, "It seems to me that there is nothing in this that is not contained in the Security Agreement. As a matter of fact," Stephen said, "there is even less contained in this statement than there is in the Security Agreement. What is it for?"

"Probably the easiest way to illustrate this," Alan said, "is by returning to the pawnbroker situation which we discussed yesterday. You remember in that situation our debtor had come in and borrowed $750 and given the pawnbroker his $1200 watch as security?"

Stephen nodded.

"Let's assume that you, as the debtor in that situation, have in fact put your watch up as collateral for the $750 loan. If you now want to go to another pawnbroker to borrow another $750 on the security of that watch, are you going to be able to do it? Certainly any pawnbroker

---

[39] *See* Section 9-615(e)(2) at footnote 35 on page 47.

who lends money on the strength of a watch is going to want to have it in his possession before he gives you the money." Alan said.

"Since the original pawnbroker has possession of the watch, you will obviously be unable to give it to a second pawnbroker as collateral for a loan. It would be highly irregular for him to loan you money in such a situation. But if he did so, he would have notice that the watch is possibly being held as collateral for another loan, or at the very least, that you couldn't produce the watch for his immediate possession."

"This little financing statement serves the identical purpose with respect to all of the property in which the Bank has a security interest. As we discussed yesterday, the bank will not take possession of your inventory and your equipment and the like. Yet, there must be a way to let subsequent lenders or potential lenders know that the collateral is subject to a security interest. If subsequent lenders did not know this, or had no way of finding out, it would be very difficult to get money from anybody, for a lender could never loan money knowing what priority he had."

Alan continued, "To eliminate this problem, the financing statement is filed by the Bank and then with the central filing system. When the Code was first enacted, business filings were sent to the Secretary of State's Office in Tallahassee. In many states, like Florida, the filing systems have been privatized, so that you now file in the Florida Secured Transactions Registry. Once the financing statement is received, it will be filed and indexed according to your name, that is, the name of your business since the business is the debtor. It will be alphabetically placed in the files under Stephens Boats,

Inc.[40] Thus, there will be on record, notice that the Bank might have a security interest in the collateral. Any subsequent lender could check these files prior to lending to find out this information. Of course when he does, he'll see the financing statement and be on notice that someone might have a security interest in the inventory. Section 9-502(d) authorizes filing the financing statement *'before a security agreement is made or a security interest otherwise attaches.'"* [41]

---

[40] Part 5 of Article 9 deals with filing. Section 9-501 states the places where financing statements must be filed. As noted, many states have privatized their filing systems.

While this is allowable for most types of collateral, there are three exceptions. First is for *'as extracted collateral'* [such as oil, gas or other minerals per Section 9-102(a)(6)] or timber to be cut; second is for a fixture filing where the subject goods are to become *fixtures* [goods that have become so related to real property that an interest in them arises under real property law per Section 9-102(a)(41)]. For these types of collateral, the place of filing the financing statement is:

(1) the office designated for the filing or recording of record of a mortgage on the related real property... Section 9-501(a)(1)(A)(B).

The place of filing for the overwhelming majority of collateral is stated in Section 9-501(a)(2) as:

(2) the office of [   ] or any office duly authorized by [   ] in all other cases, including a case in which the collateral is goods that are to become fixtures and the financing statement is not filed as a fixture filing.

The brackets in Section 9-501(a)(2) are to be filled in by the legislature of each state. For those states which have not privatized their filing system, the office of the Secretary of State will usually be the location of the filing system for non consumer filings.

The third exception deals with transmitting utilities and is covered in Section 9-501(b).

[41] Section 9-502(d) states as follows:

"You're quite right that the description of the collateral is not nearly as detailed as it is in the Security Agreement. However, if the Financing Statement, and for that matter, the Security Agreement reasonably identifies the collateral, that is all that is required under the Code."[42]

A financing statement may be filed before a security agreement is made or a security interest otherwise attaches [becomes enforceable].

[42] *Except as otherwise provided in subsections (c)(d), and (e), a description of personal or real property is sufficient, whether or not it is specific, if it reasonably identifies what is described. Section 9-108(a). See Section 9-521 in the Statutory Supplement on page 481 for a sample Financing Statement.*

In this regard, it should be pointed out that the degree of specificity of description required in a security agreement is greater than the degree of specificity required in a financing statement. Section 9-504 states:

A financing statement sufficiently indicates the collateral it covers if the financing statement provides:

(1) a description of the collateral pursuant to Section 9-108; or

(2) an indication that the financing statement covers all assets or all personal property.

While Section 9-504(1) clearly complies with the required level of description for a security agreement, subsection (2) does not. As comment 2 notes:

Note that a broad statement of this kind (e.g. "all debtors' personal property") would not be a sufficient description for purposes of a security agreement.

The reason that lack of specificity is acceptable in the financing statement and not in the security agreement can be explained by the respective function of each. The financing statement is simply to put other creditors on notice that a particular debtor has encumbered his assets [and to perfect its interest], while the security agreement is to delineate with specificity what was agreed to between the parties. A subsequent lender can review that agreement if it wants to lend despite the notice of the other security interest.

"You mean that once this Financing Statement is filed, nobody else will lend to me?" Stephen asked.

"Not at all Stephen," Alan said. "Another lender could certainly lend even though someone else has filed a financing statement covering certain collateral. In such a situation, however, the second lender will know that as a general proposition he won't be able to obtain a first priority with respect to that collateral, if the first lender takes all necessary steps to insure priority [discussed below]. And if he checks the files and there is no financing statement on file, he can lend to you knowing that he can get a first priority, even if South Dade has lent the money first.[43] This assumes, of course, that the second lender complies with all the necessary steps."

"What are the necessary steps?" Stephen asked.

"Each lender wants to make sure that his security interest is **perfected**." Alan responded. "This assures him of the highest protection he can get under the Code against subsequent lenders."

"When does perfection occur?"

"Here," said Alan, as he took out a copy of the Code. "Let me show you what the actual language of the Code says."

...[A] security interest is perfected if it has attached and all the applicable requirements for perfection in Sections 9-310 through 9-316 have been satisfied. Section 9-308(a).

Attachment, therefore, is a prerequisite for perfection. Section 9-203(a) states when attachment occurs:

---

[43] This will be discussed in an upcoming discussion between Stephen and Alan.

A security interest attaches to collateral when it becomes enforceable against the debtor with respect to the collateral, unless an agreement expressly postpones the time of attachment.

"When does it become enforceable?" replied Stephen.

"This is covered under Section 9-203(b).[44] As you can see, the first requirement stated is that value must be given, i.e. the Bank has to give you the money. Next, you must have rights in the collateral or the power to transfer rights in the collateral to a secured party which of course, you will, since you will own the boats. Finally, one of the conditions of Section 9-203(b)(3) must be met. You will have satisfied (3)(A) since you will have authenticated a security agreement that provides a description of the collateral." **Authenticate** means to sign. Section 9-102(a)(7)(A).

"OK. I see what attachment is, but that other section you showed me required more, didn't it?"

"Yes, in this situation and with respect to inventory, it requires that a financing statement be filed.[45] So, after the

---

[44] *Except as otherwise provided in subsections (c) through (i), a security interest is enforceable against the debtor and third parties with respect to the collateral only if:*

(1) value has been given;

(2) the debtor has rights in the collateral or the power to transfer rights in the collateral to a third party; and

(3) one of the following conditions is met:

(A) the debtor has authenticated a security agreement that provides a description of the collateral. . .

Section 9-203(b)(1)(2)(3)(A).

[45] Section 9-310 states when the filing of a financing statement is required to perfect a security interest. Subsection (a) to 9-310 states:

security interest has attached," Alan continued, "it becomes enforceable against third parties. But to get the highest protection, the bank would have to file a financing statement.[46] It is important to note," Alan continued, "that

---

Except as otherwise provided in subsection (b), a financing statement must be filed to perfect all security interests and agricultural liens.

Inventory is not among the exceptions listed, and therefore a financing statement must be filed to perfect that interest.

The remaining text of this footnote is in Appendix I on page 350.

[46] This higher protection follows from Sections 9-317(a)(1) and 9-322(a)(1). Section 9-317(a)(1)(2) states:

A security interest or agricultural lien is subordinate to the rights of:

(1) a person entitled to priority under Section 9-322;

(2) except as otherwise provided in subsection (e), a person that becomes a lien creditor before the earlier of the time:

(A) the security interest or agricultural lien is perfected; or

(B) one of the conditions specified in Section 9-203(b)(3) is met and a financing statement covering the collateral is filed.

One of these persons entitled to priority under Section 9-322 is a secured party who filed his financing statement before any other secured parties. This is discussed in footnote 47.

Section 9-317(a)(2), also gives priority to a lien creditor before the security interest is perfected, or before the conditions noted in Section 9-317(a)(2)(B). A lien creditor is defined under Section 9-102(a)(52):

Lien creditor means:

(A) a creditor that has acquired a lien on the property involved by attachment, levy or the like;

(B) ....

(C) ....

the time of filing is the crucial time with respect to who would take priority. That is, the first creditor to file a financing statement in a situation like this, rather than the first creditor to give value, would take priority later on."[47]

---

[47] Section 9-322(a)(1) states: . . . *[P]riority among conflicting security interests and agricultural liens in the same collateral is determined according to the following rules:*

(a) Conflicting security interests and agricultural lines rank according to priority from the time of filing or perfection. Priority dates from the earlier of the time a filing covering the collateral is first made or the security interest or agricultural lien is first perfected, if there is no period thereafter when there is neither filing nor perfection.

It is important to note Alan's statement in this connection that who lent money first is not the crucial question; rather, as indicated, whichever secured party filed the financing statement first would be entitled to priority under the rule quoted. Thus, to the extent that Stephen was able to borrow money from another lender after South Dade Bank and Stephen had filed a financing statement, South Dade Bank would have priority over the first lender regardless of when the money was loaned, assuming, of course, that Section 9-203 was complied with.

While this may seem an incorrect result, it is important to note that the second lender could very easily have checked the files and found the financing statement on file. It would thus have had access to full notice that there was a transaction going on between Stephen and the Bank. If is still chose to lend, it would be doing so at its peril.

Section 9-322 goes on to state the basic rule regarding priority of perfected over non perfected security interests:

A perfected security interest or agricultural lien has priority over a conflicting unperfected security interest or agricultural lien. Section 9-322(a)(2).

Finally, where conflicting security interests or agricultural liens are unperfected, the first to attach has priority:

The first security interest or agricultural lien to attach or become effective has priority if conflicting security interests and agricultural liens are unperfected. Section 9-322(a)(3).

"Now, with respect to the chattel paper, the Bank could perfect its interest by filing a financing statement.[48] It could also perfect by taking possession.[49] The Bank will most likely take possession of the chattel paper to prevent you from selling the paper to another lender. If you recall, we discussed this yesterday."

Stephen nodded.

"Remember," Alan said, "that if the purchaser took the paper under the circumstances set out in Section 9-330(a) or (b), he would take priority over the Bank."

"However," Alan continued, "the second lender would lose if he had knowledge *that the purchase violates the rights of the secured party.*[50] If not, i.e. if the second lender didn't know this, he would take priority over lender one. Lender one in such a situation should stamp on the paper the fact that it is subject to security interest."[51]

"Stephen, there is one other point I want to make about perfection at this time. Under paragraph 5, if you recall, the bank has a security interest in your deposit accounts. There are some different rules regarding enforceability and perfection with these accounts, and if you want me to, I will be happy to explain them to you. It's not as important as the inventory or chattel paper in my opinion, but I know you want to know as much as possible about all of this."

---

[48] *A security interest in ... chattel paper or negotiable documents may be perfected by filing.* Section 9-312(a).

[49] *[A] secured party may perfect a security interest in ... chattel paper by taking possession of the collateral.* Section 9-313(a).

[50] Of course by taking possession of the chattel paper, lender number one, South Dade Bank, would be able to prevent this type of sale to a third party except for that time period during which the debtor was in possession of the chattel paper prior to turning it over to South Dade.

[51] *See supra* note 18 at page 36.

"Thanks Alan. If it isn't too much trouble, I would like to understand this part of it. After all, the money from the business is going into that account, and I want to know as much as possible about that."

"Sure. Let's start with the definition, which is very straightforward. *"Deposit account means a demand, time, savings, passbook, or similar account maintained with a bank...."* Section 9-102(a)(29).

"The checking account of Stephen's Boats would be squarely within this definition."

"The rules regarding enforceability are identical to other security interest in some respects, but as indicated, there are some differences. Thus, the basic rules for enforceability of a security interest in a deposit account, like all collateral, are to be found in Section 9-203(b)(1)(2)(3)(A)(B)(C)(D). Therefore, as to the first two requirements, South Dade must give you value—i.e.—the loan proceeds, and you must have power to transfer rights in the collateral, which of course you will have as the owner of the deposit accounts."

"The third requirement for enforceability is where we see some variations." Alan opened his Uniform Commercial Code to Section 9-203.

"Here, let me show you the specific language."

Except as otherwise provided in subsections (c) through (i), a security interest is enforceable against the debtor and third parties with respect to the collateral only if:

(1) value has been given;

(2) the debtor has rights in the collateral or power to transfer rights in the collateral to a secured party; and

(3) one of the following conditions is met:

(A) the debtor has authenticated a security agreement that provides a description of the collateral and, if the security interest covers timber to be cut, a description of the land concerned;

(B) ....

(C) ....

(D) the collateral is deposit accounts, electronic chattel paper, investment property, or letter-of-credit rights, and the secured party has control under Section 9-104, 9-105, 9-106, or 9-107 pursuant to the debtor's security agreement.

Sections 9-203(b)(1)(2)(3)(A)(B)(C)(D).

"Regarding enforceability, South Dade will have an enforceable security interest in the deposit account once you sign the security agreement under Section 9-203(b)(3)(A). As you can see under Section 9-203(b)(3)(D) however, it could satisfy the requirement of Section 9-203(b)(3) by having 'control' of the deposit account."

Stephen interrupted. "Why would they do that if they already have an enforceable agreement under subsection (3)(A)?"

"That's a good question. The answer is very simple, and very important. The reason is to be found in Section 9-312(b)(1)."

Except as otherwise provided in Section 9-315(c) and (d) for proceeds:

*a security interest in a deposit account may be perfected **only** by control under Section 9-314.* [emphasis added]. Section 9-312(b)(1).

"Therefore, in order for South Dade to perfect its security interest in your deposit account, it must establish **control**.   The manner of establishing that control is found in Section 9-104 which is cross referenced in Section 9-314, which addresses 'Perfection by Control.'"

> *(a) secured party has control of a deposit account if:*
> *(1) the secured party is the bank with which the deposit account is maintained;*
> *(2) the debtor, secured party, and the bank have agreed in an authenticated record that the bank will comply with instructions originated by the secured party directing disposition of the funds in the deposit account without further consent by the debtor; or*
> *(3) the secured party becomes the bank's customer with respect to the deposit account. Section 9-104(a)(1)(2)(3).*

"Under subsection (a)(1), South Dade will have control since it is the secured party and the deposit account is being maintained with them."[52]
"Does this mean I can't write checks on the account without their permission? How can I run a business if I need permission to write a check?" asked Stephen.

---

[52] Footnote 52 is Appendix I on page 353

"Another good question," replied Alan, as he was hoping that Stephen's mind wouldn't wander back to the beach during his lengthy explanation.

"That specific question is answered under Section 9-104(b)."

A secured party that has satisfied subsection (a) has control, even if the debtor retains the right to direct the disposition of funds from the deposit account. Section 9-104(b).

Stephen felt fairly comfortable that he understood the mechanics of the transaction. What he was going to do was take the documents home, review the notes he had taken in his discussion with Alan, and if he had any questions he would get back to Alan later on. For now, however, he was convinced he understood enough to go forward with the transaction if Alan felt everything was in order, and accordingly, Stephen told Alan to try to set a closing for the loan during the week which had been planned, the first week of September 2005. Alan immediately telephoned Fred Luvick and asked if the closing might be confirmed for the 7th of September. Fred said that would be fine with him and the loan closing and execution of documents was set for September 7, 2005 at 2:00 p.m. at the Bank's downtown Miami branch.

The loan closing was to take place in the conference room on the seventh floor of the South Dade Bank.

Section 6

Present at the closing were Fred, Stephen, Alan and Doug. Alan brought Doug along so that Doug could start getting some experience in these types of closings. Doug, of course, was very interested in anything that had to do with the Uniform Commercial Code and thought he was pretty lucky to be going to things like loan closings. After all, he could bill the hours at a closing just as easily as he could bill the hours doing research. In fact, Doug was especially excited because sometimes they even got to bill the lunch!

The whole execution of documents took about five minutes. As soon as they got there, Fred's in house counsel realized that he had forgotten something very important. Namely, he was to have the financing statement filed a week before the actual closing so that the Bank could file the financing statement prior to disbursing the money. [The reason they wanted to do this, of course, was to insure a first priority when they finally did loan the money and the Security Agreement attached and became enforceable under Section 9-203. As soon as it attached, it would be perfected because the financing statement would have been filed.] In any event, because Alan forgot to have the financing statement filed prior to closing, Fred told them they would not disburse until the financing statement was on file (and of course, was the first one filed). The other documents, however, were duly executed.

Since it was Friday late in the afternoon, Alan asked Stephen if he would like to go for drink, but Stephen declined as he had to leave in morning for Atlanta. He was to fly out there to discuss the terms of the contract with Royal Boats, Inc. and attend a breakfast meeting with the vice president. He wanted to be rested and ready for Saturday.

PART TWO

Section 1

With the purchase of the land complete, and the loan proceeds to be disbursed shortly, Stephen was ready to finalize his arrangements with Royal. He telephoned Joe Thomas, vice president of Royal and the person with whom Stephen had been negotiating all along. Mr. Thomas was out of the office, but his secretary informed Stephen that Mr. Thomas was planning to meet Stephen the following morning at 10:00 a.m. at the Airport Inn. Stephen had prepared himself for an early morning meeting and had accordingly scheduled a flight which would get him to Atlanta at 8:30 a.m. Stephen confirmed the appointment and started thinking about how he was going to present his position at the meeting.

There were two things of primary importance to Stephen. First of all, he wanted to make sure that he always had adequate inventory on hand. He knew of situations where certain dealers were given preferential treatment by the company's main office with respect to new or popular models. Stephen wanted to make very certain that he was treated as well as the other dealers, even though his operation had not yet proven itself.

Second, Stephen did not want to be committed to a very large minimum purchase over a long period of time. In the first place, his cash position might not allow this, i.e., a required purchase of a large number of boats per month might be economically impossible for him. Also, he still hoped to work out something with Crown or Marina and wanted to have as much spare cash as possible at all times.

As usual, Joe Thomas was about five minutes early. Joe prided himself on being prompt and always eager to do business. He liked to see enthusiasm in distributors as well, and Stephen felt that it was his enthusiasm that won him the distributorship in the first place. In fact, Stephen was about 10 years younger than any other Royal distributor.

Fortunately, Joe hadn't eaten breakfast either and when he arrived he asked Stephen if he would like to go over to the restaurant and eat. The two went over to the dining room, sat down and ordered some coffee.

"You know, Joe, as we indicated before, our main concern is that we get adequate boats to cover our needs, but that we don't get stuck with a lot of boats on the lot when there is no demand for them. I would like very much to be able to adjust my purchases of boats in some way to the demand being made by my customers."

Joe said, "You know we will do our best to accommodate you, Stephen, but you must understand that we need some form of regular purchase from you or some form of binding commitment from you to purchase a certain number of our boats or else there is really no incentive to us to enter into the deal with you. To the extent that you simply want the market to take care of your needs, we would suggest to you that in that situation, the ultimate market risk would be borne by us. Unless there is some form of minimum purchase guaranteed by you, I don't think we can do business."

Stephen was prepared for this, and accordingly, he asked Joe how many boats he thought would suffice as the minimum purchase. Joe responded with an original purchase of at least $400,000 and a further commitment to purchase between 16 and 20 boats per year thereafter, at least 60% of which had a wholesale price of $24,000 or more, per year; in the alternative, a minimum purchase of $800,000 per year would be adequate. Furthermore, Joe told Stephen that he felt he would be able to adequately supply any other purchase needs upon 30 to 45 days' notice of the boat which Stephen desired.

Stephen agreed to the original purchase of $400,000 and a further purchase of a minimum of 16 boats per year from Royal. He knew going into the meeting that he would probably have to commit to some form of minimum purchase and a slightly over one-boat-per-month average was certainly not an unreasonable demand by Royal. Furthermore, Royal's agreement to supply him with any necessary boats upon 30-45 days notice took care of his other concern regarding always having an adequate inventory on hand. Joe had brought the standard Royal distributorship agreement with him which he gave to Stephen with the noted provisions already contained in the agreement.

"Why don't you take this with you, Stephen, and review it. Let me initial our agreement with respect to the minimum purchase, as well as the 45-day notice provision." Whereupon, Joe initialed the two provisions that they had just '*negotiated.*' "I'll get a letter off to you Monday if anything else comes to mind," Joe said. "In the meantime, if you have any objections, or anything you would like to discuss with respect to the agreement, please don't hesitate to give me a call. If I don't hear from you by the end of next week, I'll assume that the contract is in order."

Stephen was pleased and told Joe that he expected no problem with it and that, as a matter of fact, if Joe didn't hear from him Monday, when Stephen was planning to review it with his attorney, then he could assume that it was acceptable.

On the plane coming back, Stephen took the opportunity to review the agreement. It was a relatively short agreement styled Distributorship and Sales Agreement and read as follows:

DISTRIBUTORSHIP AND SALES AGREEMENT

WHEREAS, Stephen's Boats, Inc., a Florida corporation, is desirous of becoming a distributor of Royal Boats, Inc., a Georgia corporation; and

WHEREAS, Royal Boats, Inc., is desirous of having Stephen's Boats, Inc., become its sole distributor in the Southern District of Florida;

NOW, THEREFORE, in consideration of the mutual covenants contained herein and other good and valuable consideration receipt whereof is hereby acknowledged, the parties hereby agree as follows:

(1) Royal agrees to supply to Stephen's Boats, Inc., all boats needed by Stephen's Boats in connection with the operation of Stephen's Boats, Inc.

(2) Stephen' Boats agrees to purchase $400,000 of inventory within 30 days of the execution of this agreement;

(3) Stephen's Boats, inc., further agrees to purchase a minimum of sixteen boats per year from Royal with a wholesale price to Stephen's Boats, Inc., of not less than $24,000 each;

(4) Delivery of said boats shall be on a quarterly basis with four boats contained in each shipment;

(5) Royal agrees to supply Stephen with any additional boats he needs in the operation of Stephen's Boats, Inc., upon receipt of written notification from Stephen, containing the model and type of boat requested, 45 days in advance of the time in which he requires said boats;

(6) Stephen's Boats, Inc., will not sell the boats of any other manufacturer except Royal without the express written consent of Royal;

(7)   Boats will be shipped F.O.B Atlanta, GA by rail or truck, under a negotiable bill of lading to the order of Royal with delivery at Stephen's Boats, Inc.;

(8)   This agreement shall be governed by the laws of the State of Georgia;

(9)   Seller shall not be liable for any consequential damages which may result from non performance of this agreement;

(10) In the event buyer fails to properly perform under this agreement, buyer shall be liable to seller in the amount of $250,000 as liquidated damages;

(11) This agreement embodies the full understanding of the parties hereto, and may not be modified except in writing signed by both parties.

IN WITNESS WHEREOF, this Distributorship and Sales Agreement has been executed as of the date first above written.

Signed, Sealed and Delivered this 2nd day of September, 2005 in the presence of:

_____
Stephen's Boats, Inc.

_____
Royal Boats, Inc.

As soon as Stephen got off the plane, he telephoned Alan at his home to let him know what had happened. He told Alan that he was anxious to finalize the arrangements and wanted to get back to Royal as soon as possible. Stephen and Alan made arrangements to meet Monday morning at 9:00 a.m. in Alan's office.

After the meeting on Monday, Alan called Doug into his office. "How is your time Doug?" Alan asked.

"Well," Doug said, "I am pretty busy right now. I am doing a buy/sell agreement for Senior Partner."

"When does it have to be done?"

"He told me he would like to have it as soon as possible."

"Well, I have sort of a rush job for you," Alan said to Doug. "I really need this agreement reviewed and a memorandum on it right away."

Doug knew he was put on the spot. He knew he wanted to do Uniform Commercial Code work and that this was a great opportunity to get involved in it, but Senior Partner got very upset when any other work took priority over his. Doug didn't know what to do. He knew his billable hours were about 10% better than any associate in the law firm, but he also knew that if you got Senior Partner mad at you, it might cost you some money when salary increases were being discussed.

Alan could see the consternation on Doug's face. After all, it wasn't that long ago that Alan was in a similar position with Senior Partner. But he felt that it was important that Doug handle the problem himself. If he couldn't do the work, he should simply tell Alan.

"I can do it," Doug said.

"Are you sure?" Alan asked.

"Yes, I can get this done this afternoon and I will work late tonight if I have to finish Mr. Partner's work."

"Very good," Alan said and he handed the contract to Doug. "Please review this and tell me if it is enforceable or not under the Uniform Commercial Code. Also tell me anything else you think I ought to know. As you know, Doug, I don't know anything about the Code except for secured transactions. So, I will be relying extremely heavily on what you say in your memorandum."

Doug took the contract to his office to begin working on it.

Alan knew that his importance in the firm was growing. After all, if the same situation had presented itself only two years earlier, he probably couldn't have gotten anybody to do anything. But ever since he brought in Zipco and generated about $400,000 a year in legal fees for the firm, his status had changed. After all, he was now a partner and a had a big office with a window overlooking Biscayne Bay, and on top of that he thought to himself, hadn't he just moved into the nicest house owned by anybody in the firm? Yes, Alan knew that he had arrived. Just then, Stephen called to find out what the decision had been on the agreement.

"I just gave it to Doug, and he is researching the proposed contract right now, Stephen," Alan said. "I should be able to get back to you some time right after lunch."

After reviewing the contract, Doug dictated a memorandum to his secretary. While Doug was reviewing the memorandum, he thought to himself that it was really a pretty good job considering the circumstances under which he did it. In fact, he thought he should really bill more than three hours for it. He knew, however, that such a course of conduct would not be proper, so *of course* he only billed the three hours that he put on it. He took the memorandum to Alan who reviewed it. The memorandum read as follows:

MEMORANDUM OF LAW

To: Alan Lawyer
From: Doug Hawkins
RE: Stephen's Boats, Inc. Proposed Franchise
             Agreement from Royal
Date: September 4, 2005

QUESTIONS PRESENTED

You have asked me to review the above referenced agreement with a view toward the following:

Is the agreement enforceable under the Uniform Commercial Code?

What is the meaning of the proposed contract?

I.   **ENFORCEABILITY OF THE AGREEMENT**
       (A)   Statute of Frauds
       (B)   Indefiniteness
II.   **MEANING OF THE PROPOSED CONTRACT**
       (A)   Definition of Contract
       (B)   Definition of Agreement
III.   **TERMS SUPPLIED BY CODE**
       (A)   Missing Terms and Some General Obligations
       (B)   Warranty of Merchantability
       (C)   Proposed Contract as an Installment Contract
IV.   **SHIPMENT TERMS**
       (A)   F.O.B. Shipment Contract
       (B)   Shipment Under Reservations
V.   **DELIVERY OF GOODS**
       (A)   Bill of Lading

  (B) Person Entitled to Take Possession of Goods

  (C) Person Entitled Under the Document

I. ENFORCEABILITY OF THE AGREEMENT
  (A) Statute of Frauds
  (B) Indefiniteness

Since a sale of goods is involved in the instant situation, Article 2 of the Uniform Commercial Code applies.[53] With respect to the enforceability of this contract, two questions must be asked initially:

1. Is the contract enforceable under the statute of frauds of Article 2?

2. Does the absence of several terms in the contract render the contract unenforceable?

(A) Statute of Frauds
The basic rule for the *Statute of Frauds* is set forth in Section 2-201(1). That Section provides in pertinent part as follows:

> *[A] contract for the sale of goods for the price of $500 or more is not enforceable by way of action or defense unless there is some writing sufficient to indicate that a contract for sale has been*

---

[53] *Unless the context otherwise requires, this article* [Article 2 entitled Sales] *applies to transactions in goods* .... Section 2-102.

"Goods" means all things...which are movable at the time of identification to the contract...[and] includes the unborn young of animals and growing crops and other things attached to realty as described in the section on goods to be severed from realty (Section 2-107). Section 2-105(1)

made between the parties and signed by the party against whom enforcement is sought.

As a reading of the quoted portion of Section 2-201(1) indicates, the basic rule is that the proposed contract by Royal would not be enforceable against either Royal or Stephen's Boats, Inc., unless the writing was signed by the party against whom enforcement is sought. Thus, unless Royal signs the agreement, or one of the exceptions to the Statute of Frauds applies, Stephen will not be able to enforce the contract against Royal; conversely of course, if Stephen does not sign the agreement, Royal will not be able to enforce the agreement against Stephen.[54]

(B) Indefiniteness

Under pre Code law, the absence of certain terms considered 'necessary' to the contract, caused certain courts to declare such a contract unenforceable due to indefiniteness. Under the

---

[54] As noted, subsection 2-201(1) states the basic rule with respect to the statute of frauds. There are several exceptions to the rule there stated which will be discussed in this book. One exception, probably most applicable here, deals with goods *for which payment has been made and accepted or which have been received and accepted.* Section 2-201(3)(c).

As Comment 2 to Subsection 2-201 states in this connection:

Receipt and acceptance either of goods or of the price constitutes an unambiguous overt admission by both parties that a contract actually exists.

Thus if the proposed contract were never executed and Royal nevertheless shipped goods which were accepted, or payment was made and accepted within Subsection 2-201(3)(c), the contract would be enforceable as to the respective amount of goods or payment involved.

Uniform Commercial Code a contract will not be declared unenforceable if certain terms are absent provided certain criteria are met. Thus, Section 2-204(3) states as follows:

Even though one or more terms are left open a contract for sale does not fail for indefiniteness if the parties have intended to make a contract and there is a reasonably certain basis for giving an appropriate remedy.

Thus, the absence of certain terms in a sales contract will not result in unenforceability as long as:

(1) The parties intended to make a contract; and

(2) There is a reasonably certain basis for giving an appropriate remedy.

In the instant situation, should the proposed agreement be signed, it would be clear that there is an intention to make a contract. It is submitted that paragraphs 1, 2, 3 and 4 of the proposed agreement would supply a reasonably certain basis for giving an appropriate remedy in the event of breach by either Stephen or Royal. Hence, the contract is enforceable for Article 2 purposes.

II. MEANING OF THE PROPOSED CONTRACT
(A)   Definition of Contract
(B)   Definition of Agreement

A. Definition of Contract

In order to properly analyze the meaning of the proposed contract, it is necessary to analyze the language contained in the proposed contract in connection with several provisions of the Uniform Commercial Code. The first such provision is Section 1-201(b)(12) which defines a *"contract"* under the Code. That section states as follows:

> ***"Contract"*** *...means the total legal obligation which results from the parties' agreement as affected by this Act and any other applicable rules of law.*

It is readily apparent from reading this definition that in order to ascertain the legal obligations of the parties, one must first know what the parties' "agreement" is, since their contract is primarily the legal consequences of their agreement.

(B) Definition of Agreement

"Agreement", like contract, is a defined term under the Code. It is defined in Section 1-201(b)(3) as:

> *...the bargain of the parties in fact as found in their language or inferred from other circumstances, including course of performance, course of dealing or usage of trade as provided in Section 1-303.*

There are thus five variables set forth in Section 1-201(b)(3) which comprise the agreement and thus affect the contract:

1. *The language used by the parties;*
2. *Course of performance;*
3. *Course of dealing;*
4. *Usage of trade;*
5. *Inferences from other circumstances.*

1. The language used by the parties

As a general proposition, the language of a contract can consist of both the written language of the document and verbal language as well. However, in most situations where a written contract is created, there is a provision like the one in the present case which limits the terms of the contract to those contained in the writing. Clause 8 of the agreement, states that the full agreement is contained in the writing. Therefore, any conversations which contradict that writing would not be included in the agreement:

Terms ... set forth in a writing intended by the parties as a final expression of their agreement ...may not be contradicted by evidence of prior agreement or of a contemporaneous oral agreement ... Section 2-202(1).

However, as Section 2-202(1) goes on to state:

...[the writing] may be explained or supplemented

> *(a) by course of dealing or usage of trade or by course of performance [Section 1-303]; and*

> *(b) by evidence of consistent additional terms unless the court finds the writing to have been intended also as a complete and exclusive statement of the terms of the agreement.*

As will be presently shown, Section 2-202(1)(a) and the other variables listed in Section 1-201(b)(3) can significantly affect the actual meaning of the words used in the writing.

2. Course of Performance
The second element of the agreement is "course of performance."

> *A "**course of performance**" is a sequence of previous conduct between the parties to a particular transaction that exists if:*

> *(1) The agreement of the parties with respect to the transaction involves repeated occasions for performance by a party; and*

> *(2) the other party, with knowledge of the nature of the performance and opportunity for objection to it, accepts the performance or acquiesces in it without objection.[55]*

---

[55] Section 1-303(a)(1)(2). For those states which have not enacted revised Article 1, Course of Performance is found in Section 2-208.

As Royal and Stephen deal over a period of time under this contract, a course of performance may arise. For example, if delivery of boats to Stephen is due on the 5th of each month, but the boats do not arrive until the 11th, if Stephen *'accepts the performance or acquiesces in it without objection'* on a sufficient number of occasions, a course of performance probably will have arisen.

3. Course of Dealing

Since Stephen and Royal have never dealt with one another prior to this agreement, there can be no **course of dealing** when the parties start performing under the proposed agreement.[56]

---

[56] *A "course of dealing" is a sequence of previous conduct concerning previous transactions between the parties to a particular transaction which is fairly to be regarded as establishing a common basis of understanding for interpreting their expressions and other conduct.* Section 1-303(b).

The foregoing definition limits course of dealing to 'previous transactions between the parties'. It does not explicitly state that these need to be business transactions. I believe that it would be error to restrict the reading in that fashion. If individuals have dealt with one and other over time, certainly a 'common basis of understanding' within that section can be established.

4. Usage of Trade

A *"usage of trade"*, however, is always relevant when there is an established industry. Trade usage is defined under Section 1-303(c) which states:

> A **usage of trade** is any practice or method of dealing having such regularity of observance in place, vocation or trade as to justify an expectation that it will be observed with respect to the transaction in question The existence and scope of such a usage are to be proved as facts.....

Where the trade usage involved is contained in written trade code or similar writing, the court [rather than a jury] will interpret the writing:

> It if is established that such a usage is embodied in a written trade code or similar writing the interpretation of the writing is for the court. Section 1-303(c).

It is important at the outset to define precisely which "place, vocation or trade" is involved for obviously this will bear directly on the applicable trade usage. This question is not as easy as it might appear. For example, is the trade involved in the present situation the boating industry? Or is it the wholesale to retail level of the boating industry? In either event, the applicable trade usage will supplement the contract unless the construction of that usage cannot reasonably be construed within the written terms of the contract.[57]

5. Inferences from Other Circumstances

Section 1-201(b)(3) lists course of dealing, course of performance and usage of trade as illustrative of 'other circumstances' which impact on the meaning of the agreement. However, while these are the most common, there may be other things happening which in fact shed light on what the agreement means. These can be brought in as *'inferences from other circumstances'*.

From the foregoing discussion, it is seen that the agreement, and hence the proposed contract in the present situation, will consist primarily of the written agreement and any applicable trade usage. As Stephen and Royal perform under this contract, a course of performance might arise per Section 1-303(a)(1)(2).

---

[57] *Except as otherwise provided in subsection (f), the express terms of an agreement and any applicable course of dealing or usage of trade must be construed wherever reasonable as consistent with each other. If such a construction is unreasonable*

> *(1) express terms prevail over course of performance, course of dealing and usage trade;*

> *(2) course of performance prevails over course of dealing and usage of trade;*

> *(3) course of dealing prevails over usage of trade.*

Section 1-303(e)(1)(2)(3).

III. TERMS SUPPLIED BY THE CODE
(A)   Missing Terms and Some General Obligations
(B)   Warranty of Merchantability

*(A) Missing Terms and Some
General Obligations*

In addition to the terms noted above, various Code provisions bear directly upon the proposed agreement and give meaning thereto. In this connection the Official Comment to Subsection 2-204 notes:

> If the parties intend to enter into a binding agreement, this subsection [2-204(3)] recognizes that agreement as valid in law, despite missing terms, if there is any reasonably certain basis for granting a remedy... [This act makes] provision elsewhere for missing terms needed for performance, open price, remedies and the like.

Various missing terms, general obligations, and rules regarding construction of the contract will be supplied by Part 3 of Article 2; performance by Part 5; and remedies by Part 7 thereof.

Only the more relevant provisions of Parts 3 and 5 will be noted. The general obligations of the parties are stated in Section 2-301:

> *The obligation of the seller is to transfer and deliver and that of the buyer is to accept and pay in accordance with the contract.*

Under the first clause of the contract:

'Royal agrees to supply to Stephen's Boats, Inc., all boats needed by Stephen in connection with the operation of Stephen's Boats, Inc.'

As a result of this language, the contract involved is a **requirements contract**. As such, various rules are set in place by Section 2-306(1):

A term which measures the quantity [of goods to be supplied under the contract] by the requirements of the buyer means such actual...requirements' as may occur in good faith, except that no quantity unreasonably disproportionate to any stated estimate... may be tendered or demanded.

In the instant situation, under the terms of the proposed contract, Royal had agreed to supply all of the requirements of Stephen's Boats, Inc. Thus, as Stephen needs inventory to replace the boats he sells, i.e., when he "requires" more boats, Royal is under a duty to supply all such requirements. As a consequence, the language quoted above in Section 2-306(1) would apply.

In this regard, two things must be noted. First, the requirements which Stephen requests, must be *'actual...requirements as may occur in **good faith.'*** This requires *"honesty in fact and the observance of reasonable commercial standards of fair dealing"* by Stephen per Section 1-201(b)(20). [See footnote 58 on page 83.]

It is also important to note that under the second clause to Section 2-306(1), Stephen may not demand any number of boats which is *"unreasonably disproportionate"* to the amount of boats which he has estimated to Royal that he will need, or, in the alternative to his prior requirements. Thus, should Stephen find himself in an extremely good season and make a heavy demand on Royal, for example, 15 boats in a given month, it may well be that such a demand would be 'unreasonably disproportionate' within the above language. If, however, Stephen had gradually increased his purchase 5, 8, 10 or 12 a month, the demand for 15 boats in a given month might not be disproportionate within that section. As noted however, whatever his requirements from Royal are, however, Stephen must act in good faith.[58]

---

[58] By now, the reader may have become aware of how often the standard of good faith is mentioned in the various Code sections. Of particular significance is Section 1-304 which states:

Every contract or duty within the Uniform Commercial Code imposes an obligation of good faith in its performance or obligation.

Thus, duties imposed by the Code as well as contractual agreements between the parties must be conducted in good faith. The failure to act in 'good faith' can have a tremendous impact. As Comment 1 to Section 1-304 states:

[T]his section means that a failure to perform or enforce in good faith, a specific duty or obligation under the contract, constitutes a breach of that contract or makes unavailable, under the particular circumstances, a remedial right or power.

The definition of good faith under amended Article 1 differs significantly from its predecessor in as much as it requires [except in Article 5] 'honesty in fact and the observance of reasonable commercial standards of fair dealing' per Section 1-201(b)(20). The earlier version only requires 'honesty in fact' per Section 1-201(19).

In the case under consideration, commercial reasonableness would be required in any event since both parties are merchants, and Article 2 requires 'honesty in fact and the observance of reasonable commercial standards of fair dealing in the trade' per

Under the above contract, however, the unreasonably disproportionate language and its possible detrimental effect on Stephen will be mitigated inasmuch as Royal is under a duty to use its best efforts to supply all boats which Stephen orders. This follows from Section 2-306(2) which applies to the instant situation:

A lawful agreement by either the seller or the buyer for exclusive dealing in the kind of goods concerned imposes unless otherwise agreed an obligation by the seller to use best efforts to supply the goods and by the buyer to use best efforts to promote their sale.

Under the second "WHEREAS" clause of the proposed agreement, Stephen's Boats will be the exclusive distributor for Royal in the south Florida area. Hence, Royal must 'use best efforts' to get the boats to Stephen and Stephen must 'use best efforts' to promote the sale of the boats. These requirements should, of course, cause no problem to either party. Obviously, it is in Royal's best interests to supply all boats which Stephen needs inasmuch as sales to him will generate profits to Royal. Stephen, of course, under the terms of the agreement may not sell any other boats besides

---

Section 2-103(1)(b). The one exception to the commercial reasonableness requirement for 'good faith' under the amended version is that in Article 5, 'good faith' does not include the observance of reasonable commercial standards, but instead only requires 'honesty in fact'. Section 5-102(a)(7). While I am certain the drafters had good reason for this exclusion, I believe negating that standard in Letters of Credit is error. Nevertheless, that is the state of the law.

Royal's without express written consent from them first. This, plus the profitability of selling Royal Boats, anyway, should insure that Stephen uses his best efforts to sell those boats.

(B) Warranty of Merchantability

Another important provision which Part 3 of Article 2 will supply in the instant situation is that the goods sold by Royal to Stephen will be "merchantable." This warranty is implied when goods are sold by a merchant.[59] A **merchant** is described as one who, among other things, *'deals in goods of the kind involved.*[60] Inasmuch as Royal deals in the kind of boats involved in the contract, it would obviously be a merchant with respect to those goods. What is or is not **merchantable** is defined under Section 2-314. Under that section, the more relevant definitions in the instant situation would probably be as follows:

> *(2) Goods to be merchantable must be at least as:*
>
> > *(a) pass without objection in the trade under the contract description;*
> > *...*

---

[59] *Unless excluded or modified (Section 2-316), a warranty that the goods shall be merchantable is implied in the contract for their sale if the seller is a merchant with respect to goods of that kind.* Section 2-314(1).

[60] *"Merchant" means a person who deals in good of the kind or otherwise by his occupation holds himself out as having knowledge or skill peculiar to the practices or goods involved in the transaction...* Section 2-104(1).

(c) are fit for the ordinary purposes for which such goods are used.[61]

As you can see, in the above quoted definition, both the trade standard[62] and the ordinary purpose for which such goods are used will be the determining factors in deciding whether or not the goods are merchantable. One other thing to note is that under Subsection (3) to 2-314, implied warranties may also arise from course of dealing or usage of trade.[63]   Thus, to the extent that Royal ships Stephen boats of a certain quality over a long period of time, a course of dealing warranty might arise between Stephen and Royal that the boats shall at least be of that quality. If, thereafter, Royal should start delivering boats below the quality which were initially delivered and thereafter delivered for a long enough period of time, an argument could be made that an implied warranty from course of dealing had been breached. Similarly, if the trade has certain standards of quality, a warranty can arise from those standards.

---

[61] The full text of Subsection 2-314(2) is reprinted in the Statutory Supplement.

[62] Trade standards are an extremely strong component in any commercial setting. Those standards establish baselines from which to analyze facts in similar settings. Trade journals provide very valuable information which can be used to increase understanding and analysis of any UCC problem. Content in trade journals has impact under the definition of agreement and contract.

[63] *Unless excluded or modified (Section 2-316) other implied warranties may arise from course of dealing or usage of trade.* Section 2-314(3).

(C) Proposed Contract as an
Installment Contract

The proposed contract would be classified as an installment contract under Section 2-612(1):

*An **installment contract** is one which requires or authorizes the delivery of goods in separate lots to be separately accepted...*

As a result of this classification, the basic rule regarding Stephen's ability to reject non conforming goods is changed. In a typical situation:

...[I]f the goods or the tender of delivery fail in any respect to conform to the contract, the buyer may
   (a) reject the whole; or
   (b) accept the whole, or
   (c) accept any commercial unit or units and reject the rest.
Section 2-601(a)(b)(c).

In the installment contract situation, any non conformity must "*substantially impair the value of the installment*":

The buyer may reject any installment which is non conforming if the non conformity substantially impairs the value of that installment and cannot be cured.... Section 2-612(2).

Section 2-612(3) goes on to state:

Whenever non-conformity or default with respect to one or more installments substantially impairs the value of the whole contract there is a breach of the whole. But the aggrieved party reinstates the contract if he accepts a non conforming installment without seasonably notifying of cancellation or if he brings an action with respect only to past installments or demands performance as to future installments.

A few other points should be briefly noted. First, had the contract not called for delivery in installments, and if nothing had been said on that point, Royal would be required to deliver boats called for under the contract in a single lot; second, since there is no time limitation specified for certain action by the parties, the Code requires that any action be taken within a **reasonable time**:

Whether a time for taking action required by [the Uniform Commercial Code] is reasonable depends on the nature, purpose, and circumstances of the action. Section 1-205(a).

Parenthetically, it should be noted that the Code would supply a place of delivery if one weren't specified in the contract, and that if the parties had not agreed on a price of the goods or a method for arriving at one (highly unlikely in this situation but quite possible in certain commercial settings), and had nevertheless intended to enter a contract, the Code would supply the price.[64]

---

[64] These points of law result from Sections 2-307, 2-308, 2-309 and 2-305 respectively. (They are reproduced in full in the Statutory Supplement).

Having concluded that the contract will not fail for indefiniteness and having discussed some of the terms which the Code will supply, a discussion of the shipment terms will be undertaken.

IV.   SHIPMENT TERMS
(A)   F.O.B. Shipment Contract
(B)   Shipment Under Reservations

(A) F.O.B. Shipment Contract

The terms of shipment call for delivery by Royal F.O.B. Atlanta, shipment to be under negotiable bill of lading to the order of Royal. This type of contract is called an *F.O.B. shipment contract* under reservation. For the purpose of analysis, it will be broken down into two categories, the "F.O.B. shipment" nature of the contract and the "reservation" nature of the contract.

Section 2-319 of the Code governs F.O.B. shipment contracts. Section 2-319(1)(a) is specifically on point. That section reads as follows:

Unless otherwise agreed the term, F.O.B. (which means free on board) at a named place, even though used only in connection with the stated price, is a delivery term under which:

(a) when the term is F.O.B. the place of shipment, the seller must at that place ship the goods in the manner provided in this article (Section 2-504) and bear the expense and risk of putting them into the possession of the carrier...[65]

---

[65] As can be seen, the expense and risk of putting goods into the possession of the carrier is upon the seller in an F.O.B. shipment contract. In addition, Section 2-319(1)(a) requires that the seller ship

Thus, since the terms of the contract are F.O.B. Atlanta (the place of shipment), Royal would be under a duty to put the boats into the possession of a carrier at the expense and risk of Royal. It is very important to note in this connection that at the point in time that Royal complies with Section 2-319(1)(a), and otherwise conforms with the terms of the contract, the *risk of loss* of the boats passes on to Stephen's Boats, Inc. This derives from Section 2-509(1)(a) which states in pertinent part:

----

goods in a certain way in this type of contract. This is covered by Section 2-504 referred to in Section 2-319(1)(a) which states as follows:

> *Where the seller is required or authorized to send the goods to the buyer and the contract does not require him to deliver them at a particular destination, then unless otherwise agreed he must*
>
> *(a) put the goods in the possession of such a carrier and make such a contract for their transportation as may be reasonable having regard to the nature of the goods and other circumstances of the case; and*
>
> *(b) obtain and promptly deliver or tender in due form any document necessary to enable the buyer to obtain possession of the goods or otherwise required by the agreement or by usage of trade; and*
>
> *(c) promptly notify the buyer of the shipment.*

Section 2-504(a)(b)(c).

Requirements (a) and (c) are self-explanatory; requirements set out in Subsection (b) will be discussed later in Doug's memorandum.

Where the contract requires or authorizes the seller to ship the goods by carrier:

(a) If it does not require him to deliver them at a particular destination, the risk of loss passes to the buyer when the goods are duly delivered to the carrier...

Thus, if the boats are properly delivered by Royal to the carrier within Subsection 2-319(1)(a), and the boats are subsequently destroyed by fire or the like, that loss would fall upon Stephen's Boats, Inc.[66] Is it vital therefore, that if the terms of the contract are accepted as they are, Stephen get adequate insurance to cover the possibility of such a loss.

(B) Shipment Under Reservation

The second phase of the contract with respect to the shipment is the *shipment under reservation* provision. Shipments under reservation are covered by Section 2-505. Of particular applicability to the

---

[66] It is important to note, however, that if Royal had shipped nonconforming goods of a nature which would give Stephen a right of rejection, Royal would have been in breach of contract at the time the goods were shipped, and there would be a different result on the risk of loss matter. In such a situation, the risk of loss would not pass to Stephen. This is covered by Section 2-510(1) which states as follows:

Where a tender or delivery of goods so fails to conform to the contract as to give a right of rejection, the risk of their loss remains on the seller until cure or acceptance.

Furthermore, where goods are required to be delivered at a particular destination, risk of loss would not pass until the goods were so delivered. Section 2-509(1)(b).

proposed contract is Section 2-505(1)(a) which states in pertinent part that:

Where the seller has identified goods to the contract by or before shipment:

(a) his procurement of a negotiable bill of lading to his own order or otherwise reserves in him a security interest in the goods....

Thus, when Royal has the bill of lading (discussed below) made out to its order per the contract, it will have a security interest in the boats covered by that document. 'Security interest' is defined under Section 1-201(b)(35) and states in relevant part as follows:

"Security interest" *means an interest in personal property or fixtures which secures payment or performance of an obligation....*

The interest in the present situation would be Royal's interest in the boats. And, of course, the obligation being referred to is, Stephen's obligation to pay money as called for by the contract. In order to explain how Royal's procurement of a negotiable bill of lading to its order reserves a security interest for Royal, it is necessary to look at several provisions of Article 7 which in part deals with the movement of goods.

V. DELIVERY OF GOODS

(A) Bill of Lading

(B) Person Entitled to Take Possession of Goods; Person Entitled Under the Document.

(A) Bill of Lading[67]

When the carrier receives the boats, it will issue a bill a document known as a *bill of lading.* This document will acknowledge the carrier's possession of the boats, and in addition will contain a contract for delivery of the boats. In such a situation, the carrier is called a **bailee**.[68] The person from whom the carrier receives the goods is called the

---

[67] "Bill of Lading" means a document evidencing the receipt of goods for shipment issued by a person engaged in the business of transporting or forwarding goods.... Section 1-201(b)(6).

A bill of lading is a document of title under Section 1-201(b)(16). That section states as follows:

"Document of title" includes dock warrant, dock receipt, warehouse receipt or order for the delivery of goods, and also any other document which in the regular course of business or financing is treated as adequately evidencing that the person or possession of it is entitled to receive, hold and dispose of the document and the goods it covers. To be a document of title a document must purport to be issued by or addressed to a bailee and purport to cover goods in the bailee's possession which are either identified or are fungible portions of an identified mass.

The use of documents in commercial transactions is extremely important and will be discussed in some detail in this book. For now it should simply be borne in mind that in many situations the document is treated as the equivalent of the goods it covers and that transfer of the document or rights there under will generally be equivalent to a transfer for the goods so covered.

[68] *"Bailee" means the person who by ... bill of lading or other document of title acknowledges possession of goods and contracts to deliver them.* Section 7-102(a)(1).

consignor,[69] here, Royal. Since the contract calls for delivery to the order of Royal, Royal would also be the *consignee*.[70]

A document of title can take one of two forms. It can be **negotiable** or **non negotiable**. Section 7-104 specifies when a document is negotiable or non-negotiable:

> (a) *Except as otherwise provided in subsection (c) a document of title is negotiable if by its terms the goods are to be delivered to bearer or to the order of a named person;*
> (b) *A document of title other than one described in subsection (a) is non-negotiable.*
> (c) *A document of title is non-negotiable if, at the time it is issued, the document has a conspicuous legend, however expressed, that it is non-negotiable.*

In the instant situation, the goods are to be delivered to the order of a named person, Royal. Thus, the form of the bill of lading falls squarely within Section 7-104(a). As is obvious from the quoted definition, whether or not a bill of lading [or any document of title] is negotiable or non-negotiable is simply a matter of form. To the extent that the bill of lading does not have the proper form,

---

[69] *"Consignor" means the person named in a bill as the person from whom the goods have been received for shipment.* Section 7-102(a)(4).

[70] *"Consignee" means the person named in a bill to whom or to whose order the bill promises delivery.* Section 7-102(a)(3).

it is non-negotiable.[71] The distinction between negotiable and non-negotiable documents pervades all of Article 7. In fact, the last sentence to the first paragraph of the comments to Section 7-104 states as follows:

> *The distinction between negotiable and non-negotiable documents in this section makes the most important sub-classification employed in this article....*

There are many reasons under Article 7 as to why this is so; it is, however, beyond the scope of this memorandum to discuss all of these. In the instant situation, the question for our purposes is: how does procurement of a negotiable bill of lading to the order of Royal reserve a security interest in Royal? That is, how does Royal's procurement of a negotiable bill of lading to its order *secure payment or performance of an obligation,* per Section 1-201(b)(35). The simple straightforward answer is that the carrier would be required to deliver the boats only to Royal, inasmuch as Royal would be the holder of the negotiable document (bill of lading), and delivery to anyone else would be

---

[71] Section 7-104(c) previously quoted, states as follows:

(c) A document of title is nonnegotiable if, at the time it is issued, the document has a conspicuous legend, however expressed, that it is nonnegotiable.

This provision is contained in the newest amendments to Article 7 and is absent under Section 7-104 as it exists in those states which have not enacted the revised version. The amendment is logical insofar as it indicates a clear intent of the issuer, and presumably the consignor, that the document be treated as nonnegotiable. The importance of negotiability will be seen shortly in Doug's memorandum.

unlawful. Again, some further analysis is required to illustrate how this works under Article 7.

(B) Person Entitled to Possession of the Goods; Person Entitled under the Document

The first relevant section in dealing with this question is Section 7-403(a) which reads in pertinent part as follows:

The bailee shall deliver the goods to a person entitled under the document of title if the person complies with subsections (b) [dealing with bailee's lien] *and (c)* [surrender or notation of deliveries on document of title]....

As previously noted, the bailee in the instant situation would be the carrier, who, per Section 7-403(a) noted above, must deliver to a *"person entitled under a document,"* which is defined under Section 7-102(a)(9)) as follows:

Person entitled under the document *means the holder, in the case of a negotiable document of title, or the person to which delivery of the goods is to be made by the terms of, or pursuant to written instructions in a record under, a nonnegotiable document of title.*

As indicated, since a negotiable bill would be used here, the "person entitled under the document" would be the holder of that document. ***Holder*** is defined under Section 1-201(b)(21)(B) as *'the person in possession of a negotiable tangible document of title if the goods are deliverable to bearer or to the order of the person in possession'.*

Thus, as long as Royal maintains possession of the negotiable document of title issued to its order, Royal is the person entitled under the document as the holder of the negotiable document. Should the carrier deliver to anyone other than the holder, it would be an improper delivery for which the carrier would be liable. The carrier knows this and will only deliver to Royal or the subsequent holder of the document. Royal doesn't want the boats; it simply wants to maintain possession of the bill of lading until it gets paid.

In practice, the transaction might proceed as follows: First, Royal will ship the boats and have a negotiable bill of lading issued to its order. It will then draw a draft on Stephen's Boats, Inc.[72] The

---

[72] A 'draft' is a negotiable instrument under Article 3 of the Code. Section 3-104(e). Negotiable instruments will be discussed in detail later in the book. At this time, the draft should be conceptualized as a "check" drawn on a non-bank-here, Stephen. Thus Royal will create an instrument which looks like the following:

Atlanta, Georgia

(Date)

To: Stephen Seller, 16 Boat Lane, Miami, Florida

At Sight

Pay to the order of Royal Boats, Inc. $35,000.00

Thirty-five thousand and no/100 _____ Dollars

Per Sales/Distributorship Agreement

(Date)

M. E. Fabre

Treasurer, Royal Boats, Inc.

documents[73] will be taken to Royal's bank and indorsed[74] to that bank. The purpose of taking it to that bank is to initiate the collection process with respect to the draft and to effectuate transfer of the bill of lading to Stephen upon payment of the draft.

Part 5 of Article 4 deals with the collection of documentary drafts, and will be briefly discussed here as an aid to understanding the present transaction. The initial duty of Royal's bank is set forth in Section 4-501:

A bank which takes a documentary draft for collection must present or send the draft and accompanying documents for presentment...

---

[73] The bill of lading together with the draft is called a *"documentary draft"* since it is *"a draft to be presented for acceptance or payment if specified documents ... are to be received by the drawee or other payor before acceptance or payment of the draft."* Section 4-104(a)(6).

[74] Indorsement and delivery of the document of title (the bill of lading) will result in *"negotiation"* of the bill of lading to the bank Section 7-501(a)(1). [This section and the concept of negotiation is discussed in detail later in the book].

"Indorsement" means a signature, other than that of a signer as maker, drawer, or acceptor, that alone or accompanied by other words is made on an instrument for the purpose of negotiating the instrument.... Section 3-204(a).

Thus, when Royal's bank takes the documentary draft, it will send the documents into the collection process. When they arrive at South Dade (either directly from Royal's bank or via another bank), South Dade will inform Stephen of the arrival of the documents. Stephen will then come to the bank to examine the documents to see if the called for boats were noted therein.

If the draft requires payment by Stephen within three days, he will be required to pay before he can get the documents; otherwise his acceptance will be sufficient:

> *Unless otherwise instructed and except as provided in Article 5 a bank presenting a documentary draft:*
>
> > *(a) must deliver the documentation to the drawee on acceptance of the draft if it is payable more than three days after presentment; otherwise only on payment.* Section 4-503(a).

The *'drawee'* would be Stephen:

> ***"Drawee"** means a person ordered in a draft to make payment.* Section 3-103(a)(4).

Royal, as the person ordering Stephen to pay would be the 'drawer':

> ***"Drawer"** means a person who signs or is identified in a draft as a person ordering payment.* Section 3-103(a)(5).

If the draft is payable more than three days after presentment and Stephen properly accepts the draft as presented, he will have agreed to pay the amount specified in the draft:

> **"Acceptance"** *means the drawee's signed agreement to pay a draft as presented. It must be written on the draft and may consist of the drawee's signature alone....* Section 3-409(a).

Upon the payment, or proper acceptance by Stephen, South Dade will release the bill of lading properly endorsed to Stephen, allowing him to take delivery of the boats since he will be the holder of the negotiable bill. If he fails to pay (or in a proper case, accept) the draft, the bank will not deliver the documents to him and he will be unable to pick up the goods. Hence, by structuring the transaction in a shipment under reservation manner, Royal "secures payment" from Stephen before he can obtain possession of the boats.

* * *

When Alan finished reading Doug's memorandum, he wanted to talk to Doug. He had some questions regarding some of the things in the memo. He asked his secretary to get Doug in for him as soon as she could. About two minutes later Doug showed up. Alan raised his head and told Doug to come in.

"I enjoyed reading your memorandum and I think you did a very good job, especially in view of the time constraints you were working under. I do, however, have one or two questions I would like to ask if you have time. Do you?"

"Of course," said Doug, thinking to himself he really wouldn't mind if he didn't see Alan for awhile. After all, there *were* other partners in the firm for whom Doug was doing work. He really wasn't the personal servant of Alan, but apparently Alan didn't realize that.

"Doug, the first question I have is regarding this security interest that you talk about under Section 2-505 and the shipment under reservation and all that. It was my understanding that if you were going to have a security interest in goods you had to be under Article 9. Isn't that so? And don't you have to file a financing statement and do everything else you are supposed to do under this situation?"

"Actually, Alan, there is a section under Article 9 which deals with this type of situation. Unlike other security interests noted, however, you don't have the same requirements regarding filing and the like. Do you have a Code with you?" Doug asked, whereupon Alan reached around and gave his Code to Doug. Doug opened it to Section 9-110 which read:

A security interest arising under Section 2-505 ... is subject to this article. However, until the debtor obtains possession of the goods:

> *(1) the security interest is enforceable, even if Section 9-203(b)(3) has not been satisfied;*
> *(2) filing is not required to perfect the security interest;*
> *(3) the rights of the secured party after default by the debtor are governed by Article 2. . .; and*
> *(4) the security interest has priority over a conflicting security interest created by the debtor.*

Alan nodded and said, "Doug, I don't understand why this provision exists."

"Well," Doug said, "as you can see, all of the Article 9 requirements will apply as soon as the debtor, here Stephen, has possession of the goods. Until that time, no creditor should lend him money on the strength of those goods. On the other hand, once he takes possession, a creditor is entitled to rely on those goods as belonging to Stephen. If the files at the Florida Secured Transaction Registry showed no financing statement covering them, then a lender would lend if he were so inclined. Of course, once the seller gets paid, he doesn't care what happens and has no need to maintain security in the transaction so he won't bother filing."

"Very interesting," Alan said. "One other thing I want to ask you before you leave. I know you are busy, but you know this deal has to close as soon as possible and Stephen, I think, will be a good client for us." (Of course, the fact that Alan was getting 10% of the profits of the boat business *may* have affected his view of the importance of the file.) "That question is regarding the requirement that Stephen has to pay for the boats before he even gets to look at them. Does this mean he has no inspection rights and that if the boats are non-conforming, Stephen can't complain later on that they are defective? It seems to me that he has a real problem there. Does he?"

"No," said Doug. "Since the contract requires payment prior to inspection of the goods, Stephen relinquishes no rights of inspection or the like by making such payment[75]

---

[75] Section 2-512(2) states:

Payment [before inspection, when required by the contract] *...does not constitute an acceptance of goods or impair the buyer's right to inspect or any of his remedies.*

against conforming documents.[76] However, even if the documents conform, when the boats arrive, Royal will ·have to deliver boats which conform to the terms of the contract."[77]

"Okay," said Alan, "Stephen has to pay when the documents arrive. But," he continued, "what happens if the boats show up defective? Can he get out of the contract?"

Buyer's general right to inspect prior to payment or acceptance is recognized in Section 2-513(1):

Unless otherwise agreed and subject to subsection (3), where goods are tendered or delivered…the buyer has a right before payment or acceptance to inspect them at any reasonable place and in any reasonable manner….

[76] The requirement that Royal must tender conforming documents comes from Section 2-503(5)(a) which states:

Where the contract requires the seller to deliver documents:

(a) he must tender all such documents in correct form….

Tender through customary banking channels is sufficient…

Section 2-503(5)(b).

[77] *Tender of delivery requires that the seller put and hold conforming goods at the buyer's disposition and give the buyer any notification reasonably necessary to enable him to take delivery.* Section 2-503(1).

Section 2-503(1) goes on to state in connection with the foregoing that:

The manner, time and place of tender are determined by the agreement and this article and in particular

(a) Tender must be at a reasonable hour, and if it is of goods they must be kept available for the period reasonably necessary to enable the buyer to take possession; but

(b) Unless otherwise agreed the buyer must furnish facilities suited to the receipt of the goods.

"Of course," replied Doug, "the basic rule is that Stephen is entitled to reject goods which don't conform to the contract per Section 2-601.

And, if you recall, since this is an installment contract, he can only reject an installment when the defect '*substantially impairs the value of that installment and cannot be cured*' per Section 2-612(2)."

About this time in the discussion, Alan was wishing that he had taken the time to learn all of the Uniform Commercial Code instead of hoping it would go away.

"What does 'cure' mean?" asked Alan.

Cure is discussed under Section 2-508. "May I see your Code again?" he asked.

Alan handed his Code to Doug who opened it to Section 2-508 which states:

> *When any tender or delivery by the seller is rejected because non-conforming and the time for performance has not yet expired, the seller may reasonably notify the buyer of his intention to cure and may then, within the contract time, make a conforming tender.*

> *Where the buyer rejects a non-conforming tender which the seller had reasonable grounds to believe would be acceptable with or without money allowance, the seller may, if he seasonably notifies the buyer, have a further reasonable time to substitute a conforming tender.*

"As you can see," said Doug, "Section 2-508 contemplates two different situations. Under Subsection (1) the time for seller's performance 'has not yet expired.' Thus, if Royal is to supposed to deliver boats by a certain date, e.g. January 3, 2006 which arrive on December 15,

2005, and which are properly rejected by Stephen, Royal will have until January 3 to tender conforming goods."

"What about Subsection (2)?" asked Alan.

"As you can see," said Doug, pointing to the subsection, "if Royal *had reasonable grounds to believe the boats would be acceptable, it has a further reasonable time to substitute a conforming tender.*"

"What if they choose not to?" asked Alan.

"In that situation," responded Doug, "Stephen could do one of a few things. First of all, he could **cover.**[78] If he does that, he *may recover from the seller as damages the difference between the cost of cover and the contract price together with any incidental or consequential damages ... less expenses saved in consequence of the breach.*"[79]

"For example," said Doug, "he may be able to get lost profits.[80] If he chose to accept the boats in the condition

---

[78] *After a breach within the preceding section, the buyer may "cover" by making in good faith and without unreasonable delay, any reasonable purchase of or contract to purchase goods in substitution for those due from the seller.* Section 2-712(1).

[79] Section 2-712(2).

[80] Section 2-715(2)(a) states:

Consequential damages resulting from the seller's breach include:

(a) any loss resulting from general or particular requirements and needs of which the seller at the time of contracting has reason to know and which could not reasonably be prevented by cover or otherwise.

This has been construed to include lost profits; please note, however, Stephen has a duty to mitigate "by cover or otherwise" if reasonably possible.

they were sent, he could sue Royal for damages for breach of warranty."[81]

"Thank you very much, Doug," Alan said. "I appreciate your time." Just to make Doug feel extra good (and work harder, making Alan more money), Alan added, "I really think you are going to go places in this firm."

Now that he was completely satisfied that everything was in order, Alan telephoned Stephen. He told Stephen his opinion that the contract was in order and recommended that the agreement for sale be executed. Stephen came down that afternoon and executed the agreement which was immediately mailed to Royal.

---

[81] *The measure of damages for breach of warranty* [for accepted goods] *is the difference at the time and place of acceptance between the value of the goods accepted and the value they would have had if they had been warranted, unless special circumstances show proximate damages of a different amount.* Section 2-714(2).

Section 2

On October 14, 2005, the loan proceeds were disbursed according to the terms of the loan agreement. Accordingly, $400,000 was immediately placed in the Stephen's Boats, Inc., account at South Dade Bank. On October 24, 2005 the initial inventory of twelve boats arrived. The boats were of various sizes, ranging from a small $12,500 speedboat up to $146,000 sailboat. These boats were placed in the showroom of Stephen's Boats, Inc., along with some 500 brochures of Royal which contained a complete description of all the boats that Royal manufactured. Stephen hoped that certain customers who couldn't find exactly what they wanted in the showroom would see that the boats could be ordered.

Stephen's first month of business went rather well. Within the first ten days, he sold two of the smaller speedboats, both in the range of $16,000. In addition, he had a buyer interested in the large 44-foot sailboat. His name was Gregg Zoringo, nicknamed "Dunker" because of the famous triple twisting dunks he made when he played professional basketball with the New York Blues.

On November 7, 2005, Stephen got some good news and some bad news. The good news was that Dunker wanted to come back and take a look at the sailboat again. He had telephoned Stephen to find out if it was still there and Stephen informed him that it was. Dunker sounded very eager to buy and Stephen felt he might be able to make a really big sale. The bad news was that a gentleman by the name of Onus Primo who had purchased one of the $16,000 speedboats was starting to complain that it was not working properly. In fact, Stephen had had a phone call from Mr. Primo's lawyer informing Stephen of the complaints with respect to the boat. A letter was to follow shortly.

On the afternoon of November 7, 2005, Dunker came in. As always, he was wearing his New York Blues warm-up jacket, gym shorts and his team socks. Although

Dunker had been out of professional basketball for about eight years, he insisted on wearing his warm-up jacket or team blazer everywhere he went. In fact, even when he went out for social occasions and wore the team blazer, he left the warm-up jacket in the car.

"Stephen," Dunker said, "as you know, I am very interested in purchasing this 44-footer of yours. However, I expect to keep the boat for a long time and I really don't think I can buy this boat unless it has some modifications made on it."

"What did you have in mind?" Stephen asked.

"There are several things," said Dunker.

Stephen said, "I will be only too happy to do whatever I can, Dunker." (He insisted that everybody call him Dunker.)

"What would you like me to do?"

"Well, Stephen, first of all I would like to have the living quarters completely redesigned so that I can fit into them comfortably. After all, I am 7'2" tall and the sleeping quarters look like they were made for somebody about half my size. I would like for you to knock out the wall separating the two bedrooms below so that I can more comfortably move about. Also, I would like the steering column redesigned and raised so that I can steer standing up without having the steering wheel at my waist. Finally, and most importantly, I want this boat to reflect my playing days with the New York Blues."

"How?" Stephen asked.

"Well," Dunker said, "first of all I would like to have the outside of the boat display the team insignia of the New York Blues." He told Stephen he would like to have it painted in the team design and in addition wanted to have the face of the team mascot, the boll weevil, carved and placed around the side of the boat. That is, he wanted about ten different carvings of the boll weevil with blue eyes placed all the way around the boat. In addition, he wanted the bathroom tiled with the face of the boll weevil.

Stephen had heard that professional athletes were weird. He was trying very hard not to make a value judgment about Dunker, but tiling the bathroom in the New York Blues boll weevil insignia? Very strange, Stephen thought to himself.

"I think it is an excellent idea," Stephen said. "It will be truly a unique boat. None like it. You will be proud to own it. I do have a problem however," Stephen said.

"What's that?" Dunker asked.

"Well, I don't believe we can do all that to this particular boat at a cost that is anywhere near reasonable. What I do think we can do, however, is get a hold of the manufacturer in Atlanta and tell them exactly what you want and have them make the boat exactly to your specifications. How does that sound?"

"Great," Dunker said, "How long will it take?"

"I don't think it will take more than two months," replied Stephen. "Is that okay?"

"Certainly," Dunker said. "I'll tell you what, let's go into your office right now and make sure you have written down everything I want."

Whereupon Stephen and Dunker went into Stephen's office and basically confirmed what they had discussed outside. While Dunker was there, Stephen called the main office at Royal and placed the order for the boat. When he got off the phone, he asked Dunker if he had ordered everything that he had requested. Dunker assured Stephen that he had and Stephen told Dunker that he would get back to him as progress on the boat was reported to Stephen.

Stephen was feeling especially good at having sold a 44-footer. His profit margin on the larger boats was about 3 or 4 times as much as on the smaller boats. He figured he could make about $28,000 profit on the big boat and maybe he would be able to squeeze a few thousand dollars extra out of it for the New York Blues work, above and beyond the cost of the work to him. Bathroom tiled in boll weevil, he thought to himself. Oh well, Stephen didn't really care as long as the guy paid for the boat and Stephen could make his profit.

Inasmuch as Stephen had already concluded he was going to make $28,000 on this gentleman, he decided that perhaps he would go out and look at the sports car he had wanted to price for a long time. The new models had just come out and Stephen had been looking at the XGT-TGB-13. The XGT-TGB was as exciting a thought as boating used to be to Stephen. The thought of getting himself a new car and seeing something for all the hard work he had been putting in seemed like a really good idea.

Stephen went to three dealerships. The disparity in prices between the first two dealerships and the third one was really rather startling to Stephen. At the last dealership, Stephen was told he could have the XGT for $31,500 while the other dealerships were charging between $37,500 and $39,500. Stephen said he would like some time to think about it, even though it was a good deal, because he really hadn't been that certain that he was going to buy that day. The salesman, however, said that the only reason they were offering it at $31,500 was because they were trying to meet a quota imposed by the head dealership. If they sold this car they would have sold 12 cars in the first 10 days of the new model season which would be a really exceptional start for them.

"In other words," Stephen said, "if I don't pick it up today, I might not be able to pick it up at this price tomorrow. Is that right?"

"That's right," the dealer said. Thus, Stephen made the decision to buy the car that day.

He was told he would have to put down $10,500 in cash, plus his old car, and sign a conditional sales contract calling for payment in the amount of $650 per month for three years. Stephen, of course, was very familiar with the sales contract at this point in time as it was the type of contract under which his business was operating. He also knew that to the extent there was a security interest on the dealership's inventory at the time he bought the car, he took free of that interest, as did the people purchasing boats from his boat dealership.[82]

On the drive home, Stephen was pleased with how the car performed. Plus, it was a convertible and Stephen *knew* everyone was looking at him with envy as he drove by. He tried not to look back but he just couldn't help it. He couldn't wait to tell Alan.

As he walked to his apartment, the phone was ringing. Coincidently, it was Alan.

"Guess what I did today?" Stephen asked.

"I have something more important to ask you," Alan said.

"What's that?" Stephen said.

"Well, you know this guy George Friedman?"

"Isn't that the guy you do all the legal work for?" Stephen asked.

"Yes," said Alan. "Well, it turns out that George wants to go back to Chicago as soon as possible and he wants to sell his clothing outlet. It's a wholesale joint off the expressway."

"So?" Stephen said.

"Well, he is letting it go at a really cheap price. I was wondering if you would be interested in going in on it with me as a partner? I will do all the legal work," Alan said.

"Why do you think it is such a good deal?" Stephen asked. "Furthermore, even if it is a good deal, you know I don't have very much cash."

---

[82] *See* footnote 82 in Appendix I on page 356.

"You don't need very much cash," Alan said. "As a matter of fact, I believe we can get in it for about $18,000 cash a piece. Second, I know it is a good deal because I have handled the legal matters and financing for this company for the last eight years. It just happens that George wants out and I knew it and I told him that I might be interested. What do you think?"

"If you think it is a good deal, go ahead and include me, Alan. After all, I am in business now and if you think that this is the right move to make, then I will make it with you."

"I'll tell you what," Alan said, "I'll try to get you and myself in for about $12,500 cash apiece. George will take a long-term note for the rest of it."

"Okay, Alan," Stephen said.

"Listen," Alan said, "I'm going to try to get a hold of George right away. I'll get back to you later."

At which time Alan hung up the phone without giving Stephen the chance to tell him of the new XGT he bought. Oh well, Stephen thought, he might as well to show it to his parents because he *knew* they would be proud of him.

Section 3

In order to discuss the purchase of the wholesale outlet, Stephen and Alan set a meeting for December 21, 2005. George had to return to Chicago for some business and personal matters, and was going to go over everything with his attorney in Chicago. So, the meeting was scheduled accordingly. Stephen and Alan realized that they were starting to meet rather regularly about these various business proposals and decided to set a meeting for the first of every other month unless either one wished to cancel for some reason.

"The deal looks great," Alan said. "It looks even better than it did when we spoke before."

"Why?" Stephen asked.

"Well, I have some good news. It seems that Mr. Primo, the manager at the clothing outlet, has agreed to stay on in his present capacity if we would like him to. In addition, I have discussed the possibility of having Mr. Primo sign with us on the note and hopefully get George to take less cash from us." He told Stephen that he would work that out later.

"In any event," Stephen asked, "how much is it going to cost me to get into the deal as it is presently set?"

"Eighteen thousand dollars at the outside," Alan said. "And probably, I would say $12,000. Can you get it together?"

"I think so. But I will tell you something, I would prefer to have Mr. ... what's his name ...?"

"Mr. Primo," Alan said. "Onus Primo."

"Mr. Primo sign." Stephen stopped then for a second and asked if this guy was about 5'10" and carried a knife everywhere he went with a lot of keys hanging on it. Alan nodded.

"That's right," Stephen said. "This is the guy who bought a boat from me just after we opened and who is having trouble with it right now."

"What kind of trouble?"

"It appears that the steering was jamming when it was turned to the left. At least that is what he says. I sent Jerry out there today to look at the boat. I should hear from him tomorrow."

"Well," asked Alan, "do you not want to go in on the deal with Primo? We don't need him if you can come up with $18,000."

"No," said Stephen. "If the guy really knows the business, he will probably be good to have around. Besides, for all I know, something really is wrong with the boat, and if it is I want to fix it."

"Very good," Alan said. "By the way, I heard you bought an XGT!"

"That is one of the things I wanted to talk to you about," said Stephen. "I have been having so much trouble with the car that it spends most of its time in the shop. They keep telling me they are going to fix it and when I get it back it usually works a day or two and starts breaking down again. I can't have that," Stephen said. "I have to get to work every morning and I just can't have the car stopping on me all the time."

"Do you want the car or do you want to get rid of it?" Alan asked.

Stephen said he really enjoyed the car when it worked and he would like to get it fixed and keep it. But, he said, if it continued breaking down he would have no choice but to get rid of it. "What should I do?" he asked.

"Listen," said Alan. "I will write the dealer a letter this afternoon and see if we can get a little action on this car. If not, then you can decide what you want to do with the car."

"Thanks a lot," said Stephen. "Listen, go ahead on that deal and let me know what comes up."

"Great," said Alan. "I think we will get this car thing straightened out right away and I will get back to you early next week."

Whereupon Stephen went back to work and Alan immediately went back to the office and dictated the following letter:

Dear Dealer:

I am writing regarding an automobile sold to my client, Stephen Seller, on November 7, 2005. As you know, Mr. Seller has had consistent trouble with his XGT-TGB-13 since he purchased it, and, in fact, has had the car in the shop eight times since its purchase. On each occasion, Mr. Seller was informed by your service department that the trouble would be corrected. In fact, however, in none of the instances has the car been operative for more than 10 days at a time.

Mr. Seller cannot continue having this type of consistent problem with his automobile. He needs an automobile to get to his work and he simply cannot have an automobile that doesn't work. This is formal notice that Mr. Seller considers the car defective and that warranties made with respect to the car have been breached.[83] Mr. Seller will bring the car in at a time within the next two days to have it fixed, such time to be arranged by both of you, and should the car not thereafter become operative so that he can use it on a daily basis,

---

[83] Of course the warranty of merchantability would be applicable here since the sale to Stephen was by a merchant. In addition, express warranties would probably be made as well. These are covered by Section 2-313(1)(a)(b)(c) which are discussed in the Appendix I where footnote 83 is continued on page 360. A brief discussion of the implied warranty of fitness, and disclaiming warranties generally, is also contained there.

Mr. Seller will be forced to take appropriate legal action.

Very truly yours,
Alan Lawyer

Alan knew that this type of letter usually worked well with car manufacturers. Most of the dealerships were hesitant to get into the type of dispute which Alan's firm was prepared to engage in. After all, most of the lawyers that their dealerships were up against were sole practitioners who didn't really have the time or the manpower to bombard the other side with interrogatories and depositions. Usually, when the other side got Alan's first set of interrogatories, which was usually about 120 pages, Alan was contacted within a couple of days thereafter by their attorney. In any event, he knew he was wise to write this letter from a legal standpoint.[84]

---

[84] This is discussed in the upcoming discussion between Doug and Alan.

Section 4

On January 4, 2006, Stephen called Alan very nervously and asked him if he could meet him right away. Alan wanted to know what was wrong, but Stephen indicated that so much was wrong he just wanted to sit down with him and talk it all over. Alan asked Stephen if he would like to meet him for lunch that day and Stephen agreed to meet him at noon.

When Stephen arrived for lunch, Alan asked, "What is all the commotion about?"

"Well," said Stephen, "I have all kinds of trouble. First of all, I took the car in as you told me to and it worked for about three weeks. Then it broke down again, I took it back, it broke down again. I just don't want it anymore. I can't have the aggravation. I love the car but it is too much trouble."

"Okay," said Alan, "We'll file suit this afternoon. Now what else is bothering you?"

"Well, remember when I told you that I had sold a 44 footer to Dunker Zorringo, the basketball player?"

Alan nodded.

"Well, it seems that the guy doesn't want the boat anymore and he told me he isn't going to pay for it."

"Why doesn't he want it?"

"Don't ask me," Stephen said. "He just told me that he didn't want the boat and if I had anymore questions about it, I should contact his lawyer."

"Who's his lawyer? Did he tell you?"

"Yes," said Stephen. "I have it right here. Her name is Ms. Quickfile."

"Not Ruth Quickfile?" Alan said. "She's the one who stalks around the courthouse singing the tune 'Candyman' with the word plaintiff's man substituted for Candyman."

"I'll give her a call this afternoon," said Alan. "Don't worry about it. You can always sue him for breach of contract."

"Well, that's part of the problem," said Stephen. "We never did have a written contract."

"What?" said Alan.

"Yeah," said Stephen. "There was no written contract."

Stephen then told Alan the whole story regarding the purchase and the oral contract for the 44-foot sailboat.

"Listen," said Alan, "this afternoon I will go back and have some research done on this point. There may be some way that we can still hold him to the deal. Don't worry about it, especially since there is nothing you can do at this time. Just go take care of business. In the meantime, I will call Ruth and find out what the story is."

The last bit of news that Stephen passed along regarded the $18,000 speedboat sold to Mr. Primo. After Jerry, one of his salesmen and part-time mechanic, had checked the boat, he had reported to Stephen that it appeared to him as though the steering mechanism was defective. He called Onus that afternoon and told him that he would be glad to have the boat fixed. Mr. Primo, however, told Stephen that he didn't want the boat repaired. He said he wanted a new boat and told Stephen that he wasn't going to make any more payments on the old boat.

"Well," said Alan, "I see why you didn't want to talk about this on the phone. Let me go back to the office and see what I can work out on some of these problems. I'd just as soon not even have lunch. It seems to me I have enough to do on these three matters to keep me busy for the rest of the day."

Accordingly, Alan went back to his office to get to work on the problems that Stephen had presented him with.

When Alan got back to the office, he had his secretary get Mr. Hawkins to come in to discuss all of these problems. Doug showed up a few minutes later.

"Hi, Doug," said Alan. "I have a few problems that I would like your assistance with. Do you have time?"

Doug nodded.

"Well, the first problem concerns Stephen's new car. Have you seen that new XGT that he bought?"

"Yes," said Doug. "What's wrong with it?"

"The car has been defective ever since he picked it up. It has been in the shop at least 10 times since he got it just a few months ago. He simply has to have a car that works and he would like to get rid of this car and get his money back. What I would like to know," said Alan, "is whether or not Stephen can reject the car and stop making payments under the contract."

"First of all, as you know, if Stephen signed an agreement not to assert defenses against an assignee of the chattel paper, which he almost certainly did, he is obligated to continue making those payments if the assignment fits within the requirements of Section 9-403. [See footnote 38 in Appendix I on page 346.] In that situation, he would still have a cause of action against the seller of the XGT."

"Leaving that aside," Alan interrupted, "can Stephen reject the car?"

Well," said Doug, "the key question in that regard is whether or not Stephen has accepted the car. If, in fact he has accepted the car, he may not reject the car thereafter."

"Why is that?" Alan asked.

Doug replied, "The Code says that if goods are accepted by the buyer, he cannot thereafter reject the same goods."[85]

"Has he really accepted the car?" Alan asked. "After all, he has been complaining about the car since he first got it. He never would have kept it unless these people

---

[85] *Acceptance of goods by the buyer precludes rejection of the goods accepted....* Section 2-607(2).

told him that the defects or the problems that he was having would be fixed. That doesn't seem right to me," Alan said.

"First of all," Doug said, "the fact that he may have accepted the car does not mean that he has no remedies under the Code. In fact," Doug continued, "he still may be able to get rid of the car."

"Has he accepted?"

"**Acceptance** is defined under Section 2-606(1) in three different ways.[86] Under (1)(a) of that section he probably would not have accepted since he never said the car was conforming nor did he say he would keep it anyway. In fact, from what you've told me, he has never said it was anything but nonconforming."

"What about subsection (b)?"

"As you can see, this is determined by Section 2-602, i.e., the question of whether of not an effective rejection has been made. That section says that action constituting a rejection must be made within a reasonable time.[87] That is a question of fact which will vary according to

---

[86] *(1) Acceptance of goods occurs when the buyer:*

(a) after a reasonable opportunity to inspect the goods signifies to the seller that the goods are conforming or that he will take or retain them in spite of their non-conformity; or

(b) fails to make an effective rejection (Subsection (1) of Section 2-602), but such acceptance does not occur until the buyer has had a reasonable opportunity to inspect them; or

(c) does any act inconsistent with the seller's ownership; but if such act is wrongful as against the seller, if is an acceptance only if ratified by him. Section 2-606(1)(a)(b)(c).

[87] *Rejection of goods must be within a reasonable time after delivery or tender.* Section 2-602(1).

.....[After rejection any exercise of ownership by the buyer with respect to any commercial unit is wrongful as against the seller.... Section 2-602(2)(a).

each situation.[88] I really think that here, based upon the time that has elapsed, a reasonable time within Section 1-205 has expired. This continued use of the car, I think, would also cause you problems under Section 2-606(1)(c) since the continued use of the car was inconsistent with the seller's ownership. I really think, Alan, that a court would find that Stephen accepted the car."

"Is there anything else we can do?   What about rescission?"

"You are not allowed to rescind in this situation anymore under the Uniform Commercial Code," replied Doug. "There is, however, something much like rescission-although less cumbersome from the plaintiff's point of view and that is *revocation of acceptance,* said Doug. "Revocation of acceptance, what's that?" replied Alan.

"As its name implies, it is revoking of the acceptance made by a buyer. That is, although Stephen might be held to have accepted the car under Section 2-606, he may 'revoke his acceptance' under Section 2-608."[89]

---

[88] *Whether a time for taking action required by [the Uniform Commercial Code] is reasonable depends on the nature, purpose, and circumstances of the action.* Section 1-205(a).

Section 1-302(b) states in this regard:

....The parties, by agreement, may determine the standards by which the performance of those obligations is to measure if those standards are not manifestly unreasonable....

[89] *The buyer may revoke his acceptance of a lot or commercial unit whose non-conformity substantially impairs its value if he has accepted it:*

(a) on the reasonable assumption that its non-conformity would be cured; or

(b) without discovery of such non-conformity, if its acceptance was reasonably induced either by the difficulty of discovery

Doug flipped the pages to Section 2-608. "As you can see," said Doug, "the first question is whether or not the non-conformity here 'substantially impairs' the value of the car to Stephen. This is a question based on a subjective analysis," Doug said, "that is, based upon Stephen's needs.[90] Obviously, if he needs the car to get to work everyday and it continues to break down, its value to him is substantially impaired. Furthermore, Stephen couldn't have discovered these defects prior to acceptance. He would not have seen, simply by inspecting the car, that something like repeated engine failure would occur. He needed to drive it first. And, once he found the defects, he had the seller's assurance that they would be fixed."

"The next question facing us under the revocation section is under subjection (2).[91] As you can see, he must revoke his acceptance within a reasonable time.

"Again," Doug said, "whether or not a revocation at this time is within a reasonable time is a question of fact as it would be in a case of rejection. It seems to me, however, that in view of the fact that the seller continued to make promises that the car would be fixed, Stephen's

---

before acceptance or by the seller's assurances. Section 2-608(1)(a)(b).

[90] Comment 2 to Section 2-608 states in pertinent part:

For this purpose the test is not whether the seller had reason to know at the time of contracting; the question is whether the non-conformity is such as will in fact cause a substantial impairment of value to the buyer though the seller had no advance knowledge as to the buyer's particular circumstances.

[91] *Revocation of acceptance must occur within a reasonable time after the buyer discovers or should have discovered the ground for it and before any substantial change in condition of the goods which is not caused by their own defects. It is not effective until the buyer notifies the seller of it.* Section 2-608(2).

revocation of acceptance after the last breakdown would be within a reasonable time.

Furthermore, there is no 'substantial change in condition of the goods not caused by its own defects or otherwise.'"

"What does that mean, 'substantial change caused by its own defects?'" asked Alan.

Doug replied, "Assume, for example, you have a defective engine block. If the engine block completely goes and the inner condition of the engine substantially changes, the change would have been caused by the defects of the car itself, that is, the defective block caused the change in the engine."

"As opposed to, for example," Alan interrupted, "Stephen's ramming the car into a fire hydrant and ruining it, due to Stephen's negligence."

"Exactly," said Doug.

"In any event, as the next sentence to subsection (2) states, the revocation will not be effective until he notifies the dealer of it."

"Well," said Alan, "at least I wrote them a letter two months ago regarding the complaints about the car. I knew I should do that and..."

"Right," Doug interrupted, "because under Section 2-607(3)(a), if you don't give reasonable notification   after the discovery, or in which time he should have discovered a breach, you would be barred from any remedy.[92]   But you still must notify of a revocation per Section 2-608(2)."

---

[92] *Where a tender has been accepted:*

(a) the buyer must within a reasonable time after he discovers or should have discovered any breach notify the seller of breach or be barred from any remedy. Section 2-607(3)(a).

Stephen's repeated complaints would already have put the seller on notice, but it is always a good idea to formalize the problems in a written document.

"Listen," said Alan, "how would you like to handle this case yourself?"

Finally, Doug thought to himself, people are starting to trust me around here. My very own case. "I would love to," said Doug.

"Good," said Alan. "I would like you to do whatever you think is necessary in the case and then get back to me later on this afternoon.

"By the way," said Alan, "I would like you to prepare a memorandum for me regarding a breach of an oral contract by one of Stephen's boat purchasers."

"Oral?" asked Doug.

Alan nodded.

"Well, you had better give me the facts and I hope we can get around the Statue of Frauds problem."

Whereupon, Alan gave Doug the facts surrounding the breach by Dunker. Not only was Doug elated with the fact that the case sounded relatively easy-but he was really excited to be working on a case involving the "Big Dunker." Doug had been a fan of Dunker for years. He even thought he might get to meet him. Doug told Alan he could get a memorandum to him that afternoon when he came in to discuss the other problem with the car.

"Great," said Alan, "I will see you later."

Doug nodded, determined to do a good job on both of these matters. He could see that he was beginning to make progress in the firm. With raise time coming up in just five months, he couldn't get moving any too soon.

That afternoon Doug gave the following memorandum to Alan:

MEMORANDUM OF LAW

TO: Alan
FROM: Doug
RE: Suit Against Dunker on Oral Contract
            for Purchase of Boat
DATE: January 4, 2006

QUESTIONS PRESENTED

I. Is the oral contract between Stephen's and
    Dunker enforceable?

II. If the contract is enforceable, what course of
    action should Stephen take at this time?

III. If the contract is enforceable, what damages
     are available to Stephen?

I. Is the Contract Enforceable?

As you know, the basic rule under Section 2-201(1) is that unless there is a writing, this contract would not be enforceable against Dunker since it obviously has a value over $500. This, of course, is the same rule that we discussed in connection with the Royal Boats' contract. There are, however, exceptions to the broad rule in Section 2-201(1), one of which would be applicable here. It is set forth in Section 2-201(3)(a) which states that:

A contract which does not satisfy the requirements of subsection (1) but which is valid in other respects is enforceable

(a) if the goods are to be specially manufactured for the buyer and are not

suitable to sell to others in the ordinary course of the seller's business and the seller, before notice of repudiation is received and under circumstances which reasonably indicate that the goods are for the buyer, has made either a substantial beginning of their manufacture or commitments for their procurement.

In the instant case the following questions must thus be posed:

(a) Was the boat to be specifically manufactured for Dunker?
(b) Is the boat suitable for sale to others in the ordinary course of Stephen's business?
(c) Did Stephen make the "substantial beginning" of the manufacture of the boat or "commitments for their [its] procurement"?
(d) Was the foregoing done before notice of repudiation was received, and under circumstances which reasonably indicate that the goods are for the buyer?

In order for the contract to be enforceable under the Statute of Frauds per Section 2-201(3)(a), the questions must be answered as follows:

(a) yes; (b) no; (c) yes; (d) yes.

If Stephen's recollections of the facts are correct,[93] it seems that questions (a), (c) and (d) would supply the necessary answers.[94] The only remaining question is whether the boat is suitable for sale in the ordinary course of business.

This is a question which has never been discussed by a court on facts like the instant situation, and therefore the "proper authority" [quotes supplied by the author of this book] must come from "speculative reasoning."[95]

Inasmuch as I believe that Stephen should have the boat completed [to be discussed below], I recommend that he try to sell it at the business for some reasonable period of time prior to bringing suit. Of course, if he sells it for the right price, there will be no need to sue; and, if he can't, he'll have evidence to substantiate that fact, which would, of course, help his case under Section 2-201(3)(a) and question (b) posed above.

---

[93] Often, facts are "remembered" in such a way as to facilitate recovery in a lawsuit. I am not casting any doubts on Stephen's moral character, of course, but anyone dealing with law should be aware of this. The odds are very high that Dunker (who I also have no reason to doubt) will remember a different version of the story. He might, for example, remember telling Stephen that he was interested in buying a boat and that the call to Royal was only to get a price quote.

[94] The second question in (d) seems to be unnecessary if question (a) is answered in the affirmative.

[95] I feel strongly that it is an error to go immediately to the cases to "find out the answer to a legal question." There are no identical cases, and one can, at best, only come close to similar facts. In teaching this material, I encourage students to work with the Code first and then go to the cases if they seek case support.

II. What course of action should Stephen take at this time?

In the present situation, it is clear that Dunker has breached his contract with Stephen. Since the breach occurred prior to Dunker's required performance, it is called an ***anticipatory repudiation***.

The rules governing anticipatory repudiation are set forth in Section 2-610 which states:

> *When either party repudiates the contract with respect to a performance not yet due the loss of which will substantially impair the value of the contract to the other, the aggrieved party may*
>
> *(a) for a commercially reasonable time await performance by the repudiating party; or*
>
> *(b) resort to any remedy for breach (Section 2-703 or Section 2-711), even though he has notified the repudiating party that he would await the latter's performance and has urged retraction; and*
>
> *(c) in either case suspend his own performance or proceed in accordance with the provisions of this Article on the seller's right to identify goods to the contract notwithstanding breach or to salvage unfinished goods. Section 2-704.*

Stephen's options are thus clear; he can wait for a commercially reasonable time for Dunker to perform or resort to any available remedy for breach. If he chooses either of the above, he may suspend his own performance; in the alternative, he can proceed under the salvage provisions of Article 2.

You have informed me that the boat is roughly 70% complete and that many of the particulars requested by Dunker have in fact been completed on the boat. Because of this, I would not recommend suspending performance and waiting for Dunker to perform under Subsection (a). Subsection (b) of Section 2-610 provides Stephen the most options since it provides all general remedies available to a seller under Section 2-703:

Seller's Remedies in General

Where the buyer wrongfully rejects or revokes acceptance of goods or fails to make a payment due on or before delivery or repudiates with respect to a part or the whole, then with respect to any goods directly affected and, if the breach is of the whole contract (Section 2-612), then also with respect to the whole undelivered balance, the aggrieved seller may:

(a) withhold delivery of such goods;

(b) stop delivery by any bailee as hereafter provided (Section 2-705);

(c) proceed under the next section respecting goods still unidentified to the contract;

(d) resell and recover damages as hereafter provided (Section 2-706);

(e) recover damages for non-acceptance (Section 2-708) or in a proper case the price (Section 2-709);

(f) cancel.

On the present facts, subsections (c) through (f) are most applicable and will be briefly discussed in order.

Section 2-704(2), referred to in Section 2-703(c), deals with seller's rights regarding goods which are unfinished at the time of breach by the buyer:

Where the goods are unfinished an aggrieved seller may in the exercise of reasonable commercial judgment for the purposes of avoiding loss and of effective realization either complete the manufacture and wholly identify the goods to the contract or cease manufacture and resell for scrap or salvage value or proceed in any other reasonable manner.

Thus, Stephen has the option of having Royal cease manufacture on the boat and selling it for scrap value, or ordering Royal to complete manufacture. This must, of course, be done consistent with the purposes noted, and must be done in the exercise *of reasonable commercial judgment.* Given the fact that the boat is near completion, it is my opinion that reasonable commercial judgment would probably dictate that the boat be completed and an attempt be made to resell. In making this decision, it is my opinion that Stephen should check with Royal, find out the costs of completion and sample, if possible, any potential market for the boat in its present state as well as its completed state. Since Dunker is a famous basketball player, someone might want it for that reason alone. At the very least, I suggest the foregoing steps be taken so it can be shown that Stephen attempted to exercise reasonable commercial judgment based upon all the information available to him at the point in time in which he was required to make his decision. He should document these efforts.

In the instant situation, if Stephen chose to resell the boat after completion, he would be entitled to receive from Dunker the difference between the amount he received upon selling the boat and that called for by the contract price with Dunker, as well as other possible damages as noted below.

Subsection (1) to Section 2-706, referred to in Section 2-703(d), would be applicable to such a resale. It states in full as follows:

> *Under the conditions stated in Section 2-703 on seller's remedies, the seller may resell the goods concerned or the undelivered balance thereof. Where the resale is made in good faith and in a commercially reasonable manner, the seller may recover the difference between the resale price and a contract price together with any incidental damages allowed under the provisions of this Article (Section 2-710), but less expenses save in consequence of the buyer's breach.*

As the first sentence to the above section indicates, one of the conditions set forth in Section 2-703 must exist in order for the seller to take advantage of that section. In the instant situation, inasmuch as the buyer has repudiated with respect to all of the contract, such a situation exists. It is important to note that a resale under

Section 2-706 must be **commercially reasonable**[96] and in good faith in order for the seller to obtain the difference between the contract price and the resale price. In addition, Stephen must give the notification required by Section 2-706 prior to the sale of the boat.[97] (Incidental damages noted in Section 2-706 also recoverable in such a situation are discussed below.)

If Stephen, after reasonable attempts to sell the boat, is unable to do so, he would be able to sue Dunker for the price of the boat under Section 2-709(1)(b) (referred to in Section 2-703(e)). Section 2-709(1)(b) states as follows:

When the buyer fails to pay the price as it becomes due, the seller may recover, together with any incidental damages under the next section, the price...(b) of goods identified to the contract if the seller is unable after reasonable effort to resell them at a reasonable price, or the circumstances reasonably indicate that such effort will be unavailing.

---

[96] *Sale may be as a unit or in parcels and at any time and place on any terms but every aspect of the sale including the method, . manner, time, place and terms must be commercially reasonable.* Section 2-706(2).

[97] *Where the resale is at private sale the seller must give the buyer reasonable notification of his intention to resell.* Section 2-706(3).

Where the resale is at public sale:

...It must be made at a usual place or market for public sale if one is reasonably available and except in the case of goods which are perishable, or threaten to decline in value speedily, the seller must give the buyer reasonable notice of the time and place of the resale. Section 2-706(4)(b).

As I indicated to you, I am of the opinion that an attempt should be made to resell the boat. A reasonable attempt to resell should cause Stephen no difficulty, and as discussed earlier, such a resale attempt might meet with success simply because Dunker's reputation as a former New York Blues star. As noted however, if attempts to resell the boat are unsuccessful, Section 2-709 gives a remedy for the price.

In addition, as that section and Section 2-706 state, Stephen will be entitled to recover incidental damages under Section 2-710 such as transportation costs, shipping costs or whatever costs are reasonably incurred in the attempt to resell or effectuate resale of the boat.[98]

* * *

Just after he gave the memorandum to Alan, Alan asked Doug what he had done with regard to Stephen's car.

"I got a letter off today notifying the dealer of our intention to revoke acceptance," said Doug. "This, of course, is necessary because of the last sentence to Section 2-608(2). What I plan to do next is draft a complaint and hopefully get it filed sometime tomorrow."

"By the way," Doug continued, "it is important to note that once the revocation of acceptance occurs, Stephen will have the same duties with respect to the car as if he

---

[98] *Incidental damages to an aggrieved seller include any commercially reasonable charges, expenses or commission incurred in stopping delivery, in the transportation, care and custody of the goods after the buyer's breach, in connection with return or resale of goods or otherwise resulting from the breach. Section 2-710.*

had rejected it.[99] It is required of him that he not continue to exercise ownership over the car after he revokes his acceptance."[100]

"I have two more questions," said Alan. "You tell me that Stephen is not supposed to do anything with respect to the car. Yet he needs a car to get to work. What is he supposed to do?"

"I addressed that in the letter this morning," said Doug. "I told them that if he didn't have a car by the end of the week, he was going to have to rent a car and include that in his claim for damages against the dealership. I don't know if we can successfully recover these, but we can try."

"Very good," said Alan. "Please keep me posted on the matter."

"My second question is whether there is anything we can do in the future if anything even remotely similar to the Dunker situation presents itself."

"I don't know the extent of any communications which occurred between Dunker and Stephen or what relevant information Stephen may have had," replied Doug. "However, if Stephen had reason to believe that Dunker might not do the deal, or was legitimately concerned about that, he could have moved under Section 2-609, which deals with a party's right to **Adequate Assurance of Performance.**"

Doug opened his Code and showed Alan Section 2-609(1).

---

[99] *A buyer who so revokes has the same rights and duties with regard to the goods involved as if he rejected them.* Section 2-608(3).

[100] *After rejection any exercise of ownership by the buyer with respect to any commercial unit is wrongful as against the seller.* Section 2-602(2)(a).

A contract for sale imposes an obligation on each party that the other's expectation of receiving due performance will not be impaired. When reasonable grounds for insecurity arise with respect to the performance of either party the other may demand in writing adequate assurance of due performance and until he receives such assurance may if commercially reasonable suspend any performance for which he has not already received the agreed return.

"What would have happened if Stephen would have made a demand on Dunker, and Dunker just did nothing?" asked Alan.

"In that case, you would be under Section 2-609(4):

After receipt of a justified demand failure to provide within a reasonable time not exceeding thirty days such assurance of due performance as is adequate under the circumstances of the particular case is a repudiation of the contract.

"Very interesting. Thanks Doug. I will keep you more in the loop on what's happening with Stephens' Boats, so that if anything like this or analogous to this comes up again, you can help us figure out what to do."

Doug tried to keep from smiling, but when he heard those words from Alan—being "kept in the loop" and "help us figure out", he actually had to bite his lip so that Alan wouldn't see how excited he was. As soon as he left Alan's office, Doug smiled ear to ear!

Just after Doug left, Alan called Stephen to let him know what was going on. He told him that a letter had been written to the dealer regarding the car. With respect to Dunker, he advised him to follow advice along the lines of the memorandum Doug had written him. Stephen agreed with Alan and accordingly it was decided to complete the boat and attempt to sell it.

Section 5

On the morning of January 7, 2006, Doug came into Alan's office to let him know the good news, that is, to let him know that he had just received an offer from the people at the car dealership to settle the lawsuit on Stephen's XGT.

"Great," said Alan, "What did they offer?"

"They offered Stephen a new 2006 XGT if Stephen will pay the difference between the 2005 model wholesale price and the 2006 wholesale price, which comes to about $2,166."

"It seems like a pretty good offer to me," said Alan. "Why don't you give Stephen a call and let him know what they offered?"

Of course this elated Doug as it was only the third time he was able to call a client directly since he started work. He told Stephen what the offer was. Stephen agreed that it was a good offer and told Doug to communicate his acceptance to the dealer.

He also asked Doug to transfer the call to Alan because he had something to talk to him about.

The call was transferred and Alan picked up his phone. "It sounds like a good deal you got today Stephen. We are finally starting to make some progress around here for you. I told you we would be able to work these things out."

Stephen somewhat morosely said, "Yeah, that is really great."

"What's wrong, Stephen," Alan asked.

"I'll tell you," said Stephen. "This business is really starting to get to me. I got lawsuits with Dunker, I got sued today by Onus Primo, plus when I was going over my bank statement, I found out that a $850 sales commission check that I made out to Jerry Zamanski, my salesman, had been raised to $8,500 and my account got charged an extra $7,650. I am beginning to think this is not worth it."

"Of course it is," said Alan. "Look at how much money you have made since you have been in business. You have been open only eight months and you have grossed $467,000. These little losses and inconveniences, granted, take their toll on you, but when you think about how much you are making, you just can't worry about these other things."

"I'll tell you what," said Alan, "I am going to knock off early today. Why don't we go get a drink and discuss these things? Don't worry about the business, though, it is going well."

"Okay," said Stephen, "I will meet you at 4:00 p.m. at Randy's."

"Fine," said Alan, "talk to you later." He hung up the phone. Alan thought to himself that Stephen's business was just starting to catch on. He had already made $46,700 gross to date after only eight months in operation. This represented a very, very heavy profit for Alan inasmuch as he had only worked about $5,000 worth of billable time for Stephen's Boats. The last thing he wanted was for Stephen to leave the business when it could probably get up to a point where the business could gross several million dollars a year and Alan could take ten percent of that for doing nothing. Alan wanted Stephen to stay in business. Besides, Alan thought to himself, Stephen is sure making a lot of money and he is too young to be going to the beach every day reading books that he enjoys and doing things that he likes. He should work all the time like everybody else. Yes, it was best for him to stay in business. As a friend, not only as a lawyer and business partner who was making ten percent of everything, he would show Stephen that the right thing to do was to stay in business.

Alan was prepared to really have a heart-to-heart talk with Stephen. Amazingly, though, when Alan got to Randy's, Stephen had completely overcome his earlier problems and he was back to his enthusiastic business self. Alan was relieved that he didn't have to go through the ordeal of talking him into staying in business. Stephen did want to talk about the check problem, however, as this really bothered him.

"I just don't know what to do," Stephen said. "I have known Jerry for a long time and I can't believe that he would do anything like this."

"Did you ask him?" Alan said.

"I just couldn't," Stephen said. "Am I responsible?"

"I don't know," Alan replied. "I'll need more information before I'll know that." (Even though Alan knew next to nothing about Articles 3 and 4 under the Code, he didn't want to convey that to Stephen. Besides, thought Alan, he knew that he'd need more information even if he did know this area of law.)

"I have a friend who works at the bank," continued Alan. "I'll give him a call." Alan took out his cell phone and telephoned Joe Lewis, his friend at the bank with whom he had dealt on previous occasions. "Joe, how are you? Listen, I am calling about a small problem that my client is having with the bank."

"What can I do for you, Alan?" asked Joe.

"It seems that a check of my client's, Stephen's Boats, Inc., was raised from $850 to $8,500 and was charged to his account. I would like for you to recredit the account for the $7,650."

"Alan, you know this has to go through channels. I'll tell you what, I'll check it out for you and If I don't get back to you later on, say by about 2:30 p.m., why don't you give me a call?"

"Great," said Alan. "I'll talk to you later."

Alan told Stephen what had happened and he told him that he was confident that the bank would recredit the account. "By the way," said Alan, "as long as I have got you here, I have a question for you."

"What is that?" said Stephen.

"Well, I am set to meet with George Friedman and Mr. Primo on this closing next week. Friedman agreed to take the reduction in cash to be put up if we can get Onus Primo to sign the note. I spoke to Onus last night and he had no objections. He didn't even ask for anything which surprised me. So anyway, I know this is kind of a rough time for you, but if you could be there next Wednesday for the closing, I would really appreciate it."

"Okay," said Stephen. "I'll be there. Why don't you call me later on in the week and let me know exactly where I am supposed to be. Also, let me know how much money I am supposed to bring."

"Fine," said Alan, "I'll talk to you later."

When Alan got back to his office, he called Joe. Joe said he was sorry but the bank refused to recredit Stephen's account.

"Why?" said Alan.

"Well, we need to know other facts," said Joe.

"Like what?" asked Alan.

"What if, for example, the check was made out by Stephen in such a way that it was easy to alter? For example, what if he left the amount blank? You know in that situation," Joe continued, "we might not be obligated to recredit his account"[101]

"I see," said Alan. "Thanks for the help, anyway. I'll get back to you later on this week."

Alan telephoned Stephen to inform him of the bank's decision and to find out if Stephen had spoken to Zamanski. Stephen had, in fact, spoken to Jerry who, upon finding out what had happened, immediately called his twin brother, Harold, who had been staying with him and his wife Claudia for a week. Claudia had never

---

[101] This point is discussed in a memorandum which follows shortly.

trusted Harold and he suspected that Harold had stolen the check and raised it.

His wife informed him that his brother had left a note explaining that he was sorry he did it, but he needed the money. (Although Harold had too much "integrity" to get a job within the system, he didn't hesitate to "borrow" from anybody he could.)

When Alan got off the phone, he called Doug to discuss the check question with him. Unfortunately, Doug was out of the office, supposedly handling a motion at Circuit Court. Alan was very upset that Doug wasn't there, but being in line with the nice guy that he was, he decided that he wouldn't say anything to Doug. He would simply leave him a note with the facts of the case and ask Doug to speak to him about it in the morning.

Alan called in his secretary and asked her to take some dictation. He dictated the following message to Doug:

To: Doug
From: Alan
Re: Altered Check Question

Jerry Zamanski is a salesman at Stephen's boats. On December 21, 2005 Stephen's Boats issued an $850 commission check to Jerry. Jerry wrote 'for deposit only' on the back of the check and placed it in his desk drawer.

Jerry's identical twin brother Harold stole the check & raised it from $850 to $8,500. Harold took the altered check to East Dade Bank, where Jerry had his account.

Harold explained to the teller, that he had changed his mind on depositing the check and wanted cash for an upcoming vacation.

The teller knew Jerry very well, and had done business with him for many years and, believing

Harold to be Jerry, allowed him to cross out 'for deposit only' followed by his initials.

Harold then signed Jerry's name and was given $8,500 in cash. Two weeks later, the theft, alteration and forgery were discovered.

Stephen's bank, South Dade, has charged his account $8,500.

Jerry has asked Stephen to give him another commission check.

Stephen would like an analysis of this situation.

Particularly, Stephen wants to know whether he is responsible for the charge to his account, and whether he must reissue the commission check to Jerry.

I would appreciate it very much if you would review these facts in light of the relevant law contained in the Uniform Commercial Code. I would like a memorandum on the subject, but I am anxious to have some information as soon as possible tomorrow. If a memorandum is impractical given the time situation, please see me first thing tomorrow morning so that we can discuss this.

Incidentally, Doug, if you do write a memorandum, please describe the transaction and law completely so that when I show it to Stephen, he'll be impressed with your work.

* * *

Doug returned from Court, exhausted, at 4:30 p.m. When he read the memorandum from Alan he was furious. In the first place, it was obvious to Doug that Alan wanted this in writing tomorrow. 'If a memorandum is impractical...' 'Incidentally, Doug, please describe the transaction and law completely so that when I show it to Stephen, he'll be impressed . . .' What a bunch of bull, Doug thought to himself. Who does he think he's kidding?

And if that wasn't bad enough, Alan was making so much more money than Doug. It just wasn't fair, he thought. Some day I'll rectify these gross inequities. For now, though, he knew he would just have to do his work and wait until later on the money question. He wrote the following memorandum to Alan:

MEMORANDUM

TO: Stephen Seller,
          President of Stephen Boats

FROM: Alan Lawyer, Esq.
           Doug Hawkins, Esq.

REF: Check #: 1214949

DATE: February 3, 2006

Introduction

In order to put the Article 3 [Commercial Paper] aspects in context, some discussion of Article 4 is necessary. Article 4 of the Uniform Commercial Code deals with Bank Deposits and Collections. It contains the rules surrounding the movement of checks from the time the check is first issued until the check is paid or dishonored by the drawer's bank. In addition, it provides for certain duties on the part of a bank customer, and states when a bank may charge its customer's account. [a *customer* in part means *any person having an account with a bank.* Section 4-104(a)(5).] A discussion of all of Article 4 is beyond the scope of this memorandum. I have, however, included what I consider to be essential in order to understand the present case in context.

Overview: Part I
(A)   Characterization of Banks Involved;
(B)   Activities of Depository-Collecting Bank;
(C)   Activities of Payor Bank;
(D)   Rights of Revocation and Chargeback;
(E)   Loss of Chargeback Rights: Final Payment

ARTICLE 4 AND BANK COLLECTIONS

A. Characterization of the Banks Involved

At the outset it is important to distinguish the manner in which a particular bank is characterized for Article 4 purposes, for oftentimes different duties and liabilities will attend this classification. In fact, Article 4 is roughly broken down into various subparts based upon such classifications. In the instant case, East Dade Bank was a depository, collecting, and presenting bank; **depository** since it was the first bank to which the check was taken for collection;[102] **collecting** since it was a bank handling the item for collection (and was not the payor bank),[103] and finally as a **presenting bank** since it presented the item for payment and was not the payor bank.[104]   South Dade Bank, as the drawee, was the **payor bank**.[105]

---

[102] *"Depository bank" means the first bank to take an item even though it is also the payor bank, unless the item is presented for immediate payment over the counter.* Section 4-105(2).

[103] *"Collecting bank" means a bank handling the item for collection except the payor bank.* Section 4-105(5).

[104] *"Presenting bank" means a bank presenting an item except the payor bank.* Section 4-105(6).

[105] *"Payor bank" means a bank that is the drawee of the draft.* Section 4-105(3).

B. Activities of the Depository-Collecting Bank
1.   Provisional credits
2.   Cash Withdrawals
3.   Timely Action

Generally, when a depository-collecting bank receives an item for collection, it will not advance cash for the item. *An **Item** means an instrument or promise to pay money handled by a bank for collection or payment....* Section 4-104(a)(9). It will usually wait until final payment by the payor bank before allowing any cash to be withdrawn on the strength of the item. In order to reflect the transaction on its books, it will make a provisional entry into its customer's account [discussed more below].

Some banks will however, allow customers to draw cash in this type of situation, but that is usually because there is enough money in the account to offset the check if it doesn't clear, or the customer and the bank have an established relationship in which such advances are normal. Regardless of whether or not cash is taken back, the bank will reflect the transaction by making the noted entry in its customer's account. The presumption is that this entry is "provisional" in nature:

Unless a contrary intent clearly appears...a collecting bank ...is an agent or sub-agent of the owner of the item and any settlement given for it is provisional Section 4-201(a).

The fact that cash was given for the item prior to receiving payment from the payor bank as in the instant case does not change the provisional nature of the credit given.[106] After the depository-collecting bank provisionally credits its customer's account, it will initiate collection of the item. In performing this duty:

> *A collecting bank shall send items by reasonably prompt method taking into consideration relevant instructions, the nature of the item, the number of those items on hand, and the cost of collection involved and the method generally used by it or others to present such items.* Section 4-204(a).

The check could have been sent to a clearing house, into the Federal Reserve System [under proper circumstances], or as here, directly to the payor bank.[107] Whichever it chooses, the bank has exercised ordinary care if it takes proper action prior to its midnight deadline.[108]

---

[106] The second sentence to Section 4-201(a) states in part as follows:

> *This provision [regarding the provisional nature of a credit noted above] applies regardless of the form of endorsement or lack of endorsement and even though credit given for the item is subject to immediate withdrawal as of right **or is in fact withdrawn.** (emphasis added).*

[107] Section 4-204(b)(1) says:

(1) A collecting bank may send

   (a) any item direct to the payor bank....

[108] A collecting bank must exercise ordinary care in:

   (1) presenting an item or sending it for presentment...

Section 4-202(a)(1).

A collecting bank exercises ordinary care under subsection (a) by taking proper action before its midnight deadline

(C) Activities of the Payor Bank
1. Provisional settlement
2. Decision to Pay or Decline

Upon receipt of an item from a presenting bank, the payor bank will typically give a provisional credit to the account of the presenting bank. Thus, in the instant situation, South Dade would have provisionally credited the account East Dade has with it. After the provisional credit has been given, the payor will decide whether to pay the item based upon whatever commercially reasonable systems are in place which make that determination. If it pays the item, it will charge the customer's account [Stephen's Boats].

---

following receipt of an item, notice or settlement. Taking proper action within a reasonably longer time may constitute the exercise of ordinary care, but the bank has the burden of establishing timeliness. Section 4-202(b).

For the purpose of allowing time to process items, prove balances, and make the necessary entries on its books to determine its position for the day, a bank may fix an afternoon hour of 2:00 p.m. or later as a cutoff for the handling of money and items and the making of entries on its books.

An item or deposit of money received on any day after a cutoff hour so fixed or after close of the banking day may be treated as being received at the opening of the next banking day. Section 4-108(a)(b).

(D)   *Rights of Revocation and Charge-Back*
1.   Payor Bank and the Presenting Bank
2.   Collecting Bank and Its Customer
3.   Timely Action & Final Payment

If the payor bank decides not to pay the item, which it could do for many reasons (such as insufficient funds or what it thought to be a forged drawer's signature), it will return the item to the presenting bank. If South Dade took proper action in a timely manner, it could revoke the provisional settlement it gave East Dade:

> *If a payor bank settles for a demand item [the check]...presented   otherwise   than   for immediate payment over the counter before midnight of the banking day of receipt, the payor bank may revoke the settlement and recover the settlement if before it has made final payment...and before its midnight deadline it*
>
> *1. returns the item; or*
>
> *2. returns an image of the item, if the party to which the return is made has entered into an agreement to accept an image as a return of the item and the image is returned in accordance with that agreement; or*
>
> *3. sends a record providing notice of dishonor or nonpayment if the item is unavailable for return. Section 4-301(a)(1)(2)(3).*

As noted in Section 4-301, the payor bank must take proper action before its midnight deadline.

Midnight deadline is defined under Section 4-104(a)(10) as follows:

> ***Midnight deadline*** *with respect to a bank is midnight on its next banking day following the banking day on which it receives the relevant item or notice or from which the time for taking action commences to run, whichever is later....*

In the event that South Dade revoked the provisional settlement it gave East Dade, that bank would have revoked any provisional settlement it gave Jerry's account:

> *If a collecting bank [East Dade] has made provisional settlement with its customer for an item and itself fails by reason of dishonor...to receive settlement for the item which is or becomes final, it may revoke the settlement given by it....* Section 4-214(a).

(E) Loss of Chargeback Rights: Final Payment

> *...These rights to revoke, charge back and obtain refund terminate if and when a settlement received by the bank is or becomes final.* Section 4-214(a).

As the foregoing states, the determinative question regarding the right to revoke, charge back and obtain refund, is whether or not there had been ***final settlement*** [final payment] of the item. If that occurred, it is clear that the rights of chargeback would be gone.

On the facts as stated, two weeks passed from the issue of the check to the realization as to what had occurred. Therefore, any action taken by the Bank would have been taken many days after its 'midnight deadline' with respect to this check, which would have resulted in final payment:

An item is finally paid by a payor bank when it has ...:
(1) paid the item in cash;
(2) settled for the item without having a right to revoke the settlement under statute, clearing-house rule or agreement;
(3) made a provisional settlement for the item and failed to revoke in the time and manner permitted by statute, clearing house rule or agreement.
Section 4-215(a)(1)(2)(3).

South Dade had made a provisional settlement with East Dade, and subsequently did not revoke the settlement within the timeframe 'permitted by statute', i.e., by its midnight deadline. Therefore, South Dade will be deemed to have finally paid the item. As a result, East Dade received "final settlement" for the item.[109] As previously noted, once final payment was made, East Dade lost any rights it had to charge back Jerry's account.

The failure to charge back does not, however, affect the other rights of the bank against the customer or any other party. Section 4-214(e). In other words, East Dade still has all causes of action

---

[109] *If a provisional settlement for an item between the presenting and payor banks is made ... by debits or credits in an account between them, then to the extent that provisional debits or credits for the item are entered in accounts between the presenting and payor banks or between the presenting and successive prior collecting banks seriatim they become final upon final payment of the item by the payor bank.* Section 4-215(c).

it may have against Jerry and certainly against Harold.

With this background in place, I shall direct my attention to the facts under consideration, and various provisions of Article 3, Commercial Paper. Only the more relevant code Sections of Article 3 will be noted.[110]

Overview: Part II

(A) The Restrictive Indorsement;
(B) Person Entitled to Enforce the Instrument;
(C) The Alteration;
(D) When Payor Bank May Charge Customer's Account;

A. The Restrictive Indorsement

You have indicated that when Jerry received the check, he wrote the words "for deposit only" on the back of it. With this language, and accompanying indorsement, this would have been a *restrictive indorsement* of the check under Section 3-206(c):

> *If an instrument bears an indorsement ... using the words "for deposit" "for collection," or other words indicating a purpose of having the*

---

[110] The following discussion deals primarily with Article 3 of the Code which covers the topic of Commercial Paper. In reading this discussion a few things should be borne in mind; first, as this is the first discussions of Commercial Paper in this book, certain relevant sections are, of necessity, omitted from the discussion. While this is somewhat true of other discussions in the book, the structure and drafting of Article 3, in the writer's opinion, make the problem somewhat more acute than it would be with respect to the other articles. Second, Article 3 is covered in the next few sections, as well as later in this book, in detail. This material will give the reader additional knowledge which will apply to the present case. After finishing that material, the reader might wish to take another look at the following discussion for further analysis.

instrument collected by a bank for the indorser or for a particular account. . .[it is a restrictive indorsement].

A Depository Bank has strict duties when it receives a check which is restrictively indorsed:

A depository bank that purchases the instrument or takes it for collection when so indorsed converts the instrument unless the amount paid by the bank with respect to the instrument is received by the indorser or applied consistently with the indorsement. Section 3-206(c)(2).

Therefore, any credit given by East Dade for the check should have been "deposited" to Jerry's account. Harold clearly had no authority to alter the restrictive indorsement. Furthermore, his forged signature of Jerry is ineffective to transfer any rights in the check.[111]

---

[111] Subsection (a) to Section 3-403 states in pertinent part:

...[A]n unauthorized signature is ineffective except as the signature of the unauthorized signer in favor of a person who in good faith pays the instrument or takes it for value....

Therefore, Harold's signature was not 'effective' as Jerry's, but in fact operated as Harold's.

Furthermore, Jerry would not be liable on the instrument since neither he, nor his authorized representative signed it:

A person is not liable on an instrument unless (i) the person signed the instrument, or (ii) the person is represented by an agent or representative who signed the instrument and the signature is binding on the represented person under Section 3-402. Section 3-401(a).

B. Person Entitled to Enforce the Instrument

The only person who was entitled to enforce the instrument as it was originally made out was Jerry:

"Person entitled to enforce" an instrument means:
  i.   the holder of the instrument;
  ii.   a nonholder in possession of the instrument who is entitled to enforce the instrument; or
  iii. a person not in possession of the instrument who is entitled to enforce the instrument pursuant to *3-309* [Lost or Stolen Instruments] *or 3-418(d)* [Payment by Mistake]. Section 3-301(i)(ii)(iii).

Sections 3-301(ii)(iii) are outside the general movement of checks and in any event do not apply here. Under Section 3-301(i), the only person entitled to enforce the instrument would be the *holder*, which is defined as follows:

"Holder" means: the person in possession of a negotiable instrument that is payable either to bearer or to an identified person that is in possession. Section 1-201(b)(21)(A).

Harold was not a *bearer* of the check simply because he had possession of it:

A promise or order is payable to bearer if it:

(1) states that it is payable to bearer or to the order of bearer or otherwise indicates that the person in possession of the promise or order is entitled to payment. Section 3-109(a)(1).

The check was payable to an identified person—Jerry. While in possession, he would have been the holder, and the only person who could have that status [unless he indorsed it]. Therefore, Harold was not a holder, and hence not "entitled to enforce" the instrument.

C. The Alteration

When Harold raised the check to $8,500, he altered the item:

*"**Alteration**" means (i) an unauthorized change in an instrument that purports to modify in any respect the obligation of a party ...* Section 3-407(a).[112]

---

[112] The obligations of the drawer and endorser are set forth in Sections 3-414 and 3-415 respectively. These sections are discussed in detail later in the book but are reproduced here in case the reader wants to examine the respective obligations of drawer or indorser (in connection with the statement which was the basis for this footnote).

Obligation of Drawer:

If an unaccepted draft [e.g. a check] is dishonored, the drawer is obligated to pay the draft (i) according to its terms at the time it was issued. . . The obligation is owed to a person entitled to enforce the draft or to an indorser who paid the draft under Section 3-415. Section 3-414(b).

Obligation of the Indorser:

(a). . . [I]f an instrument is dishonored, an indorser is obliged to pay the amount due on the instrument (i) according to the

Of course, in raising the check, the obligation of the drawer was changed from $850 on the check to $8,500. The unauthorized change in the instrument [the check] purported to modify the contract of the drawer [Stephen's Boats]. Additionally, the change of the restrictive indorsement purported to modify the obligation of East Dade Bank, and was itself an alteration.

The fact that an alteration occurred in the instant situation, however, does not insure that the drawer's account may not be charged.

> *A person whose failure to exercise ordinary care substantially contributes to an alteration of an instrument or to the making of a forged signature on an instrument is precluded from asserting the alteration or the forgery against a person who, in good faith, pays the instrument or takes it for value or for collection.* Section 3-406(a).

In the present case, Stephen probably issued the check via customary business practices, and would not be within 3-406(a). If however, he would have written the check in pencil, and such conduct, were deemed '*a failure to exercise ordinary care [which] substantially contribute[d] to the alteration'* Stephen would be precluded from asserting the alteration against the bank, provided, that the bank paid in accordance with the standard set forth in Section 3-406(a).

Similarly, if Jerry were found somehow to be negligent within Section 3-406, he would be similarly

---

terms of the instrument at the time it was indorsed. . . Section 3-415(a).

precluded from asserting the alteration against his bank. [For example, would it matter if Harold had a history of theft, forgery, or was known to be in desperate need of money? These are the types of questions that are activated once you get into the facts of a particular case. Does Harold, being an identical twin, figure into this at all?]

D. When a Payor Bank May Charge Customer's Account

Part 4 of Article 4 deals with the relationship between the payor bank and its customer, here, South Dade and Stephen. Section 4-401 states when a bank may charge its customer's account and reads in relevant part as follows:

A bank may charge against the account of a customer an item that is properly payable from the account even though the charge creates an overdraft. An item is properly payable if it is authorized by the customer and is in accordance with any agreement between the customer and the bank. Section 4-401(a).

In the present situation, Stephen's Boats did not authorize payment in the amount of $8,500, nor did he authorize payment to Harold. Therefore, the item is not 'properly payable' and Stephen should have his account recredited [unless he fell within Section 3-406].

If on the other hand, *Jerry* had altered the item and taken it for collection, the indorsement would have been effective, and Stephen's account could have been charged, although not $8,500:

(d) A bank that in good faith makes payment to a holder may charge the indicated account of its customer according to:

(1) The original terms of the altered item;

(2) The terms of the completed item, even though the bank knows the item has been completed unless the bank has notice that the completion was improper.

Section 4-401(d)(1)(2).

If in fact Jerry had altered the item, Section 4-401(d)(1) would control. East Dade would have been a 'holder' within 1-201(b)(21)(A) since Jerry would have endorsed the check to its order. South Dade would have made a good faith payment to East Dade, and therefore would be entitled to enforce the instrument according to its original terms.

Among the 'original terms' of the altered item was the amount to be paid. That amount was $850 and thus, South Dade would be entitled to charge Stephen's account at least that amount.[113]

---

[113] Before leaving this case, a few other points should be briefly noted. First, South Dade Bank would have a cause of action against East Dade Bank for breaching warranties under Section 4-207(a)(1)(2)(3):

(a) A customer or collecting bank that transfers an item and receives a settlement or other consideration warrants to the transferee and to any subsequent collecting bank that:

(1) the warrantor is a person entitled to enforce the instrument;

(2) all signatures on the instrument are genuine and authorized;

(3) the item has not been altered.

It should also be noted that East Dade would have a cause of action against Harold for similar warranties under Section 3-417(a)(1)(2)(3). [See Statutory Supplement for text of these

Section 6

On February 16, 2006, per agreement, Stephen, Alan and George met at the clothing outlet to finalize the purchase of the store.[114] The details had been worked out in advance between George and Alan with the purpose of this meeting being simply to review what had been agreed upon, as well as to execute the note.

"You know," said George, "the business has been extremely profitable for me and I am sure that it will be

---

sections.] Finally, a customer of a bank, such as Stephen, is under a duty to promptly examine his bank statement to discover forgeries or alterations which must be promptly reported to the bank:

If a bank sends or makes available a statement of account or items pursuant to subsection (a), the customer must exercise reasonable promptness in examining the statement or the items to determine whether any payment was not authorized because of an alteration or an item or because a purported signature by or on behalf of the customer was not authorized. If, based on the statement of the items provided, the customer should reasonably have discovered the unauthorized payment, the customer must promptly notify the bank of the relevant facts. Section 4-406(c).

If the bank proves that the customer failed with respect to an item, to comply with the duties imposed on the customer by subsection (c), the customer is precluded from asserting against the bank:

(1) the customer's unauthorized signature or any alteration on the item, if the bank also proves that it suffered a loss by reason of the failure…. Section 4-406(d)(1).

[114] As originally enacted, Article 6 the Uniform Commercial Code, Bulk Sales, regulated various aspects of the sale of a business selling goods. One of the primary goals was to protect creditors of the seller. In 1989 the National Conference of Commissioners on Uniform State Laws concluded that Article 6 was no longer necessary and recommended its repeal by states that had enacted it. Forty-eight states followed this recommendation. Given this limited use of Article 6, it is not discussed in this book.

equally profitable for you. I am especially happy for you that Onus Primo is staying on because he has a good feel for the business and I am sure he will be a big asset to you." Reaching for his briefcase, "Here," said George, "this is the note which I had prepared." The note states as follows:

PROMISSORY NOTE

IN CONSIDERATION for the purchase of George's Clothing Outlet, the undersigned promise to pay to the order of George Friedman $800,000 in equal monthly installments commencing on April 1, 2006, and payable in an amount of $4,400.00 per month for 20 years.

This note is being given in consideration for the sale of George's Clothing Outlet as contained in a separate Sales Agreement between the undersigned entered into on even date herewith. George has retained a security interest in the inventory of George's Clothing Outlet in order to secure payment thereof.

In addition, George retains a security interest in equipment and accounts, now or hereafter acquired. The security interest referred to herein is governed by a separate Security Agreement executed between the parties to this Agreement.

Should George at any time deem himself insecure, insecurity being defined exhaustively herein as the failure of the debtor to remit two monthly installments in a row, principal and interest under this note may be accelerated.

Should such insecurity arise, and acceleration be had, the undersigned hereby authorize a confession of judgment to be entered against them. In addition, the parties hereby agree that acceleration in the circumstances just described as insecurity is an acceleration done in good faith.

It is understood that the failure of the payee to exercise any rights contained in this agreement shall not operate as a waiver or an estoppel to assert those rights at a later time.

It is further understood that the seller has warranted to the buyers that the schedule of debts attached hereto is a full and complete disclosure of all outstanding liabilities, exclusive of taxes owed to the State of Florida which the seller has incurred in connection with George's Clothing Outlet, and which may be deducted from the first monthly payment after the amount of said taxes are made known.

Furthermore, seller agrees to postpone payment of any monthly installment for thirty (30) days in the event the profitability schedule contained in the Sales Agreement executed on even date herewith is not met. In computing such profitability, excess amounts accumulated from preceding months over the guaranteed schedule will be considered towards determining whether any given monthly installment has been met.

Signed this 16 day of February, 2006.

Witnesses:

_____   _____

Gloria Diaz   Stephen Seller

                               _____

                               Alan Lawyer

                               _____

                               Onus Primo

Alan briefly reviewed the note and saw that it embodied the essential terms of the understanding between him and George. He did, however, want to make one very important change in the note. He knew if he simply asked George to make the change, George would agree. However, Stephen had become very insistent on being comfortable with these legal matters and Alan felt that if he tried to change the terms of what was supposed to be a settled agreement with George, without consulting Stephen, Stephen might hesitate to close the deal. In order to alleviate the problem, Alan decided to ask for a break so that he could discuss everything with Stephen.

"How about if we take an hour for lunch?" asked Alan.

George was somewhat surprised and asked if there was something wrong.

"No, of course not," said Alan, "It is just that Stephen and I really have not had a chance to discuss the terms of the note and I would feel more comfortable if we reviewed them briefly. After all, George" continued Alan, "it is a lot of liability."

"Fine with me," said George. "Why don't we make it a long lunch so that I can run some errands and meet back here at 2:00 p.m. I'll leave word with Onus Primo to meet us here then, too."

"Great," said Alan.

Alan and Stephen went to the coffee shop across the street from the bank. "Why did you want to take a break from the meeting?" Stephen asked. "You know that I am leaving this whole matter up to you, don't you?"

"Yes," said Alan. "When I was referring to the terms of the note, however, it occurred to me that in its present form, the note is probably negotiable. This could hurt us later on, so I would like to make it non-negotiable."

"What's negotiability?" asked Stephen.

Fortunately for Alan, Doug had explained all of this to him over the course of the last few weeks.

"A piece of commercial paper, such as this note," responded Alan, "is termed *negotiable* if it is drafted in a particular form."[115]

"Why is that so important?" Stephen asked.

"For a couple of reasons," replied Alan. "For example, if the note is negotiable and George transfers it to a third party, it is possible that the third party will obtain greater rights on the note against us than George had."

"Before explaining *that* one to me, why would George transfer the note?" asked Stephen.

"Well," said Alan, "George might decide that he prefers to have one lump sum of cash for the note as opposed to waiting for payments over a 20-year period. Accordingly, he might try to sell the note to someone."

"What does that have to do with negotiability?" interrupted Stephen.

"Well," said Alan. He paused for a moment and said, "Perhaps the best way to explain this is with an example. Assume for a moment that George decides in a year or

---

[115] The form required for a writing to be a 'negotiable instrument' is contained in Section 3-104(a)(1)(2)(3) which is reproduced in the Statutory Supplement. The requirements of these sections are discussed in the following dialogue between Alan and Stephen. *An instrument is a "note" if is a promise [to pay] and is a "draft" if is an order [to pay].* Section 3-104(e).

two that he wants a lump sum cash payment for the note. He might take the note to his bank and ask the bank if it would be interested in purchasing the note. The bank's interest in purchasing the note lies in the interest built into the note, as well as the amount of 'discount' it can get on the note. That is, if the principal amount owing on the note in two years is $720,000, anything the bank pays for the note less than $720,000 will represent the amount of discount of the note to the bank. Of course, in deciding how much to pay for the note, the bank will take into account such factors as inflation, the state of the business at the time, the projected business to be done and the like.

One thing the bank should definitely check is the form of the note, i.e., whether it is negotiable or not negotiable. If it is negotiable and the bank purchases the note under certain conditions (set forth in Section 3-302 and discussed later in this discussion), the bank is given a legal status which may give it superior rights with respect to the note, in relation to us, than George had. For example, certain claims we might have against George in a lawsuit on the note would not be assertable against the bank."

"I'm sorry Alan, but I don't understand this. What superior rights are you talking about, and how would this happen?"

"Okay, Stephen, assume for a moment that when we start operating the outlet we see that George made a mistake in calculating the amount of inventory on hand for which we would be entitled to reduce the note in a corresponding amount. If George refused to do this and the amount of the mistake was substantial enough to take a stand on, I would refuse to make any further payments to George. Of course, he would sue us. Against him we could assert the mistaken value placed on the inventory. If he sold it to the bank, however, under circumstances in which the bank becomes a **holder in due course**, the inventory error would not be assertable against the bank."[116]

"Why does that law produce such a result?" asked Stephen.

"In order to facilitate the movement of commercial paper," responded Alan, "someone purchasing such paper must know that when it is taken under certain commercial circumstances, the person or persons obligated on the paper can't refuse to make payment based on certain designated personal defenses. Otherwise, banks and interested third party lenders would not purchase this type of paper except at a correspondingly lower cost which would be almost impossible to compute in most situations."

"Okay, but what does negotiability have to do with it?"

"Here, let me show you," said Alan, as he took out his copy of the Uniform Commercial Code. He showed Stephen that under Section 3-302(a)(1) a holder in due course is first a holder[117] of an instrument. "Thus, in order for one to be a holder in due course, one must take an *instrument*." "An instrument," Alan went on to say, "is defined in Section 3-104(b) as a 'negotiable instrument.' If it is not negotiable, which is purely a matter of the form of the writing, it is not an instrument under Article 3 and there can be no holder in due course under Section 3-302."[118]

---

[116] The rights of the holder in due course are contained in Section 3-305(b), which is reproduced in footnote 116 in Appendix I on page 369. Some of the policy reasons for this result are discussed later in this discussion between Alan and Stephen.

[117] As previously noted, with respect to negotiable instruments, the 'holder' means the person in possession of a negotiable instrument that is payable either to bearer or to an identified person that is the person in possession. Section 1-201(b)(21)(A).

[118] In this connection the third paragraph to comment 2 of Section 3-104 states as follows:

"And you said that this whole question is simply a matter of form, right?" asked Stephen.

"Yes," said Alan. "Here, let me show you. You start out with Section 3-104(a). As you can see, in order to be a negotiable instrument, all of the conditions in subsection (a), (1), (2) and (3) must be met.

The first condition under Section 3-104(a), that the writing must contain an **unconditional promise** *or order to pay a fixed amount of money.* The 'unconditional promise' is not made conditional by the fact that the note mentions the underlying sales agreement, for as noted under Section 3-106, a promise or order is not made conditional by the fact that it refers to another writing.[119] Nor is the writing made non-negotiable by the fact that the note refers to the Security Agreement and various rights contained therein with respect to the collateral. Section 3-106[120] Notice, though, if the agreement stated that it was **subject to** the terms of the sales agreement, it would not be negotiable under Section 3-106(a)(ii)."[121]

An order or promise that is excluded from Article 3 because of the requirements of 3-104(a) may nevertheless be similar to a negotiable instrument in many respects. Although such a writing cannot be made a negotiable instrument within Article 3 by contract or conduct of the parties, nothing in Section 3-104 or Section 3-102 is intended to mean that in a particular case involving such a writing a court could not arrive at a result similar to the result that would follow if the writing were a negotiable instrument.

[119] *... A reference to another writing does not of itself make the promise or order conditional.* Section 3-106(a).

[120] *A promise or order is not made conditional (i) by a reference to another writing for a statement of rights with respect to collateral, prepayment, or acceleration.* Section 3-106(b).

[121] *Except as provided in this section, for the purposes of Section 3-104(a), a promise or order is unconditional **unless** it states:... (ii) that the promise or order is **subject to** or governed by another writing...* Section 3-106(a)(ii). [Emphasis added].

Stephen nodded, waiting for Alan to continue.

Alan then turned the page back to Section 3-104(a) and said, "As we've already discussed, this unconditional order or promise must be to pay a certain amount of money. I know what you are thinking," said Alan. "The fact that there is a possibility of other charges such as court costs and attorney's fees being awarded obviously would make the sum uncertain inasmuch as you will never know exactly what attorney's fees or court costs would be in a given matter. However, as you can see," Alan continued, "under Section 3-104(a), this poses no problem."[122]

"Next the instrument must be **payable on demand or at a definite time**." Section 3-104(a)(2). "This is not a demand instrument inasmuch as it is not payable *'on demand* [of the holder] *or at sight'* or otherwise within Section 3-108(a);[123] rather it is **payable at a definite**

Anyone purchasing paper which states that it is "subject to" another writing, is on notice that the piece of commercial paper involved is in effect, subrogated to the terms of the other writing. The promise on the commercial paper, in that situation, is clearly conditional on the terms and conditions in the other writing.

[122] It may seem that these allowances of provisions and references to other agreements, attorneys fees and the like would make it impossible to ever have a sum certain or unconditional promise. However, the realities of commercial practice balance the precise language of the statute and those realities. These references and various contingencies are to be distinguished from a situation where the note was 'subject to' another agreement as discussed above.

[123] *A promise or order is "payable on demand" if it (i) states that it is payable on demand or at sight, or otherwise indicates that it is payable at the will of the holder, or (ii) does not state any time of payment. Section 3-108(a).*

time.[124]   That is, it is payable in full on April 1, 2026. The fact that it is subject to acceleration does not affect this.[125]

"Does this simply mean that if he wants to he can force us to pay ahead of time?"

"No," said Alan. "First of all, Section 1-309 requires that the accelerating party must in **good faith**[126] believe *'that the prospect of payment or performance is impaired'*. That is, George must act 'honestly in fact' and with the 'observance of reasonable commercial standards' in accelerating.[127] In this case, we negotiated out what insecurity would be.[128] If we miss two monthly payments and the profitability schedule has been met during those two months, George has the right to

---

[124] *A promise or order is "payable at a definite time" if it is payable on elapse of a definite time period after sight or acceptance or at a fixed date or dates….* Section 3-108(b).

[125] *[An instrument can be "payable at a definite time' even if] subject to rights of (i) prepayment, (ii) acceleration, (iii) extension at the option of the holder, or (iv) extension of a further definite time at the option of the maker or acceptor or automatically upon or after a specified act or event.* Section 3-108(b).

[126] *A term providing that one party or his successor in interest may accelerate payment or performance or require collateral or additional collateral "at will" or "when he deems himself insecure' or in words of similar import shall be construed to mean that he shall have the power to do so only if he in good faith believes that the prospect of payment or performance is impaired….* Section 1-309.

[127] *"Good faith" means honesty in fact and the observance of reasonable commercial standards of fair dealing.* Section 3-103(a)(4).

[128] By so doing, the parties removed the definitional aspect of insecurity from the trier of fact. Section 1-302(b) permits the parties to set standards as to what constitutes good faith in their agreement as long as such standards are not manifestly unreasonable. Section 1-302(b) is discussed later in this book.

accelerate. Other than that, the terms of the agreement still bars him from doing so."

Stephen nodded.

"Finally," continued Alan, "in order to be negotiable, the instrument must be **payable to order** or **to bearer**. As you can see, the note is payable to the order of George, and is therefore order paper within Section 3-109."[129]

"I see," said Stephen. "So if it's an instrument, and someone buys it, that person is a *'holder in due course'*, right?"

"No," said Alan. "To be a holder in due course, the purchase[130] of the instrument must satisfy the requirements of Section 3-302, i.e., for value, in good faith and without notice that the instrument is overdue or has been dishonored or within the other circumstances noted in the second clause to Section 3-302(a)(2).[131] Basically, the law wants to protect purchasers of this paper who are honest, pay for the paper, and are unaware of some problem with the instrument involved. If it was purchased under all of these circumstances, *then* the purchaser would be a holder in due course and would

---

[129] *A promise or order this is not payable to bearer [Section 3-109(a)] is payable to order if it is payable (i) to the order of an identified person or (ii) to an identified person or order. A promise or order that is payable to order is payable to the identified person.* Section 3-109(b).

[130] *"Purchase" includes taking by sale, discount, negotiation, mortgage, pledge, lien, security interest, issue or re-issue, gift or any other voluntary transaction creating an interest in property.* Section 1-201(b)(29).

"Purchaser" means a person who takes by purchase. Section 1-201(b)(30).

[131] At this point, it might be useful for the reader to reread footnote 116 which is contained in Appendix I beginning on page 369.

cut off personal defenses such as the mistaken value of the inventory."[132]

"I see," said Stephen. "What are you going to do to prevent this?"

"I am simply going to ask George if we can stick in a term that makes this note **subject to** the terms of our sales agreement, which would therefore impair negotiability under Section 3-106(a)(ii)."

"I know you are probably tired of explaining these things to me, but why does this affect negotiability when stating the agreement doesn't?"

"Of course I don't get tired of answering these questions for you, Stephen. After all, I'm your lawyer." (And I'm getting ten percent of everything you make, Alan thought to himself.)

"There are two main purposes for the negotiability requirements. We've already discussed one, i.e., that a purchaser taking the instrument under circumstances which make him a holder in due course knows that the obligor or obligors can't assert certain defenses against him. This of course will facilitate the movement of this paper and provide capital to the seller of the paper. The other purpose is the certainty of the promise contained in a negotiable piece of paper. That is, there is a definite promise to pay a definite amount at a definite time.

---

[132] The reader might also which to review the text of Sections, 3-303, 3-304, and 3-306, which are reproduced in the Statutory Supplement.

Now, when the paper says it is 'subject to' another agreement, it is clear that the promise contained in the writing is not definite. Rather, it could be partially or totally defeated by terms contained in the other agreement. A person purchasing paper in such a situation should know this. In addition, the obligor is probably counting on this provision to keep the payee from transferring the paper to a purchaser who becomes a holder in due course. Primarily because of those reasons, the Code does not give negotiable status to such paper."

After the discussion, Alan and Stephen returned to meet with George. As was expected, Onus Primo also showed up and was there to sign the note as had been worked out between Alan and George. After they all sat down, Alan asked George if he would mind making the change he had discussed with Stephen.

"Of course not," said George. Whereupon George made the change on the note which was initialed by George, Alan, Stephen and Onus.

"Great," said Alan.

Stephen and Alan signed at the bottom of the note where it said makers. Onus also signed the note just below Alan's signature.[133]

---

[133] Onus Primo's signature in this situation would be 'for accommodation' under Section 3-419(a):

> *If an instrument is issued for value given for the benefit of a party to the instrument ("accommodated party") and another party to the instrument (accommodation party") signs the instrument for the purpose of incurring liability on the instrument without being a direct beneficiary of the value given for the instrument, the instrument is signed by the accommodation party "for accommodation."*

Unknown to everyone in the meeting, Onus Primo was delighted to sign the note in any capacity. The only reason Onus was signing it was so he would put himself in a position to steal from the company, milk it for all it was worth and then leave town. He didn't mind signing the note at all; in fact, it was a chance he had long been waiting for. For the twelve years that Onus worked a 60-hour week, George paid him a measly $325 a week. Finally, he thought to himself, I can get even with that miser.

Section 7

Stephen felt completely recovered from the ordeals of just a short period ago, and as he sat back in his reclining chair, he felt like a businessman. First of all, the boat business was definitely off to a great start. He was having no trouble meeting his payments to the South Dade Bank and each day he would take any proceeds which he received over to the bank. Bank personnel even knew his name! Most important of all to Stephen was the purchase of the outlet. It made him feel really important to be able to say that he was in the clothing business as well as in the boat business. He had dreams of entering into even more businesses and starting to accumulate wealth. Perhaps Grandfather was right, he thought to himself. As he sat back smoking his cigar, he was confident he would soon be smoking $10 cigars. Maybe someday, he wouldn't even need to look at the price.

One of the reasons Stephen was so excited was that he had landed the Crown account earlier in the week. In fact, the previous day he had placed an order to Crown Boats for six boats, ranging from $22,500 in value up to $58,000 in value. He felt that these boats were comparable to the Royal Boats which he currently held in the showroom. He figured that the disparity in prices which existed between Crown Boats and Royal Boats, when the boats were sitting side by side with one another, would create a sense of competition in the showroom and would give him an appearance of objectivity.

He felt that he would be able to sell the Crown Boats more easily because of the Royal stock which was also available. He did feel, however, that he would be able to move the Royal Boats at pretty much the same pace at which they had been going. Royal Boats was, of course, one of those well known "name brands" which people tended to buy regardless of the fact that another boat was just as good and priced less expensively. Thus, he hoped to be able to get the person who was not just interested in buying brand names to try the Crown line while at the same time continue to keep the customer who was only interested in purchasing the name brand.

Just when Stephen was beginning to fantasize about money, the phone rang. Crown was on the line and wanted to discuss the payment terms of a sales agreement which they would enter into with Stephen if a long-term arrangement was to be agreed upon. Stephen had contemplated payment by certified check which South Dade Bank would give him under the future advance clause of the security agreement.[134]

Crown was not enthused with the idea and requested that Stephen get a letter of credit issued on behalf of Crown for all boats shipped. Stephen didn't know what a letter of credit was but told Crown that he would take the

---

[134] When a drawer of a check issues that instrument, the bank is not liable on it at that point:

(1) A check or other draft does not of itself operate as an assignment of any funds in the hands of the drawee available for its payment, and the drawee is not liable on the instrument until he accepts it. Section 3-408.

In a certified check situation the bank has accepted the check. *"Certified check" means a check accepted by the bank on which it is drawn...* Section 3-409(d).

In either situation, *"Acceptance" means the drawee's signed agreement to pay a draft as presented. It must be written on the draft and may consist of the drawee's signature alone....* Section 3-409(a).

A certified check would be preferable to Crown since the bank would be liable on the check at the time Crown received possession of the check, as opposed to a regular check situation in which the bank would not be liable until presentment and final payment by the bank.

matter up with his attorney that day and would get back to them shortly.

As soon as he got off the phone, Stephen called Alan to find out what a letter of credit was. Alan was on his way to court and didn't have time to discuss it. Stephen asked if he could come down the following morning to talk about it. Alan apologetically told Stephen that he would still be in court. Stephen became rather upset because he wanted to close the Crown deal as soon as possible. Alan said that he would dictate a memo to him and have it emailed to Stephen's Boats that afternoon or evening if that would be okay. Reluctantly, Stephen agreed.

As soon as Alan got off the phone with Stephen he called Doug. He told Doug about the purchase of the boats by Stephen's Boats, Inc., from Crown. He asked Doug if he would be so kind as to draft a memorandum to Stephen under the name of Alan to explain this transaction. Stephen was very insistent about getting it, Alan explained, and just did not have time to do it because he had to be in court the following morning and had a lot of preparation to do. Doug, somewhat overworked, reluctantly agreed to do it. Of course, he did not communicate his reluctance to Alan.

MEMORANDUM

TO: Stephen
FROM: Alan
RE: Letter of Credit Transaction
            with Crown
DATE: April 24, 2006

Article 5 of the Uniform Commercial Code deals with letters of credit. A ***letter of credit*** is defined under Section 5-102(a)(10) as *"a definite undertaking...by an issuer to a beneficiary at the request or for the account of an applicant...to honor a documentary presentation by payment..."*[135] Thus the following must be present:

1. A definite undertaking by an issuer to a beneficiary;
2. The undertaking must be at the request, or for the account of an applicant;
3. The undertaking made by the issuer is to 'honor a documentary presentation by payment.'

A brief hypothetical will be presented to illustrate the operation of Section 5-102(a)(10) noted above.

Let's assume for a moment that Crown's contract with Stephen's Boats is for the purchase of two $45,000 Model X speedboats, and that, as they have done in their upcoming transaction,

---

[135] *"Letter of credit" means a definite undertaking that satisfies the requirements of Section 5-104 [Formal Requirements] by an issuer to a beneficiary at the request or for the account of an applicant... to honor a documentary presentation by payment or delivery of an item for value.* Section 5-102(a)(10).

Crown requests payment by letter of credit. Stephen's agrees and approaches South Dade Bank who commits to *'make a definite undertaking'* to Crown Boats that if Crown complies with the terms of the letter of credit, South Dade will *honor 'a documentary presentation by payment '* to Crown.

The bank, in issuing the letter of credit, would be the ***issuer***.[136] Crown, as the party *'entitled to have its complying presentation honored'* [i.e., to get paid] would be called the ***beneficiary***.[137] Stephen, as a person causing the bank to issue a credit, would be called the ***applicant***.[138]

In the hypothesized transaction, the letter of credit will require at a minimum that Crown submit documentation to South Dade which shows that Crown shipped the called for boats as well as a properly drawn draft in the called for amount. The bill of lading, as a document of title, would be within the definition of a *document* under Article 5.[139] Delivery of that document with the called for

---

[136] *"Issuer" means a bank or other person that issues a letter of credit...* Section 5-102(a)(9).

[137] *"Beneficiary" means a person who under the terms of a letter of credit is entitled to have its complying presentation honored. The term includes a person to whom drawing rights have been transferred under a transferable letter of credit.* Section 5-102(a)(3).

[138] *"Applicant" means a person at whose request or for whose account a letter of credit is issued....* Section 5-102(a)(2).

[139] The draft and bill of lading constitute a 'document' under Section 5-102(a)(6):

Document means draft or other demand, document of title ... or other record, statement, or representation of fact, law, right or opinions .... which is capable of being examined for purposes of compliance with the terms and conditions of the letter of credit.

draft to South Dade for the purpose of being paid, would be a presentation under Section 5-102(a)(12):

> ***Presentation*** *means delivery of a document to an issuer ...for honor or giving value under a letter of credit.*

Once South Dade is satisfied that these documents are in order, South Dade will honor the draft presented by paying the amount specified therein to Crown.

The letter of credit in the example noted might read as follows:

To: Crown Boats

Gentlemen:

This is to advise you that irrevocable letter of credit number 343 has been issued in your favor on behalf of our customer, Stephen's Boats, Inc. You are authorized to draw a sight draft on Stephen's Boats, under this letter of credit, in the amount of $90,000 upon presentation of the following to South Dade Bank: a bill of lading showing shipment of two 28' Model X speed boats to Stephen's Boats and a draft drawn as stated above. These documents must be submitted by June 30, 2006.

Signed,

_____
South Dade Bank, Issuer

The example of the letter of credit given above is illustrative. Under Article 5 of the Code there is no particular form needed in order to have an enforceable letter of credit other than the fact that it be in the form of a 'record' and properly authenticated. Section 5-104(i)(ii). **Record** *means information that is inscribed on a tangible medium, or that is stored in an electronic or other medium and is retrievable in perceivable form."* Section 5-102(a)(14).

As you can see, the essence of the transaction is that Crown must submit documentation showing that the called for boats have been shipped [as evidenced by the bill of lading].

Once South Dade sends the letter to Crown, it becomes enforceable.[140] Although the above letter of credit calls for an "irrevocable" letter of credit, it is not necessary to so state, for in the absence of language to the contrary, the irrevocable nature would be presumed.[141] Once a letter of credit is issued, the rights of the parties to the letter of credit cannot be changed without the parties consent.[142] If however, there are changes, no

---

[140] *A letter of credit is issued and becomes enforceable according to its terms against the issuer when the issuer sends or otherwise transmits it to the person requested to advise or to the beneficiary.* Section 5-106(a).

[141] *A letter of credit is revocable only if it so provides. Id.*

[142] *After a letter of credit is issued, rights and obligations of a beneficiary, applicant, confirmer, and issuer are not affected by an amendment or cancellation to which that person has not consented except to the extent the letter of credit provides that it is revocable or that the issuer may amend or cancel the letter of credit without that consent.* Section 5-106(b).

consideration is required. Nor is any consideration required for the initial issue of the letter of credit:

> *Consideration is not required to issue, amend, transfer or cancel a letter of credit, advice or confirmation.* Section 5-105.

When South Dade issues the letter of credit, it could send notification to the First National Bank of Mobile, Crown's bank, rather than directly to Crown. If it does and that bank notifies Crown of the letter of credit, First National Bank of Mobile would be an *'adviser'*:

> **Advisor** *means a person who...notifies or requests another adviser to notify the beneficiary that a letter of credit has been issued....* Section 5-102(a)(1).

As an adviser, it is not obligated to honor a presentation or give value:

> *An adviser that is not a confirmer is not obligated to honor or give value for a presentation.* Section 5-107(c).

Rather:

> *An advisor undertakes to the issuer and to the beneficiary accurately to advise the terms of the letter of credit, confirmation, amendment, or advice received by that person and undertakes to the beneficiary to check the apparent authenticity of the request to advise.* Section 5-107(c).

If, however, First National engaged to Crown that it would *honor* the letter of credit upon presentation of the called for documents, or that South Dade would honor such a presentation, First National would become a **confirmer** and, as such, [would] *'undertake... to honor a presentation under a letter of credit issued by another.'* Section 5-102(a)(4). As a confirmer First National would be *'directly obligated on...[the] letter of credit and has the rights and obligations of an issuer to the extent of its confirmation.'* Section 5-107(a).

For purposes of the hypothetical, I shall assume that First National was an adviser, and that upon receipt of this letter of credit it notified Crown by sending a copy of the letter to Crown. After receiving the letter of credit, Crown will be ready to proceed. It knows with relative certainty that upon compliance with the terms of the letter of credit [i.e. the documents are in order] it will be paid by South Dade Bank in the called for amount.[143] Crown will thus take the two boats

---

[143] This rule is contained in the first clause to Section 5-108(a):

Except as otherwise provided in Section 5-109 [dealing with fraud and forgery] an issuer shall honor a presentation that ... appears on its face strictly to comply with the terms and conditions of the letter of credit.

For a wrongful dishonor:

The beneficiary...may recover from the issuer the amount that is the subject of the dishonor or repudiation. Section 5-111(a)...

That section goes on to state:

...[T]he claimant may also recover incidental but not consequential damages.

The comments to Section 5-111 suggest that "[Since compensatory damages are not allowed] *a fortiori* punitive and

called for in the letter of credit to a carrier, either rail or truck. The carrier will issue a "bill of lading" to Crown which will describe the boats shipped and contain the carrier's contract to deliver pursuant to the terms contained therein.[144]

After it receives the bill of lading, Crown will take the bill of lading and a draft for $90,000 to First National who will forward the documents to South Dade Bank. South Dade Bank will examine the documents in accordance with standards used in the industry to see whether they conform with the terms of the letter of credit.[145]

Three things should be noted in this connection: first, as stated previously, if the documents conform to those called for by the letter of credit, the issuer must make payment to the beneficiary [absent fraud or forgery as previously discussed]; second, as Section 5-108(a) indicates, the focus of the bank is whether or not the presentation *'appears on its face strictly to comply with the terms and conditions of the letter of credit.'*[146]

---

exemplary damages are excluded". The same comment noted above goes on to state that: 'however, this section does not bar recovery of consequential or even punitive damages for breach of statutory or common law duties arising outside this article."

The balance of footnote 143 is in Appendix I on page 372.

[144] A more detailed discussion of bills of lading appears later in this book. For now, the reader may wish to review footnote 67 at page 93

[145] *[In examining a presentation] An issuer shall observe standard practice of financial institutions that regularly issue letters of credit.* Section 5-108(e).

[146] The bank is facilitating the transaction by creating the payment mechanism via a letter of credit. As a financing agency, it does not want to be concerned with the underlying contract; it wants

Finally, an issuer has a reasonable time after presentation, but not beyond the end of the seventh business day after its receipt of the documents to decide whether or not to honor Section 5-107(b).[147]

It is thus seen that the basic mechanics of the letter of credit in the hypothetical situation given are as follows:

1. Stephen gets his bank to issue a letter of credit to Crown;
2. Crown ships the called for goods and obtains proper documentation thereof (as specified in the letter of credit). In addition, Crown will draw a draft on Stephen in the specified amount;
3. Crown takes the documents to First National Bank of Mobile which sends the same to South Dade;

---

to be able to discharge its duty by reviewing documents which, if in proper form, show that the transaction in question has been performed properly and that payment is appropriately due. If the documents are not in order, then no payment is due.

[147] If it does not honor the presentation it is required *'to give notice to the presenter of discrepancies in the presentation [not later than the seventh business day following receipt.]'* Section 5-108(b)(3).

4. South Dade will examine the documents to ascertain whether or not they comply with the terms of the letter of credit;

5. If the documents are in order, South Dade will make payment to First National (who will probably just credit Crown's account);

6. South Dade will debit Stephen's account, if payment has not already been made by Stephen.

***

This memorandum was emailed to Stephen who received it the next morning in the mail. After reading the memorandum he was fairly certain that the bank would not have any reservations about entering into the letter of credit transaction requested by Crown. Of course, they were obligated to give him this money under the terms of the security agreement if he obtained the Crown or Marina account, and he figured that it wouldn't matter to them how he got it., i.e., whether his account was credited or whether the bank gave it to him under the letter of credit.

He knew Alan was in court and would be unavailable to help him secure the letter of credit from the bank. He therefore called Doug as he realized that Doug was fairly familiar with Uniform Commercial Code transactions and asked Doug if he could spare some time that day to meet with South Dade Bank officials to try to get this letter of credit. Doug was elated with the prospect of finally starting to deal with clients face to face. He told Stephen he would have no trouble getting together with him that day. He made the necessary calls and a meeting was set for that afternoon at the bank.

Section 8

At the meeting, Stephen explained why he wanted to enter into the letter of credit arrangement with Crown, and, of course, told the bank that pursuant to the terms of the Security Agreement and Loan Agreement, they were obligated to advance him $400,000. He told them that he hoped that they would not mind doing this in the form of a letter of credit. The bank agreed and drafted the following letter to Crown:

Gentlemen:

This is to advise you that irrevocable letter of credit No. 2377 had been issued in your favor on behalf of our customer, Stephen's Boats, Inc. You are authorized to draw up to $400,000 under this letter of credit. All drafts presented under this letter of credit are to be accompanied by a negotiable bill of lading to the order of Stephen's Boats describing all Crown Boats shipped thereunder. At no time shall any draft or shipment of boats exceed $150,000 without a prior written approval of South Dade Bank. Drafts must be presented by December 21, 2006.

Very truly yours,

South Dade Bank

As per agreement with Stephen, Doug was to stop by the bank the next morning to review the terms of the letter of credit before it was sent to Crown. While he was there, he happened to get into a discussion about the Uniform Commercial Code with one of the bank vice presidents, Fred Houstrant. The vice-president was very impressed with the way it seemed Doug knew the Code and asked Doug if their firm would be interested in representing the bank in a problem involving a suit against the bank by one of its depositors. Needless to say, the prospect of bringing in the bank as a client absolutely thrilled Doug. After all, he had been out of law school for only a year and a half and if he could bring in a client the size of South Dade Bank, one that the firm had been trying to get for five years, he would certainly endear himself to the firm and would be in a better position to be financially rewarded. Doug tried to be cool about it, but of course conveyed his enthusiasm to Fred who knew that Doug would love such an opportunity.

"Very good," Fred said, "I will dictate a statement of facts to my secretary who will get that, plus any other information you need, out to you this afternoon."

Doug was overjoyed as he went back to the office. As soon as he got there, he went to see Alan to tell him about the events of the day. Alan, however, was not yet back from the hearing so Doug telephoned Stephen, and told him that he had reviewed the letter of credit, that everything was in order and recommended that it be sent out. Stephen was pleased and told Doug to go ahead and have it done. Just then, Alan came back and Doug went to his office. Before Doug could say anything about what had happened with the bank, Alan started talking to him about the hearing that morning and that the judge had given him 24 hours to prepare a memorandum in support of his client's position. He needed Doug's help because he was really strapped for time at this point.

"I will give you a quick recitation of the facts," Alan said, "and then I want you to get on this right away. I want you to drop everything else which you have because I need this first thing in the morning."

Doug, totally swamped with work and somewhat disappointed that he didn't get a chance to tell Alan the news, had seen Alan like this before and decided that he had better listen to what he said, do his work, and somehow manage to do the other things when he had time.

"What are the facts?" Doug asked.

Alan said that the problem was one of commercial paper under Article 3 and essentially involved the following fact situation:

Alan's client not too long ago was at one of the exclusive garage sales in the estate area of South Miami. The items being sold were not the type typically found at a garage sale. It appears that Alan's client had purchased a sculpture for which she had written a check in the amount of $7,000. She thought it was a Bónbón original. It turned out, however, that when she got the sculpture home, her husband told her that it was a fake. Shocked as she was, she immediately called her friend, Lúis, who was an art expert. He came over to examine the sculpture. After an examination by Lúis was concluded, Lúis said that he had no choice but to agree with her husband and this was not an original Bónbón, but in fact a fake. Immediately, she telephoned Alan who advised her to stop payment on the check. This she had done.[148] Now she was being sued by Peter Dandley, the nephew of the former owner of the sculpture.

---

[148] Section 4-403 deals with the customer's right to stop payment of a check, duration of oral and written stop orders, as well as stating the burden of proof with respect to establishing loss when the bank fails to follow a binding stop order. It states in relevant part as follows:

(a) A customer or any person authorized to draw on the account... may stop payment of any item drawn on the customer's account... by an order to the bank describing the item with reasonable certainty received at a time and in a manner that affords the bank a reasonable opportunity to act to act on it before any action by the bank with respect to the item described in Section 4-303...

"How did he get the check?" Doug asked.

"What do you mean?" Alan said.

"Did he pay for it?" Doug replied.

"I have no idea" said Alan, and then somewhat indignantly added "and how could that make a difference anyway?"

Doug could not believe what he was hearing. Rather than explain it, he asked Alan to find out if Dandley paid for the check, and if so, how much.

"Okay," Doug said, "what do you want me to do with it now?"

"Dandley has moved for summary judgment and I need a memorandum in opposition to it. But," continued Alan, "Lulu, my client, does not want to say Stephanie knew the sculpture was a fake or in any way impugn her character. You see, they're good personal friends, and she says she doesn't want to risk ruining their friendship. So what I need is a memorandum which shows Dandley isn't entitled to the motion as a matter of law. And Doug, this is Judge Touten, so lay it out *very* clearly. He hates to get reversed."

"Okay," said Doug, "I'll get on it right away, but I will need the information I requested as soon as possible. By the way, I have some good news for you first."

"What's that?" Alan asked.

"Well, you know you have been trying to get South Dade Bank as a client for quite a few years?"

"We have been trying to get some of their work, yes," said Alan.

(b) A stop payment order is effective for six months, but it lapses 14 calendar days if the original order was oral and not confirmed in a record within that time.....

(3) The burden of establishing the fact and amount of loss resulting from the payment of an item contrary to a stop payment order... is on the customer....

"Well, today South Dade asked the firm to represent them, me particularly, in a big banking problem that came up."

"Why did they pick you?" Alan asked.

Doug proceeded to explain to him that he was over there on the letter of credit matter for Stephen, and that while he was there, he became involved in a discussion with the vice-president and he simply asked him to represent them. Alan was extremely pleased with this, although he was a little nervous that Doug went to the bank alone. He asked Doug when he was supposed to start on it. Doug told Alan that he was supposed to receive something in from the bank first thing in the morning as it was going out in today's mail.

"Are you going to have time to handle this memorandum for me adequately?" Alan asked, "because if you aren't, I would rather get someone else to do it and leave you free to do the South Dade Bank thing. We have been trying to get them for six or seven years and I would hate very much for anything to go wrong." (As important as the hearing was to Alan, hardly anything was more important to him than bringing new business to the firm.)

"Well," Doug said, "the material is not going to come until tomorrow and I can get a memorandum to you pretty quickly on this one. The problem is if you want me to look up case law, I am just not going to have that much time to do that, but I will be able to get you the memorandum."

"Doug, I need case law or I don't think we've got a chance."

"Don't worry, Alan," said Doug, "I'll get one of the law clerks to look up the cases after I've finished the memorandum. He'll be able to work off that."[149]

---

[149] There are several annotative services which contain decisions of courts under the UCC. I find the Uniform Commercial

"So, I'll tell you what," Doug continued, "I'll draft the memorandum for you and give you a copy of the draft and while you are reviewing it, I will get a clerk to find case support for it."

"Very good," Alan said, "and remember, Doug, I don't want anything to happen to the South Dade Bank matter, so if you get tied up, let me know and I will get someone else on it."

"Okay," Doug said, whereupon Doug went back to his office to begin dictating a memorandum on the case presented to him by Alan.

One of the reasons Alan was so busy was because he was trying to meet with officials of West Dade Bank to try to secure a loan for new inventory for the clothing outlet. He tried to get Stephen to meet him over there but Stephen simply did not have time. The first shipment from Crown was due to arrive that day and he wanted to be on hand for that. Furthermore, Stephen's brother, a cattle rancher from Texas, had come to town. He had come because he was interested in getting involved in wholesale fruit distribution in the Dallas-Ft. Worth area.

Whenever he came to town, Stephen spent all of his time with "Duke" as he was known by all of his friends and family, so he and Duke and the rest of the family were all set to go out to dinner that evening.

At Alan's meeting with West Dade, he expressed a need on behalf of the outlet to borrow $240,000. Alan explained that he wanted this money in order to insure that the outlet would be ready for the influx of college

---

Code Reporting Service to be of the greatest value and ease of use. The index is keyed to Code sections so that one knowing the relevant sections can access the cases quickly. Also, cases are sometimes reported in the UCC Reporting Service that are not reported elsewhere. My UCC education was predicated upon the belief that the answer was always in the statute, and this service was designed for quick retrieval of relevant case law.

students which started sometime around Thanksgiving and ended sometime at the end of April. He explained that he felt if they got on the stick now and stocked a really good inventory, they could beat the market by having an advance fashion selection. (Alan prided himself on being quite "hip" when it came to clothes, After all, he *could* go two weeks without wearing the same suit or shirt.)

Jerry Thompson, who was negotiating this loan with Alan, expressed a few concerns. First of all, he knew that George already had a security interest in the inventory and equipment which he took back as part of the agreement when he sold the business. Second, the bank was concerned that, because of George's interest, they would be subordinate all the way around and feared that, should something happen to the business, they, West Dade, would be out of luck.

Alan explained that this was not necessarily so. "First of all," Alan said, "$90,000 of the money is going to be used to purchase equipment." This equipment would be used to process the new design of jeans which they had in mind. Alan told Jerry that he was positive that if the transaction was structured properly, West Dade could get first priority with respect to the equipment. "Furthermore," Alan continued, "the transaction could be set up in such a way as to give you first priority even as to the inventory." This really surprised Jerry, but he said nothing and allowed Alan to continue. He went on to say that if the bank was interested in financing their accounts receivable, Alan would try to get George to agree to subordinate his interest to that of the bank.

"All of what you are saying sounds pretty good," Jerry indicated. "I'll tell you what," he said, "why don't you go back to your office and write us an opinion letter embodying the things which you said to me today regarding our priority in the equipment and inventory and how we can effectuate these priorities. When I get the letter, I will have our in-house counsel review it and if he agrees with you, we can sit down and talk about the $240,000 loan."

"Great," said Alan. Whereupon he shook Jerry's hand and went back to the office. There he found the memorandum from Doug which discussed the sculpture case:

MEMORANDUM OF LAW

TO: Alan
FROM: Doug
RE: The Sculpture Case
DATE: May 3, 2007

Facts
The facts may be briefly stated as follows:
1. Lulu purchased a sculpture from Stephanie and made payment by check;
2. Stephanie transferred the check to Dandley, her nephew, as a gift for his birthday;
3. At the time of the transfer, she indorsed the check to the order of Dandely;
4. The sculpture was represented by Stephanie to be a Bónbón original but in fact turned out not to be such;
5. Lulu stopped payment on the check;
6. Dandley took the check to Lulu's bank for payment;
7. Lulu's bank refused to pay;
8. Dandley has sued Lulu on her drawer's contract;
9. Dandley is claiming the legal status of a holder in due course;
10. Upon the basis of this status, Dandley is claiming that any problems with regard to

the sculpture are not pertinent to him in the enforcement of Lulu's obligation to pay him on the check;

11. Dandley has moved for summary judgment.

Question Presented

Is Dandley entitled to enforce payment of the check against Lulu?

Discussion

To adequately answer the foregoing question, some basic analysis will first be undertaken. The approach will be as follows:

(a) Issue, Indorsement and Transfer of the Check
(b) The Obligation of the Drawer
(c) Person Entitled to Enforce an Instrument
(d) Dandley's Rights Under the Check

(a) Issue, Indorsement and Transfer of the Check

Under Section 3-104(f) a **check** is defined as:

(i) a draft, other than a documentary draft, payable on demand and drawn on a bank or

(ii) a cashier's check or teller's check..."

When Lulu gave the check to Stephanie, there was an *issue* of the check under Article 3.

Issue occurred because it was the 'first delivery of an instrument...by the drawer...to a holder...for the purpose of giving rights on the instrument to any person.' Section 3-105(a).

A ***holder*** with respect to a negotiable instrument, *means the person in possession of a negotiable instrument that is payable either to bearer or to an identified person that is the person in possession.* Section 1-201(b)(21)(A). Lulu was the original holder.

When Lulu transferred the check to Dandley, she indorsed it with the words, *'pay to the order of Dandley'* above her signature. The check was thus 'specially indorsed' to Dandley:

> *If an indorsement is made by the holder of an instrument...and the indorsement identifies a person to whom it makes the instrument payable, it is a **"special indorsement"**....* Section 3-205(a).[150]

Since Dandley was the special indorsee and had possession of the check indorsed to his order, he was a 'holder' within Section 1-201(b)(21), as a person in possession of the check, now payable to him by reason of Lulu's special endorsement. He has maintained possession and is still a holder at this time. The impact of this status will be discussed following an analysis of Lulu's obligations as drawer of the check.

---

[150] That subsection goes on to state:

Any instrument specially endorsed becomes payable to the order of the special endorsee and may be further negotiated only by his endorsement.

(b) The Obligation of the Drawer

Lulu is the **drawer** of the check as ...*'a person who signs...ordering payment.'* Section 3-103(a)(5). As such, Lulu assumes the obligation set forth in Section 3-414(b):

> *If an unaccepted draft is dishonored, the drawer is obligated to pay the draft (i) according to its terms...at the time it first came into possession of a holder.... The obligation is owed to a person entitled to enforce the draft....*

As is clearly seen from Section 3-414(b) above, Lulu's obligation would not kick in until the check [a **draft** per Section 3-104(e)] was dishonored. In addition, the person seeking to hold the drawer to his obligation must be *'a person entitled to enforce the draft'.*

Therefore, the first question is whether or not the 'unaccepted draft' [the check] was dishonored. Dishonor of a negotiable instrument is governed by Section 3-502. In this case, Section 3-502(b)(2) would govern and states as follows:

> *If a draft is payable on demand and paragraph (1) does not apply* [for checks not presented for immediate payment over the counter] *the draft is dishonored if presentment for payment is duly made to the drawee and the draft is not paid on the day of presentment.*

Therefore, in order to answer the question of whether there was dishonor, we must determine whether or not Dandley's attempt to cash the check was a 'presentment'.

"Presentment" means a demand made by or on behalf of a person entitled to enforce an instrument (i) to pay the instrument made to the drawee... Section 3-501(a).

Dandley clearly demanded payment by the bank. So the question becomes whether Dandley was *'a person entitled to enforce the instrument.'*

(c) Person Entitled to Enforce the Instrument

A **person entitled to enforce** an instrument, for purposes of this case, is *'the holder of the instrument'*. Section 3-301(i). It has already been established that Dandley was a holder, and therefore he is a person entitled to enforce the check. The bank's refusal to pay the check on the day of presentment is a dishonor of the check per 3-502(b)(2).

(d) Dandley's Rights Under the Check

Since all of the prerequisites of Section 3-414(b) have been met, Dandley can bring a cause of action against Lulu on her drawer's obligation, and seek enforcement of the check *'according to its terms ...at the time it first came into possession of a holder.'* In this case, that would be $7,000.

Lulu's defense to that cause of action would be the fact that the sculpture was not as it was represented to be. While Lulu is not alleging fraud by Stephanie, she is clearly stating that she did not get what she paid for. Nor is Stephanie disputing that. It is Dandley's position that any dispute about the quality of the sculpture is between Stephanie and Lulu. He bases this position on his claim that he is a 'holder in due course' and therefore takes the check free of any personal defenses that might exist on the underlying obligation.

The requirements for becoming a 'holder in due course' are stated in Section 3-302. I shall assume that the check was in perfect order physically so that so that any such issues noted in Section 3-302 are not present in this case. I will further assume that the check was originally taken by Stephanie 'in good faith' and without notice of any kind under Section 3-302(a)(2). The question is whether or not Stephanie gave value for the check.

Value is defined under Section 3-303. Under subsection (a)(1):

(a) An instrument is issued or transferred for value if:

(1) the instrument is issued or transferred for a promise of performance, to the extent the promise has been performed.

In the case under consideration, the check was issued to Stephanie, for her promise to deliver a Bónbón original. She delivered a fake. She did not perform her promise. If Stephanie had sued Lulu on the check, she would have been subject to a defense of failure of consideration under Section 3-303(b):

"Consideration" means any consideration sufficient to support a simple contract. The drawer or maker of an instrument has a defense if the instrument is issued without consideration.

You have indicated that Dandley received the check as a birthday gift. He was therefore, a transferee of the check getting the rights of the transferor, Stephanie.[151]   He did not pay for the check, nor was any other value given. It was simply 'negotiated' to him[152] and he became the holder of the check, and as noted, a *'person entitled to enforce payment'*, in precisely the same position as Stephanie would be. If Stephanie were to have brought a cause of action against Lulu on the check, Lulu would have the defense noted in Section 3-303(b)..."*The drawer...of an instrument has a defense if the instrument is issued without consideration.*" Stephanie's transfer of the check to Dandley does not change the result of an action against Lulu on her drawer's contract.[153]

---

[151] *Transfer of an instrument... vests in the transferee any right of the transferor to enforce the instrument.....* Section 3-203(b).

[152] *"Negotiation" means a transfer of possession, whether voluntary or involuntary, of an instrument by a person other than the issuer to a person who thereby becomes a holder.* Section 3-201(a).

[153] This is to be distinguished from a situation where the transferee gave value to the transferor and otherwise complied with the requirements of Section 3-302. For example, if Dandley gave Lulu $7,000 for the check, took the check in good faith and had no notice per 3-302(a)(2), Dandley would be an holder in due course in his own right (as opposed to a mere transferee) and would not be subject to the defense of failure of consideration.

Section 9

After Stephen added the Royal Boats account, the size of his inventory doubled. While this delighted Stephen, it required some adjustments in his day to day operations. One of his concerns was that he wasn't able to get all of the boats cleaned in time for the start of business each day. He had hired two young men when he opened Stephen's Boats for the sole purpose of washing the boats and getting them ready to be shown each day. Thad and Reggie were good workers, but there was no way they could handle the new volume between the two of them.

Stephen was faced with not having all the boats as immaculate as he wanted them or hiring two more employees to clean and polish the boats so that all would be ready at the start of business each day. The first option was clearly unacceptable. People spending top dollar for a boat expect it to look great in the showroom and he knew it would hurt business if he got away from what he called his *SSS Look* [Stephen Seller Superman Look]. On the other hand, the cost of hiring two more employees just to maintain the look of the boats was almost as unacceptable. Stephen had quickly learned how expensive it was to employ personnel.

Alan had suggested that Stephen purchase and install a machine to do the washing. Alan also suggested that this might even allow Stephen to fire Thad and Reggie, freeing up more capital. Stephen was amazed at how callous Alan could be at times, and he would not consider firing his loyal workers. He also knew that he could not afford to purchase a $200,000 machine for cleaning and polishing the boats.

After discussing the matter with Alan, Stephen called Doug and asked him if he had any suggestions. Doug of course, was thrilled to get a direct call from Stephen. Even though they were friends, Doug knew that all calls into the firm were recorded, along with the client's name.

He also knew that the every time a client called an associate, even on something a partner was working on, it looked good at raise time.

"I know what you mean about the enormous cost of buying a new machine", Doug had told Stephen. "But there are other options. First, as you know, you can buy the machine on time and wouldn't have to put out the full $200,000 at this time. All you would need is a down payment."

"I realize that Doug," said Stephen, "but even in that situation, I would need to come up with at least $20,000 cash which I just don't have at this time. My money is already tied up in my inventory, payroll and taxes. Plus, I have so much debt, that the thought of adding any more really concerns me. I guess I could look for a used piece of equipment and see if I can negotiate a good deal. What do you think Doug?"

"I don't think you should purchase used equipment. It will still be expensive and who knows how the equipment has been handled. You are relatively new in business Stephen and you have done everything first class up to now. I wouldn't change that by purchasing used goods."

"Have you considered leasing the equipment?"

"Actually, it never crossed my mind" replied Stephen. "Leasing sounds like a good idea, but I know absolutely nothing about leases—who has what rights, what the various options are, and all the rest of it. I do not want to get into a situation where I am not well informed and properly protected. Can you put something together for me so that I can understand this better?"

Doug was thrilled that Stephen had asked him directly to work on a legal matter pertaining to the business. But he was also concerned. If he said "yes" to Stephen's request, he was afraid that Alan would go berserk. After all, no associate was allowed to accept work without speaking to a partner first! On the other hand, he did not want to say that he needed Alan's permission to commit to working on the matter either.

"Of course I can my man. I am Mr. UCC and leases of personal property are governed by the Uniform Commercial Code. When do you want it done?"

Stephen replied: "How about a week from Friday? I am going to Key West until Wednesday afternoon. Got to unwind from all the stress!"

Within moments after Doug returned to the office, he was summoned to Alan's office. After inviting Doug to have a seat, Alan went behind his desk and looked at Doug and said: "Do you have anything to tell me?"(Silence.)

"Well?"

Doug looked down for a second, then at Alan and said, "I had a nice lunch with Stephen."

Alan said nothing, but Doug knew he was furious. So, in the hopes of soothing Alan, Doug said: "When Stephen asked me to 'put something together for him' on leases, something in me just said 'Yes!' Now I realize I should have spoken with you first."

"That would have been a good idea 'Mr. UCC'."

Just as Alan was preparing to launch on Doug, Stephen called Alan to advise him of his decision to lease rather than purchase equipment to wash, wax and otherwise maintain his boats, particularly his large boats, some of which exceeded sixty feet. After conducting a thorough search, he decided on the Aqua Magic Centrex, a large structure through which the boats could be pulled on a heavy diesel engine truck. The cost for the machine was listed at $212,397, plus taxes. In the event Stephen chose to purchase the machine, Stephen's Boats would be required to put twenty percent down, roughly, $43,000, plus pay sales tax and other fees, and sign a conditional sales contract for forty-eight months giving Aqua Magic Centrex a security interest in the equipment.

On the other hand, if he leased the equipment, Stephen would be required to make a down payment of $7,200 and sign a forty-eight month lease. Stephen had also learned that there were several important financial considerations which he wanted clearly spelled out before he made his decision.

As soon as Doug left his office, Alan called Dempsey Watson, a tax attorney with his firm, and asked him to come down for a moment.

When Dempsey arrived, Alan welcomed him with much enthusiasm and the obligatory "Would you like something to drink?" Since Alan was a partner, he had his own little refrigerator in his office, and could offer a nice variety of drinks.

Dempsey passed, and Alan asked him what he knew about leases.

"I know that from a business standpoint, leasing is sometimes preferable to buying. There are certain tax advantages to leasing, such as deducting rent as a business expense and typically a much lower down payment on a lease than a purchase."

Alan continued, "Do you know anything about the law governing leases? That is Article 2A of the Uniform Commercial Code?"

"You're in luck" replied Dempsey. "I just completed an online course on Leases. You need 56 hours of logged time, and you get three law school credits once you pass the exam. It is a computer-generated course, with oversight by Lance Gilbright, who teaches the UCC at the University of Miami School of Law. If you want to check it out, just go the University of Miami website, online education."

"Thanks Dempsey. Give my best to Dempsey Junior and the Mrs. Let's get together soon." And Dempsey was gone.

Alan was determined to handle this matter himself. He had heard rumors that people were saying that Doug was doing all the UCC work for the firm and Alan felt that he was not getting the credit he deserved. He would show them. He would show everyone.

With that fearless resolve he signed up for the course on leasing, and began immediately.

ONLINE TRAINING

He knew that Leases was a lot like Sales, and hadn't he gotten a B+ in Sales? Didn't he have Elias Sunshine for Commercial Law?

As he opened the course, he noticed three options. One was for a preformatted curriculum that took the reader through Article 2A via problems and explanations. The second option was for the student to type in facts and receive a computer generated response, or when appropriate, a reviewer response. The third option was a combination of the two approaches. Alan selected the latter approach. After typing in his name and course Code, he selected the preformatted curriculum to gain an initial understanding of the area.

OLR [Online Response]: Welcome to Leases under the Uniform Commercial Code. A working knowledge of Sales is a prerequisite to this course. Please select your topic.

Alan selected *Overview*.

A. OVERVIEW

OLR: Article 2A, entitled Leases, is designed to '*cover any transaction, regardless of form, that creates a lease*' [in goods]. Section 2A-102.

Bringing leases within the purview of the Uniform Commercial Code was discussed for many years before the drafters undertook its writing and enactment. With the dramatic increase in leasing activity during the past twenty years, it has become increasingly important to have a predictable, uniform body of law on the subject.

Article 2A is modeled upon Article 2, Sales. An overwhelming majority of the sections in Article 2A have identical, or virtually identical language of their Article 2 counterpart, and will be interpreted in the same manner as in Sales.

Beginning with some of the basic terms and conditions, the overlap between the Lease and Sales provisions is immediately apparent. In many cases this includes the statutory numbers as well. The reader is encouraged to refer to **The Uniform Commercial Code Made Easy** by Robert LeVine for related discussion. Even though I am simply a computer, I, as well as other computers I have communicated with, recommend this book to anyone seeking an understanding of the Uniform Commercial Code.

B. SOME BASIC TERMS AND DEFINITIONS

OLR: A hypothetical lease will be introduced to facilitate a review of the basic terms and definitions:

Babylon Medical Group, Inc. is a Florida Corporation with twenty-eight offices on the Gulf Coast.

In order to improve office efficiency, Babylon has decided to replace all of its old copy machines with new, state of the art equipment.

After thoroughly researching available equipment, Babylon decides to enter into a lease agreement with Professional Copy Service whereby Babylon would lease the twenty-eight machines.

The lease reads as follows:

AGREEMENT

WHEREAS, Babyon Medical Group, a Florida corporation, is desirous of leasing twenty-eight (28) Strantum Mydex Compact copy machines from Professional Copy Service, a Georgia corporation; and

WHEREAS, Professional Copy Service Inc., has agreed to lease said machines to Babylon Medical Group, under the terms and conditions stated herein:

NOW, THEREFORE, in consideration of the mutual covenants contained herein and other good and valuable consideration receipt whereof is hereby acknowledged, the parties hereby agree as follows:

1. Professional Copy service agrees to lease to Babylon Medical Group, twenty-eight (28) Strantum Mydex compact copy machines;
2. The copy machines to be leased under this agreement will be described by model and serial number on an addendum to this Master Lease Agreement prior to its execution;
3. The duration of each lease between Professional Copy Service and Babylon Medical Group will be for 24 months;
4. Lessee agrees to maintain the quality of the leased goods through regular maintenance and upkeep;

5. Lessor agrees that lessee shall have the complete, uninterrupted use of the leased goods;

6. Lessor agrees to furnish copy machines which will produce high quality copies of the type described in the manufacturers' warranty;

7. Delivery of said copy machines shall be on a quarterly basis with six machines contained in each shipment;

8. Babylon Medical Group will not sublease or transfer any interest in the copy machines which are the subject matter of this lease;

9. Payment will be on the first of each month beginning September 1, 2006 at a base rate of $150 per machine;

10. Payment shall be due in one lump sum on the payment date specified above for all machines delivered under this lease at the time payment is due;

11. This agreement shall be governed by the laws of the State of Georgia;

12. Professional Copy Service shall not be liable for any consequential damages which may result from non performance of this agreement;

13. In the event lessee fails to properly perform under this agreement, lessee shall be liable to seller in the amount of $25,000 as liquidated damages;

14. This agreement embodies the full understanding of the parties hereto, and may not be modified except in writing signed by both parties.

IN WITNESS WHEREOF, this Lease Agreement has been executed as of the date first above written.

Signed, Sealed and Delivered in the presence of:

_____
Babylon Medical Group, Inc.

_____
Professional Copy Service, Inc.

OLR: The agreement between Babylon Medical Group and Professional Copy Service creates a lease:

> A **lease** 'means a transfer of the right to possession and use of goods for a period in return for consideration....' Section 2A-103(1)(j).

Babylon Medical Group is the **lessee**, as '[the] person who acquires the right to possession and use of goods under a lease'. Unless the context clearly indicates otherwise, the term includes a sublessee. Section 2A-103(1)(n).

Professional Copy Service is the **lessor** as '[the] person who transfers the right to possession and use of goods under a lease. Unless the context clearly indicates otherwise, the term includes a sublessor.' Section 2A-103(1)(p).

C. LEASE AGREEMENT

OLR: The agreement between Babylon Medical Group and Professional Copy Service is a **Lease Agreement,** which...

> means the bargain, with respect to the lease, of the lessor and the lessee in fact, as found in their

language or inferred from other circumstances including course of performance, course of dealing, or usage of trade as provided in Section 1-103.

Unless the context clearly indicates otherwise, the term includes a sublease agreement. Section 2A-103(1)(k).

There are thus five variables set forth in Section 2A-103(1)(k):

1. The language used by the parties;
2. Course of performance;
3. Course of dealing;
4. Usage of trade;
5. Inferences from other circumstances

1. The Language Used by the Parties

While in some situations, verbal language may be included under the "language" provision that would not be the case in the instant situation. This result is mandated by clause 13 of the agreement, which states that the full agreement is contained in the writing. Therefore, any conversations which contradict that writing would not be included in the agreement:

Terms with respect to which the confirmatory memoranda of the parties agree or which are otherwise set forth in a writing intended by the parties as a final expression of their agreement with respect to such terms as are included therein may not be contradicted by evidence of prior agreement or of a contemporaneous oral agreement… Section 2A-202.

However, as Section 2A-202 goes on to state:
*[however, the writings] may be **explained or supplemented***

(a) by course of dealing or usage of trade or by course of performance; and
(b) by evidence of consistent additional terms unless the court finds the record to have been intended also as a complete and exclusive statement of the terms of the agreement. Section 2A-202(a)(b) [Emphasis added]

As will be presently shown, Section 2A-202(a)(b) and the other variables listed in Section 2A-103(1)(k) can have a dramatic impact on the interpretation of the written language of the contract.

2. Course of Performance

Course of performance, as its name implies, requires some conduct by the parties to the contract before it comes into play. Unlike course of dealing, however, course of performance focuses on the transaction then ongoing:

*(a) A "**course of performance**" is a sequence of previous conduct between the parties "**to a particular transaction**" that exists if:*
    (1) The agreement of the parties with respect to the transaction involves repeated occasions for performance by a party; and
    (2) the other party, with knowledge of the nature of the performance and opportunity for objection to it, accepts the performance or acquiesces in it without objection. Section 1-303(a)(1)(2). [Emphasis added.]

As Babylon Medical Group and Professional Copy Service deal over a period of time under this contract, a course of performance may arise. For example, the rental payment is due on the first of each month. If Babylon makes payment on the 7th of each month, and Professional Copy Service *'accepts the performance or acquiesces in it without objection'* on a sufficient number of occasions, a course of performance may have arisen which could have the effect making payment on the 7th of the month valid.

Those states which have not enacted revised Article 1 have a course of performance provision in Section 2A-207.

3. Course of Dealing

Once the language has been identified, course of dealing must be looked at:

*A "**course of dealing**" is a sequence of previous conduct concerning previous transactions between the parties to a particular transaction which is fairly to be regarded as establishing a common basis of understanding for interpreting their expressions and other conduct.* Section 1-303(b).

Since this is the first time that Babylon Medical Group and Professional Copy Service have dealt with one and other, there can be no course of dealing. [In this regard, please see footnote 56].

4. Usage of Trade

Usage of trade, however, is always relevant when there is an established industry. That term is defined under Section 1-303(c) which states:

*A "**usage of trade**" is any practice or method of dealing having such regularity of observance in* *place, vocation or trade as to justify an expectation that it will be observed with respect to the transaction in question The existence and scope of such a usage are to be proved as facts....*

Where the trade usage involved is contained in a written trade code or similar writing, Section 1-303(c) provides that the court [rather than a jury] will interpret the writing:

It if is established that such a usage is embodied in a written trade code or similar writing the interpretation of the writing is for the court.

It is important at the outset to define precisely which "place, vocation or trade" is involved for obviously this will bear directly on the applicable trade usage. This question is not as easy as it might appear. For example, is the trade involved in the present situation the copy machine industry? Or is it the copy machine industry for small personalized machines? Or is it something else? Regardless of how the trade is defined, the applicable trade usage will supplement the contract unless the construction of that usage cannot reasonably be construed within the written terms of the contract. If such construction is unreasonable, there are certain specific rules of interpretation which control.[154]

---

[154] *Except as otherwise provided in subsection (f), the express terms of an agreement and any applicable course of performance, course of dealing, or usage of trade must be construed whenever reasonable as consistent with each other. If such construction is unreasonable:*

    (1) express terms prevail over course of performance, course of dealing, and usage of trade;

    (2) course of performance prevails over course of dealing and usage of trade;

5. Inferences From Other Circumstances

Section 2A-103(1)(k) lists course of dealing, course of performance and usage of trade as illustrative of 'other circumstances' which impact on the meaning of the agreement. However, while these are the most common, there may be other things happening which in fact shed light on what the agreement means. These can be brought in as *'inferences from other circumstances'.*

From the foregoing discussion, it is seen that the agreement, and hence the proposed contract in the present situation, will consist primarily of the written agreement and any applicable trade usage. As Babylon Medical Group and Professional Copy Service perform under this contract, a course of performance might arise per Section 1-303(a)(1)(2).

D. LEASE CONTRACT

OLR: The legal effect of lease agreement is the **Lease contract** *which means the total legal obligation that results from the lease agreement as determined by the [Uniform Commercial Code] as supplemented by any other applicable rules of law. Unless the context clearly indicates otherwise, the term includes a sublease contract.* Section 2A-103(1)(l).

With the exception of the lease terminology, this language is identical to the definition of contract in Section 1-201(b)(12) and should be interpreted accordingly.

---

(3) course of dealing prevails over usage of trade.

Section 1-103(e)(1)(2)(3).

Other applicable rules of law would include everything listed under Section 1-103(b):

Unless displaced by a particular provision of [the Uniform Commercial Code], the principles of law and equity, including the law merchant and the law relative to capacity to contract, principal and agent, estoppel, fraud, misrepresentation, duress, coercion, mistake, bankruptcy, and other validating or invalidating cause supplement its provisions.

ALAN: What does this mean? Is it important?

OLR: The enactment of the Uniform Commercial Code made some major changes in the areas of law effected by its enactment. The essence of Section 1-103(b) is that with the exception of these specific changes, all of the provisions of the UCC are supplemented by the other principles of law and equity. The principles listed are illustrative, but clearly demonstrate the enormous reach of Section 1-103(b).

Section 1-103(b) is tremendously important under the UCC. It allows a party to bring in enormous bodies of law and legal principles in any situation which is covered by any substantive Article of the UCC.

E. FORMATION & CONSTRUCTION OF
LEASE CONTRACT

1. Statute of Frauds

OLR: The Statute of Frauds rule is contained in Section 2A-201.

Although certain provisions of this section and the Statute of Frauds for Sales under Section 2-201 are identical, there are some important distinctions:

(1) The dollar amount for which a writing is required;
(2) A description of the goods leased;
(3) Statement of lease term.

The basic rule regarding the need for a writing is stated in Section 2A-201(1)(a)(b):

(1) A lease is not enforceable by way of action or defense unless:

> *(a) the total payments to be made under the lease contract, excluding payments for options to renew or buy, are less than $1,000; or*

> *(b) there is a writing, signed by the party against whom enforcement is sought or by that party's authorized agent, sufficient to indicate that a lease contract has been made between the parties and to describe the goods leased and the lease term.*

The total payments in the lease between Babylon Medical Group and Professional Copy Service are in excess of $1,000 and as a result, subsection (a) of Section 2A-201 does not apply. Therefore, the requirements of Section 2A-201(b) are activated. Once both parties have signed the lease, either could enforce it against the other. The writing is sufficient to indicate that a lease has been made between Babylon Medical Group and Professional Copy Service, so the remaining requirements for enforceability are that the item or items being leased are described and that the lease term is indicated.

The description required by Section 2A-201(1)(b) is sufficient *'...if it reasonably identifies what is described.'* Section 2A-201(2). The description which will be contained in the lease addendum "reasonably identifies" the copy machines.

If there was a mistake in the lease agreement regarding the lease term or the quantity of goods involved, that would not, in and of itself, render the agreement unenforceable:

A writing is not insufficient because it omits or incorrectly states a term agreed upon, but the lease contract is not enforceable under subsection (1)(b) beyond the lease term and the quantity of goods shown in the record. Section 2A-201(3).

If, for example, the lease agreement between Babylon Medical Group and Professional Copy Service listed the term as being 12 months as opposed 24 as had been agreed, it would still be enforceable, but only for 12 months.

There are exceptions to the writing requirement which are stated in subsections 2A-201(4)(a)(b)(c). Exceptions for specially manufactured goods are covered by 2A-201(4)(a); various admissions of the lease by 2A-201(4)(b), and *with respect to goods that have been received and accepted by the lessee* under Section 2A-201(4)(c).

With the exception of the lease terminology, this language for the exceptions noted above is virtually identical to the exceptions under the Statute of Frauds for Sales in Section 2-201(3)(a)(b)(c), and should be interpreted accordingly.[155]

---

[155] Author's note: The oral agreement between Dunker and Stephen for the purchase of Dunker's custom made boat is completely applicable to the exception noted for specially manufactured goods.

For purposes of the discussion, in this footnote it is to be assumed that Stephen's agreement with Dunker was for the lease of the customized boat to Dunker for $650.00 per month, as opposed to a sale.

The basic rule under Section 2A-201(1) is that unless there is a writing, this contract would not be enforceable against Dunker since it obviously has a value over $1,000. This, of course, is the same rule that we discussed in connection with the Royal Boat contract. There are, however, exceptions to the broad rule in Section 2A-201(1), one of which would be applicable here. It is set forth in Section 2A-201(4)(a) and states that:

A contract which does not satisfy the requirements of subsection (1) but which is valid in other respects is enforceable:

(a) if the goods are to be specifically manufactured or obtained for the lessee and are not suitable to for lease or sale to others in the ordinary course of the lessor's business and the lessor, before notice of repudiation is received and under circumstances that reasonably indicate that the goods are for the lessee, has made either a substantial beginning of their manufacture or commitments for their procurement.

In the instant case the following questions must thus be posed:

Was the boat to be specifically manufactured for Dunker?

Is the boat suitable for lease or sale to others in the ordinary course of Stephen's business?

2. General Formation of Lease Contract

A contract under Article 2A can be consummated in the same general manner as Article 2: [Formation in General].

A lease contract may be made in any manner sufficient to show agreement, including offer and acceptance, conduct by both parties which recognizes the existence of a lease contract, the interaction of electronic agents, and the interaction of an electronic agent and an individual. Section 2A-204(1).

Furthermore:

Unless otherwise unambiguously indicated by the language or circumstances, an offer to make a lease contract must be construed as inviting acceptance in any manner and by any medium reasonable in the circumstances. Section 2A-206(1).

Did Stephen make the "substantial beginning" of the manufacture of the boat or "commitments for their procurement"?

Was the foregoing done before notice of repudiation was received, and under circumstances which reasonably indicate that the goods are for the buyer?

In order for the contract to be enforceable under the Statute of Frauds per Section 2A-201(4)(a), the questions must be answered as follows:

(a) yes; (b) no; (c) yes; (d) yes.

OLR: After the 2A-203-2A-208 sequence, comes the first major distinction between a lease and sales transaction, for the type of lease contemplated in Section 2A-209 involves a transaction known as a *Finance Lease.*

Alan had no idea what a finance lease was, but he knew from his conversations at trade shows and business gatherings, that finance leases were a popular item. Alan turned to Section 2A-209 and followed the cross references in that section to Section 2A-103(1)(l) which defines a finance lease. As he started to read the section, he began to get a headache. He didn't have a clue as to what Section 2A-103(1)(l) was about, and as much as he didn't want to, he knew he was going to have to ask Doug for some help. That could wait until later. For now, he would focus on more of the basics.

OLR: Part 3 of Article 2A is entitled **EFFECT OF LEASE CONTRACT.** Section 2A-301 states that:

Except as otherwise provided in this Article, a lease contract is effective and enforceable according to its terms between the parties, against purchasers of the goods and against creditors of the parties.

OLR: The basic rule stated in 2A-301 reflects the freedom of contract policy stated in Article 1 and which is pervasive throughout the Code. In addition to the parallel freedom of contract provisions in Article 1, Article 9 and Article 2 have very similar provisions.

ALAN: What are some of the standard terms in a lease contract, and what do they mean?

OLR: A lease agreement, like any contract can be very simple and straight-forward or it can be complex and detailed. Some lease transactions involve enormous sums of money and documents have been drafted by knowledgeable lawyers to cover a universe of contingencies.

The Lease Agreement between Babylon Medical Group and Professional Copy Service provides provisions which would typically be found in most leases.

1. **Professional Copy service agrees to lease to Babylon Medical Group, twenty-eight (28) Strantum Mydex Compact copy machines;**

2. **The copy machines to be leased under this agreement will be described by model and serial number on an addendum prior to the execution of this Master Lease Agreement;**

OLR: As noted previously, a description of the goods leased is required by the Statute of Frauds, and therefore will be included in any properly drafted lease. The description must "reasonably describe what is being leased" The description in clauses #1 & #2 satisfy these requirements.

3. The duration of each lease between Professional Copy Service and Babylon Medical Group will be for 24 months;

OLR: As noted previously, the lease term is required by the Statute of Frauds, and therefore will be included in any properly drafted lease. The duration is stated above.

4. Lessee agrees to maintain the quality of the leased goods through regular maintenance and upkeep;

OLR: Unlike a sale, the lessor of goods has a residual interest in the goods leased, and therefore has a significant stake in the quality of the goods after the lease agreement is executed and the leased goods are transferred. By requiring sufficient maintenance and upkeep of the goods, lessor has contractually solidified this goal.

ALAN: What happens if the lessor becomes concerned about getting paid or the upkeep of the leased goods?

OLR: If either the lessor or lessee is concerned about a particular performance under the lease, the concerned party may be able to move under Section 2A-401(2):

If reasonable grounds for insecurity arise with respect to the performance of either party, the insecure party may demand in writing adequate assurance of due performance....
Furthermore, 'a repudiation of the lease contract occurs if assurance of due performance adequate under the circumstances of the particular case is

not provided to the insecure party within a reasonable time, not to exceed thirty days after a receipt of a demand by the other party.' Section 2A-401(2).

5. Lessor agrees that lessee shall have the complete, uninterrupted use of the leased goods;

OLR: As will be discussed below, the warranties for Leases and Sales, as well as the disclaimers of those warranties are virtually identical. There is however, one major distinction, and that is reflected in clause 5 above, and codified in Section 2A-211(1):

There is in a lease contract a warranty that for the lease term no person holds a claim to or interest in the goods that arose from an act or omission of the lessor, other than by way of infringement or the like, which will interfere with the lessee's enjoyment of its leasehold interest.

In addition,

...[T]here is in a lease contract by a lessor who is a merchant regularly dealing in goods of the kind a warranty that the goods are delivered free of the rightful claim of any person by way of infringement or the like. Section 2A-211(2).

Under the first clause, the lessor is not a merchant, and therefore does not make an infringement warranty. Under the second clause, there is a warranty against infringement when the lessor is a merchant.

In either situation, however,

> ...*[A] lessee who furnishes specifications to a lessor or supplier shall hold the lessor and the supplier harmless against any claim by way of infringement or the like that arises out of compliance with the specifications.* Section 2A-211(3).

6. Lessor agrees to furnish copy machines which will produce quality copies of the type and level described in the manufacturers' product catalog.

OLR: The warranty provisions of Article 2A are, for the most part identical to Article 2, and are to be interpreted accordingly.

Express Warranties
Section 2A-210 for Leases corresponds to Section 2-313 under Sales.

Implied Warranty of Merchantability
Section 2A-212 for Leases corresponds to Section 2-314 for Sales.

Implied Warranty of Fitness for Particular Purpose

Section 2A-213 for Leases corresponds to Section 2-315 for Sales

Exclusion or Modification of Warranties.

Sections 2A-214 for Leases and corresponds to 2-316 of Sales.[156]

[There are special warranty provisions for finance leases which will be discussed later in this discussion].

> **7. Delivery of said copy machines shall be on a quarterly basis with seven machines contained in each shipment;**

OLR: The proposed lease contract would be classified as an *Installment Lease Contract* under Section 2A-103(1)(i):

> ***Installment lease contract*** *means a lease contract that authorizes or requires the delivery of goods in separate lots to be separately accepted even though the lease contract contains a clause "each delivery is a separate lease" or its equivalent.*

As a result of this classification, the basic rule regarding Babylon Medical Group's ability to reject non conforming goods is changed. In a typical situation:

---

[156] The warranties noted, as well as exclusions of warranties are discussed in detail in footnote 83 at page 115 in connection with Sales, and apply with full force in Leases.

...[I]f the goods or the tender or delivery fail in any respect to conform to the lease contract, the lessee may reject or accept the goods or accept any commercial unit or units and reject the rest of the goods Section 2A-509(1).

In the installment lease contract situation, any non conformity must "*substantially impair the value of the installment*" before the lessee can reject:

Under an installment lease contract a lessee may reject any delivery that is non conforming if the non conformity substantially impairs the value of that delivery and cannot be cured or the nonconformity is a defect in the required documents; but if the nonconformity does not fall within subsection (2) [breach of the whole contract] and the lessor or the supplier gives adequate assurance of its cure, the lessee must accept that delivery. Section 2A-510(1).

ALAN*:* What is 'cure'?

OLR: The *cure* provisions of Article 2A, provide an opportunity for a lessor or supplier to tender conforming goods which have been rejected by the lessee:

If any tender or delivery by the lessor or supplier is rejected because nonconforming and the time for performance has not yet expired, the lessor or supplier may seasonably notify the lessee of the lessor's or supplier's intention to cure and may then make a conforming tender of delivery within the time provided in the lease contract.

Section 2A-513(1).

ALAN*:* I have two questions. First, what is a supplier? Second, what if the time for performance has expired?

OLR: A supplier is the party to a finance lease who supplies goods to be leased. [This is discussed shortly in a conversation about finance leases between Doug and Alan.]

If the time for performance under the lease has expired, the lessor may still substitute a conforming tender under the circumstances set forth in Section 2A-513(2):

If the lessee rejects a nonconforming tender that the lessor or the supplier had reasonable grounds to believe would be acceptable with or without money allowance, the lessor or supplier may have a further reasonable time to substitute a conforming tender if he [or she] seasonably notifies the lessee.

8. Lessee is prohibited from transferring any interest or possession or use of the leased goods to any other party.

OLR: Clause number eight, prohibiting the lessee from transferring his interest in the leased goods, is the first clause where major difficulties arise among students when analyzing Code provisions activated by this language.

Analysis begins with Section 2A-303(2) which, among other things, deals with the transfer of an interest in leased goods, by either party to the lease. Subsection 2 to 2A-303 states in relevant part as follows:

> *....[A] provision in a lease agreement which (i) prohibits the voluntary or involuntary transfer... of an interest of a party under the lease contract or of the lessor's residual interest in the goods, or (ii) makes such a transfer an event of default, gives rise to the rights and remedies provided in subsection (4). but, a transfer that is prohibited or is an event of default under the lease agreement* **is otherwise effective.** [Emphasis added].

ALAN: How can it be effective if it is an event of default?

OLR: As between the parties to the original lease, it would be an event of default, giving rise to appropriate rights on the Default provisions in Article 2A. However, the non breaching party may choose not to declare a default because of the transfer. If, for example, the transfer is to a new lessee [the sublessee] deemed suitable by the lessor, there is no economic reason to declare a default, even though such a transfer is described as an event of default under the lease. Such a transfer would be 'otherwise effective.'

In such a situation:

*...[the] sublessee from the lessee of goods under an existing lease contract obtains, to the extent of the interest transferred, the leasehold interest in the goods that the lessee had or had power to transfer, and...takes **subject to** the existing lease contract.....* Section 2A-305(1).

ALAN: Can you give me an example of the application of Section 2A-305(1)?

OLR: Assume for a moment, that six months into the lease, Babylon Medical Group came to the conclusion that the lease payments were far more expensive than the actual use of the equipment warranted. Perhaps they started to do everything online and virtually eliminated the need to copy.

Accordingly, Babylon Medical Group decided to sublease the copy machines to Happy Law Group, for the exact same rental as they were paying Professional Copy Service.

At the moment Babylon Medical Group subleased the copiers, they were in breach of the lease agreement for which Professional could declare them in default. However, Babylon Medical Group may have continued to make the monthly payments, or Happy Law Group may have contacted Professional and agreed to make the payments directly. If Professional was content to allow the sublease to stand, the sublease is "otherwise effective" under 2A-303(2), and Happy Law Group would take the copiers "subject to" the existing lease.

There is a different result if the original lessee was a merchant dealing in goods like the ones being leased, and subsequently leased the goods to a sublessee in the ordinary course of business. In that situation, the sublessee would take free of the existing lease:

> ...[A] sublessee in the ordinary course of business from a lessee that is a merchant dealing in goods of that kind to which the goods were entrusted by the lessor obtains, to the extent of the interest transferred, all of the lessor's and lessee's rights to the goods, and takes free of the existing lease contract. Section 2A-305(2).

Such a sublessee has every right to believe that the merchant lessor dealing in goods of the kind has the authority to lease goods in his inventory. Accordingly, the sublessee takes free of the existing lease contract.

ALAN: Can you give me an example of how that would work in the hypothetical between Professional and Babylon?

OLR: There are three requirements:

1. Lessee must be a 'merchant dealing in the goods of that kind;' [e.g. instead of being Babylon Medical Group, they may have been Babylon Office Supplies];
2. The sublease between the lessee [Babylon] and the sublessee [Happy Law Group] must be 'in the ordinary course of business';
3. The copy machines must have been 'entrusted' to the lessee by the lessor.

Since Babylon Office Supply, for purposes of this hypothetical, is in the business of leasing and selling copy machines as part of its business, it would be a **merchant**, per Section 2-104(1), cross referenced in

Section 2A-103(3). If Happy Law Group leases the copiers from Babylon Office Supplies:

> '... *in good faith, and without knowledge that the lease...is in violation of the ownership rights or ...leasehold interest of a third party in the goods, leases in the ordinary course from a person in the business of...leasing goods of that kind...*

they would be **lessees in the ordinary course of business** per Section 2A-103(1)(o). In the hypothetical, the sublessee would be included within the definition of lessee per Section 2A-103(1)(n), and there would be a sublessee in the ordinary course of business.

The final requirement is that the copier was 'entrusted' to the lessee by the lessor.

> **Entrusting** *includes any delivery and any acquiescence in retention of possession... Section 2-403(3) [applicable to Article 2A by reason of Section 2A-103(3)].*

Since Professional Copy Machines delivered the copiers to Babylon for their use, there would clearly be an entrustment.

ALAN: How would 2A-304 apply in this situation?

OLR: That section applies to subsequent leases of leased goods by the *lessor*, rather than the lessee.

ALAN: How can that happen?

OLR: A lessor may have represented to a third party that he had certain goods available to lease, when in fact they were already leased. If a subsequent lease was

consummated with that third party, that party would take
... '**subject to** *the existing lease contract*' per Section
2A-304(1).

There is a different result if the lessor entering the
subsequent lease is a merchant in possession of the
leased goods to whom the goods were entrusted by the
existing lessee, and who deals in goods of the kind.

ALAN: Why would the lessor have possession of
goods leased by its lessee?

OLR: The lessee may have entered into a lease
contract, and for some reason delayed pick up of the
goods, or the lessee may have returned goods to the
lessor for repair. In that situation, the subsequent lessee
will take free and clear of the existing lease:

> *A subsequent lessee in the ordinary course of
> business from a lessor who is a merchant dealing
> in the goods of that kind to whom the goods were
> entrusted by the existing lessee of that lessor
> before the interest of the subsequent lessee
> became enforceable against that lessor obtains, to
> the extent of the leasehold interest transferred, all
> of that lessor's and the existing lessee's rights to
> the goods, and takes free of the existing lease
> contract.* Section 2A-304(2).

OLR: This mirrors the rule of 2A-305(2) as regards
the subsequent lease. If the lessee leaves the goods
leased on the premises of the original lessor who
satisfies the definitional requirement noted above, there
would an entrustment under Section 2-403(3).

Similarly, if the subsequent lease was within the
definition of Section 2A-103(1)(o) noted above, the lease

would be in the ordinary course of business. In such a situation, the good faith lessee in the ordinary course of business has every right to rely on the lessor's ability to transfer full interest in the goods. By entrusting the goods to the lessor, the original lessee is the party which appropriately should suffer the consequences. The original lessee still has a cause of action against the lessor.

9. Payment will be on the first of each month beginning September 1, 2006 at a base rate of $150 per machine.

OLR: Provisions 9 is simple, direct and obvious. The lessee needs to pay the monthly rent for the leased goods on the stated date. It is important to analyze this term, and all terms under the lease contract, in light of the totality of the definition of lease agreement in Section 2A-103(1)(k), which includes course of performance, course of dealing and usage of trade as noted above. As noted earlier, rent is due on the first of each month. If Babylon and the lessee paid it on the 7th of each month for most of the lease term, with no objection by the Professional Copy Service, the course of performance between the parties may have modified the actual date on which payment was due.

10. This agreement shall be governed by the laws of the State of Georgia.

OLR: Under Section 1-301, within certain stated exceptions, parties involved in multistate transactions have the ability to choose the law which will govern their transaction:

Except as otherwise provided in this section, when a transaction bears a reasonable relation to the state and also another state...the parties may agree that the law either of this state or such other state...shall govern their rights and duties. Section 1-301(a).

In analyzing the importance of this section one must remember that each state reviews the text of the Uniform Commercial Code and will make certain amendments particular to their state. For example there are three options to the third party beneficiary warranty provisions of Section 2A-216 in the Official Text of the UCC. The differences are significant in each version. Thus to the extent states have different sections enacted, the selection of a state law to govern would be significant on the warranty matters presented in Section 2A-216.

11. Professional Copy Service shall not be liable for any consequential damages which may result from non performance of this agreement.

OLR: Under Section 2A-503 parties to a lease contract may limit their remedies, as long as the criteria of that section are met:

Except as otherwise provided in this Article, the lease agreement may include rights and remedies for default in addition to or in substitution for those provided in this Article and may limit or alter the measure of damages recoverable under this Article. Section 2A-503(1).

As noted however, the rights conferred by Section 2A-503(1) are not absolute. Article 2A limits the rights in some situations by 'otherwise providing'. One such situation is noted in Section 2A-503(3):

Consequential damages may be liquidated under Section 2A-504, or may otherwise be limited, altered or excluded unless the limitation, alteration or exclusion is unconscionable. Limitation, alteration, or exclusion of consequential damages for injury to the person in the case of consumer goods is prima facie unconscionable, but limitation where the loss is commercial is not prima facie unconscionable.

12. In the event lessee fails to properly perform under this agreement, lessee shall be liable to seller in the amount of $25,000 as liquidated damages:

OLR: A party's right to liquidate damages is governed by Section 2A-504:

Damages payable by either party for default, or any other act or omission, including indemnity for loss or diminution of anticipated tax benefits or loss or damage to the lessor's residual interest, may be liquidated in the lease agreement but only in an amount or by a formula that is reasonable in light of the then anticipated harm caused by the default or other act or omission. Section 2A-504(1).

There are however, certain limitations. As previously noted under Section 2A-503, the limitation, alteration, and exclusion of consequential damages for personal injury in consumer leases is prima facie unconscionable.

Furthermore, Section 2A-504(2) provides:

If the lease agreement provides for liquidated damages, and such provision does not comply with subsection (1), or such provision is an exclusive or limited remedy that circumstances cause to fail of its essential purpose, remedy may be had a provided by this Article.

ALAN: Would you explain Sections 2A-306 & 2A-307?

OLR: Leased goods may need to be repaired or serviced by a third party at some time during the lease term. Materials may also need to be furnished. Section 2A-306 states:

If a person in the ordinary course of its business furnishes services or materials with respect to goods subject to a lease contract, a lien upon those goods in the possession of that person given by statute or rule of law takes priority over any interest of the lessor or lessee under the lease contract...'

This is an exception to the general rule that *'a creditor of a lessee takes subject to the lease contract'.* Section 2A-307(1).

A creditor of a lessor *also 'takes subject to the lease contract unless the creditor holds a lien that attached to the goods before the lease contract became enforceable.'* Section 2A-307(2).

[END OF ONLINE TRAINING]

Alan was fairly comfortable with what he had learned up to this point. The fact that the Lease provisions which the course had presented were nearly identical to the Sales materials he knew, made him confident about his ability to get a good handle on the Article 2A. Then he remembered: Finance Leases.

As much as he didn't want to do so, he called Doug for help in understanding what a finance lease was all about.

Doug told him he would come to Alan's office in a few minutes. On the one hand, he was pleased that Alan came to him for legal advice on the UCC. On the other hand, Alan seems to have forgotten that Doug had other partners to work for besides Alan. Doug was confident that when the bonuses came out at the end of the year, he would be well remembered. So, he put on his smiling face and walked into Alan's office.

"Having a little trouble with finance leases Alan? I remember when I first looked at those sections, it didn't make much sense. But at the end of the day, it is really quite simple. As you will see, most of the confusion comes from terminology and the unique relationship of the parties through the transactional stage."

Doug continued, "Before we start working on the finance lease matter, I want to be certain that you are one hundred percent clear on the difference between a 'true lease' and a 'lease intended as security'. I know you had Professor Sunshine for Sales, and I assume that he went over this, but it is so important that I need to bring it up before we go forward with finance leases."

Alan had no idea what Doug was talking about. "Doug, Professor Sunshine was one of the best UCC minds in the country. Leases weren't even enacted when I went to law school."

Doug thought to himself, 'Irrelevant. The true lease question should have been covered in either Sales or Secured Transactions.' But he knew that Alan thought Professor Sunshine was a legend so he said nothing about the obvious, and responded "I forgot Alan. We studied this at length when I was at Miami. It is very important, so let's take a minute to go over this, and then we can discuss finance leases."

"Implicit in the question I asked you about a 'true lease' and a 'lease intended as security' is the reality that all documents which are labeled 'leases' are not in fact true leases."

Alan interrupted. "Why would someone call their agreement a lease if it wasn't one?"

"As you know, there are different tax consequences with respect to leased goods and goods which have been sold, either for the full price, or under a conditional sales contract. Rental payments are deductible as an ongoing business expense, whereas payments under a conditional sales contract, other than the interest portion, are not. In addition, if goods are purchased, the buyer has a depreciation allowance which is not the case in a lease. Of particular importance to the lessor of goods, is that in the event of bankruptcy by the lessee, the 'true lessor' can get his goods back."

"OK. I understand that part of it. How can I tell if a particular Lease Agreement is a 'true lease' or a 'lease intended as security?'"

"Can I see your Code for a second?"

Alan turned around and retrieved his UCC from his shelf and handed it to Doug.

Doug opened the Code to Section 1-201(b)(35). "As you can see, the basic definition of a security interest is contained in the first sentence. *Security interest means an interest in personal property or fixtures which secures payment or performance of an obligation."*

After several sentences of exclusionary language, the last sentence of Section 1-201(b)(35) addresses the issue, by way of cross reference, of whether a transaction is a lease, or is a transaction which creates a security interest: *"Whether a transaction in the form of a lease creates a 'security interest' is determined pursuant to Section 1-203."*

"So now we have to look at Section 1-203. Subsection (a) to Section 1-203 states: *"Whether a transaction in the form of a lease creates a security interest is determined by the facts of each case."*

"Section 1-203(b) however, states a set of criteria which create a conclusive presumption that the transaction under consideration is in fact a security interest:

A transaction in the form of a lease creates a security interest if the consideration that the lessee is to pay the lessor for the right to possession and use of the goods is an obligation for the term of the lease not subject to termination by the lessee and:

1. *The original term of the lease is equal to or greater than the remaining economic life of the goods;*
2. *The lessee is bound to renew the lease for the remaining economic life of the goods and is to become the owner of the goods;*
3. *The lessee has an option to renew the lease for the remaining economic life of the lease for no additional consideration or nominal consideration upon compliance with the lease agreement; or*

> *4. The lessee has an option to become the owner of the goods for no additional consideration or for nominal consideration upon compliance with the lease agreement."*

"So, there are three criteria needed to make a transaction a security interest rather than a lease. First, the lessee must be obligated to pay the stated consideration [rental payment] for the full term of the lease; second, the lessee cannot terminate the lease, and finally, one of the contingencies listed in paragraphs 1-4 of Section 1-203(b) must be met. If those three occurrences exist, the transaction is a security interest, not a lease, regardless of the label."

"As you can see, the essence of the transaction under Section 1-203(b)(1)(2)(3)(4) is that the so called lessee is, in reality purchasing the goods involved. The economic life of the goods is used up under subsection (a)(1); there is a mandatory renewal which has the same effect under (a)(2); there is a renewal option under(a)(3) for no additional consideration or nominal consideration, which basically means the goods involved have been fully paid for; and the same basic concept under (a)(4)."

"Subsection (c) to 1-203 provides a list of contingencies which, in and of themselves, do not give rise to a conclusive presumption of a security interest, even though they might be indicia of ownership; subsection (d) provides a definition of **nominal consideration** for purposes of subsections (b)(3)(4), and subsection (e) provides guidelines for determining *'remaining economic life of the goods'* and **fair market value of the goods** for purposes of subsection (b).

That's more than we need to get into now, but you should look them over."[157]

---

[157] Section 1-203(c)(d) & (e) state as follows:

(c) A transaction in the form of a lease does not create a security interest merely because:

    (1) the present value of the consideration the lessee is obligated to pay the lessor for the right to possession and use of the goods is substantially equal to or is greater than the fair market value of the goods at the time the lease is entered into;

    (2) the lessee assumes the risk of loss of the goods;

    (3) the lessee agrees to pay with respect to the goods, taxes, insurance, filing, recording, or registration fees, or service or maintenance costs;

    (4) the lessee has the option to renew the lease or to become owner of the goods;

    (5) the lessee has the option to renew the lease for a fixed rent that is equal to or greater than the reasonably predictable fair market value of the goods for the term of the renewal at the time the option is to be performed; or

    (6) the lessee has an option to become the owner of the goods for a fixed price that is equal to or greater than the reasonably predictable fair market value of the goods at the time the option is to be performed.

(d) Additional consideration is nominal if it is less than the lessee's reasonably predictable cost of performing under the lease agreement if the option is not exercised. Additional consideration is not nominal if:

    (1) when the option to renew the lease is granted to the lessee, the rent stated to be the fair market rent for the use of the goods for the term of the renewal determined at the time the option is to be performed;

    (2) when the option to become the owner of the goods is granted to the lessee, the price is stated to be the fair market value of the goods at the time the option is to be performed.

"The main point of all of this is to be aware of the fact that simply because people call a document a lease, and use terminology of a lease, does not make it a lease."

Alan responded with a comment and a question. "I understand the basics Doug, and thank you for bringing this to my attention. What happens in the event that it is not a lease?'"

"In that event, Article 2 will apply to the Sales aspects of the transaction, and Article 9 to the secured transactions aspects of the transaction. Remember, in order for any security interest to be enforceable, the requirements of 9-203 must be satisfied. I also advise lessors to file a financing statement just to be safe."

"Doesn't that make it look like a Secured Transaction?"

"No. It is just a precautionary filing under Section 9-505 which has no effect on the ultimate determination of the classification of the transaction."

"Now, unless you have any other questions, let's move on to finance leases."

"Sounds good to me Doug," Alan said.

"Before we look at the definition of a finance lease, I want to call your attention to the fact that the transactional aspects require three parties, the 'supplier' of the goods; the 'finance lessor' of the goods; and the 'lessee' of the goods involved. [These terms will be discussed in detail shortly.] The essence of the transaction is that the supplier provides the leased goods to the lessee, with the finance lessor becoming the ultimate owner and lessor of the goods leased. As implied in the term 'finance lease', the finance lessor is

---

(e) The "remaining economic life of the goods" and "reasonably predictable" fair market rent, fair market value, or cost of performing under the lease agreement must be determined with reference to the facts and circumstances at the time the transaction is entered into.

involved in the transaction as a financing agency, and has little involvement in the underlying transaction between the lessee and the supplier.

Let's start our analysis by taking a look at the statutory definition of a *Finance Lease* under Section 2A-103(1)(g). There are three requirements for a valid finance lease. The first two requirements unique to the finance lease, are stated under Section 2A-103(1)(g)(i)(ii):

> **Finance lease** means a lease with respect to which:
>
> i.   *The lessor does not select, manufacture, or supply the goods;*
> ii. *the lessor acquires the goods or right to possession of and use of goods in connection with the lease...."*

Alan interrupted Doug. "That's part of what confuses me. How can a finance lessor lease goods it doesn't 'select, make, manufacture or supply' and furthermore, goods that it has no interest except in connection with the lease?"

"Remember what I told you. The finance lessor is in the deal solely as a financier. As you will see, there are a number of special rules which apply uniquely in the finance lease situation which reflect the role of the finance lessor. For example, the finance lessor's role regarding warranties, and general obligations is very limited. The finance lessor is not concerned with the business of leasing goods, but with the business of collecting rents. Hence, the finance lessor *'does not select, manufacture, or supply goods'* and has no rights in the goods except *'in connection with the lease'*."

"Doug, how would this apply in our situation? I know that Stephen has talked to a guy named Tommy Caloussa from Aqua Magic Centrex. Stephen likes some machine in their inventory, and I guess he and Tommy got into discussions about leasing the equipment. Tommy said something about doing a finance lease rather than a straight lease. Something about getting its money at the front end of the lease, but that Stephen would still be protected in the event that anything went wrong. How does this work?"

"As you know," replied Doug, "in a typical lease situation, the lessor leases goods to a lessee for a certain term for an agreed price. The total lease term has a value of the total number of payments times that lease term, and the relationship is played out each month when the lessee pays the lessor. In this standard lease transaction, the lessor owns the goods being leased at the time the lease is entered into, and remains the owner throughout the lease term.

In a finance lease however, the 'would be lessor' sells the goods involved to the finance lessor.   At the point at which the finance lessor purchases the goods, the 'would be lessor' becomes the 'supplier.'"

Supplier means a person from which a lessor buys or leases goods to be leased under a finance lease. Section 2A-103(1)(x).

Doug continued: "When the finance lessor purchases the goods from the supplier, that entity is paid in full, and has a lump sum amount of capital for whatever she or he wishes to do with it. The finance lessor would receive rent payments from which it would make its profit."

"It is also possible, that the lessee would enter into a straight lease with the owner/lessor of goods, who would then assign the lease to the finance lessor at a discount. The discount reflects the finance lessor's profit. If for example, you had a thirty six month lease at $4,000 per month you have a face value of $144,000. A third party might purchase the lease for $120,000 and would profit by the difference between the full value of the lease term and the discounted value, with appropriate calculations for inflation. The finance lessor could then enter into a subsequent lease or sublease with the lessee, or simply become a sublessor under the assignment."

"The first transaction, in which the finance lessor purchases the goods involved is the more likely, but either way would create a finance lease if the requirements of 2A-103(1)(g) are satisfied. In any event, there is a high probability that Tommy knows of a company that would like to be involved in the transaction from the financial end—i.e. to either buy the goods involved and subsequently lease them, or to purchase the lease at a discounted rate, enter into a subsequent lease or sublease with the lessee and collect rent payments."

"That would be Friendly Financial", replied Alan. "Apparently, Aqua Magic has an ongoing relationship with them."

Doug continued. "Before we get deeper into the mechanics of the transaction, let's identify the parties. In the first situation, this is relatively easy. Stephen's boats would be the lessee." [Section 2A-103(1)(n)]. "Aqua Marine would be the supplier, and Friendly Financial would be the finance lessor. Again, assuming all of Section 2A-103(1)(g) are complied with."   [The remaining requirements will be discussed shortly].

"Identifying the legal role of the parties when the lease is assigned or sold is a bit more confusing, particularly since these roles will change as the transaction progresses. It is most helpful to look at the two basic levels of the transaction."

"The first level of the transaction occurs when Stephen commits to leasing the equipment. At this initial contact, Stephen will be dealing with Aqua Marine and would enter into a lease with them making Stephen the lessee and Aqua Marine the lessor."

"The confusion arises because at the time Aqua Marine enters the lease, it is the lessor, but the ultimate lessor, the one being referred to in 2A-103(1)(x), is the finance lessor.

"In this situation, Aqua Marine would enter into a lease agreement with Stephen's Boats, and subsequently sell or assign all of its rights and interest under that lease to Friendly Financial upon payment of the discounted value of the lease. Once Friendly has paid off the lease, Aqua Marine's rights as lessor will be simultaneously assigned to Friendly, who will become the finance lessor, assuming all requirements of Section 2A-103(1)(g) have been met."

"In either situation, the finance lease transaction is beneficial to all of the parties. First, it will result in a lump sum payment to Aqua Marine as reflected in the price of the goods sold to the finance lessor, or of the amount due under the lease, appropriately discounted. As noted earlier, this is beneficial to Aqua Marine since it receives a lump sum payment, rather than collecting monthly rents and can immediately use that money for business purposes."

"Friendly Financial on the other hand will gladly take the monthly check with a very nice interest rate. Having carefully scrutinized Stephen's business, and getting a personal guarantee on the lease, they know they will get a very good return. In the unlikely event that Stephen couldn't pay, they know they could get the equipment back and sell it, and if necessary, they could collect the balance via his personal guarantee."

"And of course, Stephen is happy because he has the equipment he needs. So, the transactional structure favors everybody, for reasons unique to their situation."

"Before we look at the final requirement of a valid finance lease, I believe it would be helpful to review the first two requirements under section 2A-103(1)(g) discussed above," Doug said. "As you can see, the transaction complies with both provisions. First, Friendly Financial did not *'select, manufacture, or supply the goods';* second, Friendly Financial *'acquired the goods or the right to possession and use of the goods in connection with the lease.'"*

"How are you holding up Alan?" Doug could see that Alan was tired and hoped that they could finish in the morning. Doug had a major project for Dimit Wellscone, the managing partner of the firm.

"We need to keep going" blurted Alan. "I am meeting with Stephen tomorrow for lunch, and I want to have this down cold."

With that response, Doug knew this was going to take awhile and would be over only when Alan was comfortable with his knowledge level. So, he continued.

"Once the first two requirements of Section 2A-103(1)(g) have been met, there is only one remaining requirement. This requires one of the four events stated under 2A-103(1)(g)(iii) to occur. The first three of these events have one major similarity: they all require the lessee to have access to or a clear understanding of the terms of the contract between the finance lessor and the manufacturer/supplier. The primary reason [to be discussed in more detail below] is that the representations and warranties made by the supplier to the finance lessor regarding the goods involved, pass directly to the lessee. In other words, whatever warranties and representations that Aqua Marine makes to Friendly Financial as to the goods involved, will pass directly to Stephen's Boats upon consummation of the finance lease."

Subsection (l)(iii)(A), requires that before signing the lease contract the lessee receives a copy of the contract by which the lessor acquires the goods or the right to possession and use of the goods. Under subsection (l)(iii)(B) the requirement for such review is more strongly stated in that it requires "the lessees approval" of that contract. Subsection (l)(iii)(C), which has more detail, states, as a precondition that:

the lessee, before signing the lease agreement, receives an accurate and complete statement designating the promises and warranties and any disclaimers of warranties, limitations or modifications of remedies, or liquidated damages, including those of a third party, such as the manufacturer of the goods, provided to the lessor by the person supplying the goods in connection with or as part of the contract by which the lessor acquired the goods or the right to possession and use of the goods.

"So basically, the lessee has the opportunity to review the contract between the supplier and finance lessor. Is that correct", asked Alan?

"Yes" replied Doug. "As I said a moment ago, this is very important because Article 2A creates a relationship between the finance lessee and supplier making the finance lessee a beneficiary of the supplier's promises to the finance lessor." [This is discussed in detail shortly.]

All of a sudden, Alan got it. "Doug, you did an excellent job of explaining the basics to me. I think I will do some further work by myself, and if necessary, we can meet tomorrow morning."

Great thought Doug. Why don't I just sleep here? "Glad to be of assistance Alan. It is great working with you!"

Alan was pretty excited with how much he was learning. He got what he needed from Doug on the finance lease question. Now back to his online course. He was determined to show Stephen and everyone else that he didn't need Doug. Well, aside from the finance lease matter. He was going back to the online course, and if necessary, he would get what he needed from

Doug tomorrow. And if he felt like it, he could always call Doug at home.

Alan went back to the menu of the online course and selected Warranties. The categories listed were General Warranty Provisions and Finance Lease warranty provisions. Alan typed in the basic facts of the transaction between Stephen, Aqua Marine and Friendly Financial.

ALAN: Would you explain the warranties in the transaction in the foregoing situation?

FINANCE LEASE WARRANTY PROVISIONS

OLR: It is not surprising that the finance lessor's warranty involvement is different than a standard lease. In a standard lease, the lessor will often be the manufacturer of the goods, and if not the manufacturer, will be a dealership or have some type of relationship with whomever is supplying the goods to be leased. Such a lessor will also be the owner of the goods prior to the standard lease.

A finance lessor, is not in the same position. The finance lessor, by definition cannot be the manufacturer of the goods, and per Section 2A-103(1)(g), does not have the goods or rights until prior to the lease in question. The only involvement is financial.

The Uniform Commercial Code recognizes this reality in three ways. First, the Code requires that the finance lessor *'does not select, manufacture or supply the goods'* per Section 2A-103(1)(g)(i). Second, the finance lessor must acquire *'the goods or the right to possession and use of the goods in connection with the lease'* per Section 2A-103(1)(g)(ii). Third, one of the criteria of Section 2A-103(l)(g)(iii) must be met. The essence of the latter provisions is that the potential lessee has access to the contract between the supplier and the finance lessor. The reason the latter requirement is so important, is that the finance lessee is the beneficiary of any warranties which the supplier has made to the finance lessor.

In this regard, Section 2A-209(1) states as follows:

> *The benefit of a supplier's promises to the lessor under the supply contract and of all warranties, whether express or implied...extends to the lessee to the extent of a lessee's leasehold interest under a finance lease related to the supply contract....*

In this case, as noted, Aqua Marine Centrex would be the '*supplier*' and the contract between Aqua Marine and Friendly Financial would be the '*Supply contract*' referred to above.

> ***Supply contract*** *means a contract under which a lessor buys or leases goods to be leased.* Section 2A-103(1)(y).

Therefore, the finance lessee [Stephen's Boats] will have the benefit of all warranties made by the supplier [Aqua Marine] to the finance lessor [Friendly Financial]. Since Stephen will have full knowledge of these promises by reason of one of the subsections 2A-103(l)(g)(iii), he is in a position to determine whether or not he is adequately protected, and hence whether to go forward with the deal.

ALAN: Is there anything which specifically limits the liability of the finance lessor, or is it just inferred from Section 2A-209?

OLR: Yes, there are specific sections dealing with these issues. Section 2A-212 deals with the implied warranty of merchantability. Subsection (1) to that section states:

> ***Except in a finance lease,*** *a warranty that the goods shall be merchantable is implied in a lease contract if the lessor is a merchant with respect to goods of that kind.* [Emphasis added]

Under Section 2A-213, which deals with an implied warranty of fitness for a particular purpose, there is a similar provision:

> ***Except in a finance lease,*** *if the lessor at the time the lease contract is made has reason to know of any particular purpose for which the goods are required and that the lessee is relying on the lessor's skill or judgment to select or furnish suitable goods, there is in the lease contract an implied warranty that the goods will be fit for that purpose.* [Emphasis added]

ALAN: What are some of the other differences between the standard lease and the finance lease?

OLR: Another distinction between the finance lease and the traditional lease is that in a traditional lease, is that unless otherwise agreed, the risk of loss to the goods remains with the owner/lessor. This is not the case with a finance lease:

> ***Except in the case of a finance lease,*** *risk of loss is retained by the lessor and does not pass to the lessee.* ***In the case of a finance***

lease, risk of loss passes to the lessee.
Section 2A-219(1).[158] [Emphasis added.]

ALAN: What is the rule of 2A-407?

OLR: Subsection (1) of 2A-407 sets forth the basic rule regarding the irrevocability in a finance lease:

> *In the case of a finance lease that is not a consumer lease the lessee's promises under the lease contract become irrevocable and*

---

[158] When the risk of loss passes to lessee, and the time of passage is not stated, 2A-219(2)(a)(b)(i)(ii) provides specific rules for when risk of loss passes. Under shipment contracts, risk of loss will pass to the lessee upon proper delivery to the carrier:

(a) If the lease contract requires or authorizes the goods to be shipped by carrier

(i) and it does not require delivery at a particular destination, the risk of loss passes to the lessee when the goods are duly delivered to a carrier.

Under a destination contract subsection (a)(ii) to Section 2A-219 states:

[I]f it does require delivery at a particular destination and the goods are there duly tendered while in possession of the carrier, the risk of loss passes to the lessee when the goods are there duly so tendered as to enable the lessee to take possession.

Another section which has relevance is Section 2A-220:

Where the risk of loss is to pass to the lessee and the time of passage is not stated:

(a) If a tender of delivery of goods so fails to conform to the lease contract as to give a right of rejection, the risk of their loss remains with the lessor, or, in the case of a finance lease, the supplier, until cure or acceptance. Section 2A-220(1)(a).

independent upon the lessee's acceptance of the goods.

ALAN: Irrevocable and independent from what?

OLR: Irrevocable and independent from the warranties and other agreements which run from the supplier to the lessee.

ALAN: Does that mean that if the leased goods don't work properly, that the lessee still has to make payments?

OLR: Yes. Once a finance lessee has accepted the goods. Section 2A-407(2)(a)(b):

A promise that has become irrevocable and independent under subsection (1):

(a) is effective and enforceable between the parties, and by or against third parties including assignees of third parties; and

(b) is not subject to cancellation, termination, repudiation, excuse, or substitution without the consent of the party to whom the promise runs.

By now, Alan was exhausted and felt that he couldn't learn any more tonight. He planned to get up early the next morning, get back to his online course and finish the material.

The following morning Alan got up at 4:30 a.m. and was online working on the course by 5:15 a.m. He was meeting with Stephen at 12:00 p.m. He wanted to get through the material as quickly as possible, so he started by asking the computer to identify any remaining parallel provisions in Article 2 and Article 2A that hadn't been discussed yet.

At this point Alan was confident that he understood enough to go forward with his meeting with Stephen. He hadn't gone over the Default provisions contained in Part 5 of Article 2A, but he figured that would not come up in meeting with Stephen, and he needed at least an hour of sleep before he sat down with Stephen. He wanted to be alert for his 10:00 a.m. meeting.

When he awoke from his nap, Alan was confident that he was ready. "As if I need an associate to handle my UCC matters" he said to himself, as he put on one of his power suits. As he adjusted his tie, he continued "I am Alan Lawyer! I am ready."

His meeting with Stephen was proceeding very smoothly. He was amazed at how conversant he was in the lease provisions, and was about to wrap up the meeting when Stephen said "Thanks for your time Alan. But before you go, I need to understand what happens if something goes wrong. I learned a lot from the car experience, and I don't want to go into this lease without understanding the full transaction, particularly if there are problems."

Alan began to perspire profusely. Stephen asked if anything was wrong. To which Alan replied "You know Stephen, I have been practicing law for almost twenty years. As I think back on my career, I really wish the partners would have given me more responsibility as an associate. They did crack the whip on billing hours, but I don't think I spoke to a client without supervision for almost four years."

"So if it's all the same to you, I'd like to give Doug the opportunity to speak to you directly about the matters you have just raised.[159] He has been a good associate, and I want to let him spread his wings."

"No problem Alan", replied Stephen.

"Great" said Alan. "I'll have Doug give you a call this afternoon." With that, Alan stood up, shook Stephen's hand and headed over to Randy's.

---

[159] The Default provisions of Article 2A are discussed in Appendix II on page 413.

Section 10

Doug came to work early the next morning to be sure to get the bank letter as soon as it came in. When it did, Doug was overjoyed. He took it with him to the coffee room hoping *someone* would ask him what he was reading. As he sipped his morning coffee, he read the following letter:

Dear Doug:

Enclosed please find a copy of a memorandum sent to Mr. Ron Nichols, our vice-president in charge of the legal department. This sets forth the facts of the lawsuit which we discussed yesterday. Should you have any questions, please contact Mr. Nichols or myself.

Very truly yours,

Fred Houstrant

MEMORANDUM

TO: Ron Nichols, Esq.
FROM: Sandra Oronski
RE: Burger Czar check matter

On February 20, 2006, we were informed of the following facts by Alfredo Thomas, vice-president and secretary of Burger Czar:

On Friday January 5, 2006, Burger Czar received a shipment of beef patties from Butcherama, Inc. for which a postdated check in the amount of $12,000 was given (it was postdated to allow time for a deposit to clear).

The check was signed by Thomas in his corporate capacity as treasurer. Sometime shortly thereafter, Butcherama was robbed, the check being taken along with some $27,000 in cash.

On Monday morning, January 8, 2006, a man posing as Brad Garcia, treasurer of Butcherama, presented what appeared to be a proper identification (probably taken in the robbery) and cashed the check at Central Dade Bank where Burger Czar maintained its account.

When Butcherama found out that the check had been taken, it notified Burger Czar immediately who thereupon notified us. It was, of course, too late as the check had already been cashed.

Burger Czar is demanding that its account be recredited.[160]

---

[160] See footnote 160 in Appendix I on page 374.

Section 11

When Alan got back to the office, he thought about going home to his family early that night. His wife Donna had been reminding him of what he said when he was in law school and clerking about how nobody cared about anything except work, work, work (and of course, compensation therefore). "Not me," Alan used to say. "I intend to keep my work in perspective."

Maybe I will go home, thought Alan – until he remembered that this loan was important to his clothing business. Alan then thought to himself how great it would be in 15 years when he could cut back with the knowledge of financial security (Alan wasn't worried about inflation – just dollars). Donna will be pleased when we can just sit back and watch it come in, he thought.

With that thought, he drafted a letter to Mr. Jerry Thompson which read as follows:

Dear Jerry:

As we discussed this morning, George's Clothing Outlet would like funding from the bank in the amount of $240,000. You expressed some concern as to whether or not the bank's position from a creditor's standpoint would be adequately protected if the loan were given because George Friedman, the former owner, retained a security interest in the inventory, equipment and accounts receivable.

As I indicated to you this morning, I am of the opinion that it is possible for the bank to obtain priority with respect to the equipment which the outlet would like to buy with part of the loan proceeds, as well as a certain type of priority with respect to the inventory. In addition it is my opinion that if George agrees to subordinate his interest in the accounts receivable to the bank, such an agreement would be enforceable and would give the bank priority with respect to the accounts receivable.

Purchase Money Security Interest in Equipment

As you know, the basic rule regarding priority of creditors with respect to a security interest in collateral is the "first to file rule." That is, if filing rather than possession is the method for perfection, that party which first files its financing statement with the Florida Secured Transaction Registry will take priority with respect to someone subsequently lending against the same property [assuming, of course, all of the requisites of Section 9-203 are met]. As we discussed this morning, the bank is concerned that since George has a financing statement on file with respect to the equipment "now or hereafter acquired," the bank could not take priority for any loans made for the purchase of equipment.

There is a special circumstance envisioned by the Code where the "first to file" rule is somewhat altered. Specifically, I am referring to the rule set forth in Section 9-324(a), which states as follows:

> ...[A] perfected purchase money security interest in goods other than inventory...has priority over a conflicting security interest in the same goods...if the purchase – money security interest is perfected when the debtor receives possession of the collateral or within 20 days thereafter.

As can be seen from the foregoing, if the bank obtains a purchase money security interest in the *equipment* (an "other than inventory collateral"), it will obtain priority over George's security interest in equipment 'i.e. in *equipment now or hereinafter acquired'* if the bank perfects its security interest in the equipment when the clothing outlet *receives possession of the collateral* [the equipment] *or within twenty days thereafter…* The essence of the 'purchase money concept' is implied in its name. The money given by the lender is for the purchase of specific property.

Before you can have a purchase money security interest, several requirements must be met. First, you must have purchase-money-collateral under Section 9-103(b)(1):

A security interest in goods is a purchase-money security interest;

(1) to the extent that the goods are purchase-money collateral with respect to that security interest;

So the first requirement is that the goods involved [the equipment] is "purchase money collateral":

"[P]urchase-money collateral" means goods or software that secures a purchase-money obligation incurred with respect to that collateral'. Section 9-103(a)(1).

A "Purchase-money obligation" means an obligation of an obligor incurred as all or part of the price of the collateral or for value given to enable the debtor to acquire rights in or use of the collateral if the value is in fact so used. Section 9-103(a)(2).

The purchase-money obligation would exist when South Dade gives us the funds [value] to buy the equipment, provided the money was used accordingly. Of course, the bank can insure this by direct payment to the supplier, by an appropriately drafted letter of credit with the supplier as the beneficiary, or other methods which insure that the value given by the bank is used to buy the equipment. The obligation to repay would be secured by the equipment and would therefore be 'purchase-money collateral'. Therefore, the transaction would be a 'purchase-money security interest'.

As long as the bank has perfected its security interest at the time George's Clothing Outlet receives the equipment, or within twenty days thereafter, it would have priority regarding the specific piece of equipment involved.

There is a similar, although not identical, provision with respect to inventory. That is Section 9-324(b) which reads as follows:

...[A] perfected purchase money security interest in inventory, has priority over a conflicting security interest in the same inventory, has priority over a conflicting security interest in chattel paper or an instrument constituting proceeds of the inventory and ...except as otherwise provided in Section 9-327, also has priority in identifiable cash proceeds of the inventory to the extent the identifiable cash proceeds are received on or before the delivery of the inventory to a buyer, if:

1. *the purchase money security interest is perfected at the time the debtor receives possession of the inventory;*
2. *the purchase money secured party sends an authenticated notification to the holder of the conflicting security interest;*
3. *the holder of the conflicting interest receives the notification within five years before the debtor receives possession of the inventory; and*
4. *the notification states that the person sending the notification has or expects to acquire a purchase money security interest in inventory of the debtor and describes the inventory.*

It is thus seen that the bank can in fact have a purchase-money priority within Section 9-324(b). Of course, it must initially obtain a perfected purchase money interest at the time we receive the inventory per Section 9-324(b)(1). It can obtain a purchase money security interest in exactly the same manner described above.

If it wants to insure that the funds are used to acquire the inventory, the bank can easily insure that by the same type of payment mechanisms noted above. If, in addition, the bank gave notification to George within Section 9-324(b)(2)(3)(4) and complied with the other requirements the bank would take priority with respect to the inventory as well as the chattel paper, an instrument or cash proceeds of inventory as noted in subsection (b). As the section indicates, the priority given there applies to chattel paper, instruments and identifiable cash proceeds which the outlet receives upon sale of the inventory *prior* to the time that the inventory is delivered to a buyer.

The final concern that the bank expressed today was with respect to priority of accounts receivable. As I indicated to you, I am of the opinion that if George were to agree to subordinate his accounts receivable interest, the Bank would take priority with respect to the accounts receivable. The right to subordinate priority is explicitly state in Section 9-339:

> *This Article does not preclude subordination by agreement by a person entitled to priority.*

Thus, upon George's agreement to subordinate his interest to the banks, the bank would take priority with respect to the accounts receivable. It is thus seen that if the bank complies with the Code provisions noted above and the subordination agreement can be reached with George, the bank will have the protection it desires.

Should you have any questions with respect to any of the foregoing, please do not hesitate to call me. I'll talk to you soon.

Very truly yours,

Alan Lawyer[161]

---

[161] See footnote 161 in Appendix I on page 376.

Well, Alan thought, a pretty good letter if I do say so myself (and of course he often did). He was feeling kind of confident now with things going so well in the business world as well as the legal practice. With Stephen now having become active with Crown as well as Royal, the likelihood of increased profits continued to grow. As a matter of fact, Alan had been looking at houses in a very exclusive section of south Dade County. If things continued to go as well as they had been going, Alan thought, he would show everybody how successful he was by buying an even bigger house than he had now!

Just then, Stephen called.

"Hi Stephen," Alan said. "I think we are going to be able to get the loan on the Outlet. We are really starting to roll."

"We have trouble," said Stephen.

"What's wrong?" said Alan.

"I got a telephone call today from the vice-president of Royal Boats. One of their representatives, when he came down last week, saw the Crown boats in the showroom. He didn't say anything to me at the time, but apparently went back and told Joe that they were there, sitting side by side with the Royal Boats, and it appeared to be hurting sales."

"What did you tell him?" asked Alan.

"I told him he was wrong to think that the sales were being hurt. I told him that if he wanted to check the books, he would find that business had, if anything, increased for the Royal account since we put on the Crown Boats."

"What did he say to that?" asked Alan.

"He said he didn't care about the books. He said he wanted the Crown boats out of the showroom within 24 hours and if they weren't taken off, he promised us a lawsuit within a week."

"He said that we violated the terms of our agreement with him by entering into this deal."

"What about the letter we wrote them?" Alan stated. "We told them ahead of time that we were going to do this. Why didn't they object?"

"I forgot to even mention it, but he told me that we were in breach of contract and that if we didn't get the boats out of the showroom within 24 hours he was going to sue us. What am I supposed to do Alan?"

"Stephen, we wrote him a letter requesting permission to do this before you finalized the agreements with Crown, and if he is going to fight about it now after we have been committed to Crown, I don't think we have any choice but to fight the thing."

"That's what I thought" said Stephen. "I just wanted to make certain that I understood your feelings on the matter. By the way, are we in breach of contract?"

"Well," Alan said, "you know as well as I do that there was a term in the original contract prohibiting us from putting other boats in the showroom. But we asked their permission to do so. They never answered the letter we sent, so as far as I can tell we are entitled to do just what we did."

"Okay," said Stephen. "I just wanted to let you know what was coming up."

"Thanks," said Alan. "I appreciate it."

Whereupon Stephen hung up and Alan started thinking less about a house in south Dade and more about how much work was going to be involved if a lawsuit were undertaken by Royal against Stephen. He realized that the free ride he had been getting from Stephen might possibly be about to end. This disturbed him immensely.

He telephoned Doug to see if he could help him with a lawsuit undertaken by Royal against Stephen.

"Not right away," said Doug. "Of course I will if you want, but I am currently writing an opinion letter to the

Bank with respect to that Article 3 question they presented to me a few weeks ago."

"Oh," said Alan. "I forgot all about it. How long do you think it is going to take you?"

"Probably most of today and most of tomorrow," said Doug.

"I don't need you right away on this other thing, anyway. As a matter of fact, the lawsuit hasn't been filed yet, but from what Stephen says to me, it looks like it may be filed within the week."

"I will have plenty of time by the end of the week."

"Great," said Alan. "Why don't you come in after you finish the opinion letter. I would like to hear what you are doing for the bank, anyway. We'll talk about this other mater then, too."

Section 12

Stephen was really pleased to see his older brother, Duke, again. It had been a long time. In fact, Stephen hadn't seen the Duke since 2004. Stephen hoped that Duke would finally call him Stephen instead of the nicknames Duke always came up with. Stephen hated the latest more than any. Ever since Duke went to Texas eight years ago he had called Stephen "little brother."

Duke was pretty proud of his younger brother inasmuch as Stephen had finally done something constructive. His mother no longer just bragged about Duke! For Stephen it was a moment he thought would never come. He had been trying to step out of the shadow of his brother for a long time and it appeared that he finally had made it. Stephen was especially proud of himself when he took Duke for a ride in his XGT.

"Stephen," said Duke, "we are going to have to get up first thing in the morning so that we can get up to Orlando to take a look at some of those groves."

"What do you have in mind?"

"Well, little brother, I have got a mind to enter into the wholesale orange business in the Dallas-Ft. Worth area. What I figure I will do on this trip is scout out some land, take out an option on it and purchase some oranges to see exactly what is involved in the wholesale distribution of these things."

Stephen, feeling pretty impressed with his own knowledge of business matters, asked: "Are you going to have anyone finance this operation?"

Duke tried to hold back his amazement. He had never heard Stephen use words such as "finance an operation" before. "Well, of course," said Duke, "If I purchase an interest in a grove up here, I am going to take out a mortgage on it if the cost exceeds $400,000. As far as any financing of the actual operations, I believe

I have enough liquid assets to comfortably run the operation."

"Duke, lets go to bed early so we can be refreshed and ready for the 7:00 a.m. flight to Orlando," said Stephen.

"Very good," said Duke.

The next morning Stephen and Duke arrived in Orlando at 8:10 a.m. They rented a car and Duke pulled out a list of four groves that he wanted to see.

After spending the day looking at various groves, Duke decided on the one that he wanted to buy. He asked the seller if he could get a one-year option on the grove, that is, if he could have the right to purchase the grove in one year from the date of entering into the option. He offered to pay Jeremy Alaconte, the owner of the orange grove, $8,000 for the option. Jeremy agreed to give Duke the option.

In addition, Duke entered into a contract with Jeremy to purchase 20 carloads of oranges which were then on the tree and were set to be harvested within the next six weeks. Duke arranged for the seller to contact Stephen when the oranges were about to be picked. Duke would tell Stephen exactly what he wanted to be done with the oranges. Duke hoped that by getting Stephen slightly involved in the business, he would be able to have Stephen conduct most of his orange business in Florida, at least with respect to the small items, while doing the bigger things himself in the Dallas – Ft. Worth area. If Stephen could prove himself, Duke would allow him to assume more responsibility as time went on.

After Duke obtained his option from Jeremy, he contacted his attorney about negotiating the purchase of the orange grove. Duke offered to pay the agreed purchase price of $850,000.00 with a corporate check. Jeremy however, had been watching a television special on fraudulent transactions and was not about to sign over his orange grove until he had his money in hand.

Plus, Duke was from Texas, and Jeremy *never* trusted anyone who wore a cowboy hat.

Jeremy told Duke that the only way he would sell him the orange grove was if payment was made by way of wire transfer. He learned in a television special that wire transfers were the surest and safest way to be paid. Duke told Jeremy that a wire transfer would be fine, and that he would get right on it.

Duke was no stranger to wire transfers, and had been doing them for quite some time. As he told Stephen, "You know little brother, I'm on fire when it comes to wire." Duke called Bamford Pussar Jones, his comptroller and instructed Bam to execute a wire transfer on behalf of Duke's Enterprises, to Jeremy in the amount of $850,000 and have it ready to go when he returned home.

Bam contacted Jeremy by phone to find out where Jeremy wanted the money order directed. After he was advised to send the wire transfer to Orange Grove Bank, Bam emailed his contact at Texas Trust, where Duke's Enterprises had its account, and advised him that the funds were going to be wired to Jeremy's account at Orange Grove Trust.

Now that the wire transfer was set in motion, Jeremy thought he better contact his attorney to get a more solid understanding of Electronic Funds Transfers. He called Lemont Burnsgrass and requested a memorandum on the subject:[162]

While all of this was going on in Orlando, things were happening in Miami at the same time. First of all, Alan was able to close his loan with the bank. After in-house counsel read his opinion with respect to the purchase money security interest in equipment and inventory and got George Friedman's agreement to subordinate his

---

[162] *See* footnote 162 in Appendix I on page 381.

interest in the accounts, the bank decided that the deal would be a good one to enter into. The security agreement with the bank read as follows:

WHEREAS, George's Clothing Outlet (hereinafter referred to as "Debtor"), is desirous of borrowing money from West Dade Bank (hereinafter referred to as the "Secured Party"); and

WHEREAS, the Secured Party is desirous of lending said monies to Debtor; and

WHEREAS, Debtor has made application to the secured party for a loan in the amount of $240,000; and

WHEREAS, Secured Party has agreed to loan Debtor $240,000;

NOW, THEREFORE,

In consideration of the money to be loaned to the Debtor and the Loan Agreement entered into on even date herewith the Debtor hereby grants to the Secured Party a security interest in the following collateral:

(1) A purchase money security interest in all inventory acquired with the loan proceeds of the above referenced loan;
(2) A purchase money security interest in one Electrex Seam machine, said machine to be purchased from part of the proceeds of the loan contained herein;
(3) A security interest in all of he accounts of George's Clothing Outlet, said security interest in those accounts to be a first

priority security interest by reason of the subordination agreement entered into between the Secured Party and George Friedman;

(4) A security interest in all proceeds received by the Debtor from the sale of any collateral which is the subject of the security interest contained herein;

(5) A security interest in all stock owned by the individual debtors in the corporate debtor.

Debtor further agrees:

(1) To make a daily accounting to the Secured Party for all proceeds received in connection with George's Clothing Outlet;

(2) That Debtor will not further encumber any property that is the subject of this Secured Party's security interest without the express prior written consent of the Secured Party.

Witnesses:

_____

GEORGE'S CLOTHING OUTLET

_____

WEST DADE BANK
By: _____
SECURED PARTY

Section 13

Unknown to Alan at the time of the closing, Onus Primo was starting to prepare for the kill. Onus had planned to leave by now and had, in fact, already bilked the company out of some $46,000. He had done this by creating fictitious sellers of clothing and making checks payable to the fictitious parties, cashing the checks and keeping the proceeds for himself. This was not too difficult inasmuch as he was in charge of balancing the books as well as drawing checks for the outlet. Thus, the only thing he had to do was to make certain that he was always able to meet the legitimate expenses of the business and steal as much as possible. Although he had planned to leave by now, when he found out that Alan was going to borrow and additional $240,000, he figured he might as well stick around and steal as much of that as he could. Accordingly, he was waiting to find out how the proceeds of the loan were going to be disbursed by the bank in order to determine whether or not he could take any of it.

When Alan came back to the clothing outlet, he found Onus going through some inventory. Of course, Alan was in an extremely good mood and said, "Guess what, Onus?"

"What?"

"We got the money," said Alan with a big grin.

Wrong, thought Onus to himself, I got the money, dummy. "Great," said Onus. "That is just what this business needs, a few more dollars pumped into it. Trying to be casual, Onus asked: "Is the money simply going to be put in the corporate account?"

"No," said Alan, "the bank is trying to make sure that it gets a special kind of security interest in the property so they are going to make payment directly to the parties we are buying things from. That is, all except for $35,000 of it which we are going to use to fix up certain things on the premises. Why do you ask?" Alan said.

"The less I have to do with the books the better," responded Onus. "If I only have to deal with $35,000 of it, it just seems easier." Of course he was disappointed that he couldn't steal the whole $240,000, but he felt that a $35,000 "tip" would be a nice way to end his career at the old clothing outlet.

"You know," said Alan, "I am really glad you stuck around, Onus. There is one thing I am really good at and that's judging people. I knew when I first met you that you would be great to keep in this business. But I'll tell you something else," said Alan, "effective next month, you are going to be making $360 a week. How does that grab you?"

Onus Primo thought to himself, not nearly as grabbed as you will be when you look at the books, "Oh, how kind of you," he said, thinking to himself that not only would he enjoy getting even with Friedman, but he was starting to enjoy the prospects of getting even with Alan. Initially, he had felt some regret about taking a guy he didn't know over the coals, but the more he got to know Alan, the better he felt about it. In any event, as soon as the $35,000 was deposited to the account, he created five fictitious accounts and ran the $35,000 through those accounts.

Section 14

When Stephen and Duke got back to the Miami airport, Stephen asked Duke if he would like to take a ride to see his boat business, "Of course," said Duke.

Duke walked around the showroom, then looked at Stephen and said, "You know, little brother, you certainly have come a long way. I would like to get you involved in this orange business of mine if you are interested. I think you have quite a future as a businessman."

Stephen was really pleased that Duke thought enough of him to involve him in the orange business and he accepted Duke's offer. He then asked Duke what he believed to be the major reason for his success.

"Hard work, Stephen," said the Duke. "I have worked for most of the last 20 years, sometimes as much as 20 hours a day, to get where I am. One of these days, I am going to sit back and enjoy it."

"You know, Duke, that is one of the things that bothers me about this business. You never seem to have enough time to do all the things you wanted to do before you went into business. I used to have time to go to the beach a lot; I stayed in good shape and was pretty happy. Now, I hardly ever get to the beach, and when I do, I can't keep my mind on anything but the business. Is this normal?"

"Of course," said the Duke. "That means that you are 'into your business.' If it were any different you would never make it."

Stephen felt a little better. He had always thought that when you finally made a lot of money you would be happy. Hearing Duke's reassurances, and knowing from his own experiences that many people he saw daily were in the same situation, made him feel better. He wondered if it would ever get better.

While Stephen was showing Duke around the showroom, Jerry came up to him and gave him an envelope that had come for him that day. The return address had the Clerk of the Circuit Court on it. Stephen opened it and found out that he was being sued by Royal Boats, Inc. The Complaint read as follows:

COMES NOW the Plaintiff by and through its undersigned attorneys and moves this Court as follows:

1. This is an action at law in excess of $15,000.
2. The Plaintiff is a corporation organized under the laws of the State of Georgia and doing business in the State of Florida.
3. Defendant is a Florida corporation doing business under the name of Stephen's Boats, Inc.
4. On or about September 2, 2005, Plaintiff and Defendant entered into a Distributorship Contract, whereby Defendant was to sell boats for Plaintiff as its exclusive distributor in the Southern District of Florida. A copy of said Contract is attached hereto and made a part hereof as Plaintiff's Exhibit "A."
5. As set forth in Paragraph 4, the Defendant was prohibited from selling the boats of any other manufacturer except those of the Plaintiff without the express written consent of the Plaintiff.
6. Beginning on March 3, 2006, upon information and belief, Defendant began selling the boats of Crown, Inc., said sale being without the written consent of Royal.
7. The sale of these boats by Defendant has resulted in a breach of the Contract attached hereto previously referred to and made a part hereof as Plaintiff's Exhibit "A."

8. Plaintiff has been damaged in excess of $15,000.

WHEREFORE, Plaintiff demands judgment against Defendant in the amount of $250,000.00 and in addition seeks cancellation of the Contract it entered into with Defendant.

By:_____
Lawton James Winston IV, Esq.
Comely, Hopkins, Midsmith
& Winston, PA

Stephen could feel the knot in his stomach as he read the Complaint. He was really beginning to wonder if it was worth it. After all, the lawsuit was going on with respect to the raised check, now this lawsuit, and who knew what else was going to happen.

Duke noticed Stephen's consternation and said, "What's wrong, little brother?"

Stephen handed him the Complaint.

"Is this all that's bothering you?" he asked. "Why, little brother, I get sued all the time in my business. If you're not getting sued, you're not doing business. That's what I always say," said Duke.

"But what if you lose? I can't afford to lose a major lawsuit at this time in my business career."

"Oh, these things always get settled," said Duke. "Besides, didn't you tell me that Alan was doing the legal work for free?"

"Yeah," said Stephen nodding. "But I still have to answer interrogatories, have my deposition taken, and go through all sorts of other aggravation while these things go on."

"Don't worry about it, little brother. We are going to make us some big money in the orange business and that will take your mind off all these little troubles. What do you say we go get a bite to eat so we can discuss how I want to handle this orange business transaction."

Stephen and Duke went over to Randy's and they ordered a drink. Stephen was no longer drinking piña coladas and he told the waiter he wanted a double vodka martini straight up and very dry. Duke realized that his little brother was under some stress to be drinking this way at such an early age. After all, Duke thought to himself, I didn't become a marginal alcoholic until I was 35. "I'll have the same," said Duke.

"Well, little brother," said Duke, "let's talk about the orange business. What I would like to do is this. As you know, I ordered 20 carloads of oranges today from the seller to be harvested in about six weeks. When they are harvested, I may not have a buyer yet. In the event that I don't, I would like you to have the oranges stored at a warehouse in Orlando."

"Sure," said Stephen. "What do I have to do?"

"Well, first thing I want you to do is check with the various warehouses in the area and see what kind of deal you can get with respect to storing these things. Then, after you have gotten me the best deal you can, I would like you to store the oranges and have a negotiable warehouse receipt issued to your order."

"Wait a minute," said Stephen, "I don't understand this warehouse receipt stuff. You'd better explain it all very slowly to me."

"I'll tell you what," said Duke. "As long as you have agreed to do it, why don't I have my attorney write you a short note as to how the operation will work? I don't know this too well either. I am simply quoting what he told me. I'll get back to you shortly after I return to Dallas. Let's have a drink now, little brother; forget about all these businesses and problems, and let's talk about the old days."

The old days, Stephen thought. The beach, the sun, the boating, the piña coladas, the ocean. "Yeah, let's talk about the old days," said Stephen.

Whereupon Duke began telling the old football stories which Stephen had heard 17 times before....

Section 15

A month went by without any events of significance. An answer had been filed in the *Royal v. Stephen* case basically denying everything that Royal had alleged. Furthermore, the Complaint set forth an affirmative defense based upon the earlier letter written to Royal. Stephen really was hoping that the lawsuit would be settled without going to court. He certainly didn't want to have to deal with that.

Regarding the orange deal, he got the following letter from his brother's attorney:

Dear Stephen:

Duke told me that you have consented to become involved in his orange business. He is very pleased, I might add, to have you in the business and has always spoken highly of you.

I have enclosed for your review a brief article on warehouse operations under the Uniform Commercial Code. I did some editing for purposes of your gaining a better understanding of your involvement with Duke. I would like you to review this material, try to gain an understanding of it, and then call me at your earliest convenience. We can then discuss any questions which you might have as well as the specifics of our transaction.

Very truly yours,

Vincent John Thomas, III

P.S. I wrote the enclosed article when I was a student of Professor Boola's. Can you believe he didn't even give me a footnote?

Warehouse Receipts Under the Uniform Commercial Code

By: Professor Darius Boola

Article 7 of the Uniform Commercial Code deals with Documents of Title. A *"document of title"*

> 'means a record (1) that in the regular course of business or financing is treated as adequately evidencing that the person in possession or control of the record is entitled to receive, hold and dispose of the record and the goods the record covers and (2) that purports to be issued by or addressed to a bailee and to cover goods in the bailee's possession which are either identified or are fungible portions of an identified mass... Section 1-201(b)(16).

The two documents of title which are the major focus of Article 7 are Warehouse Receipts and Bills of Lading. Part 2 of Article 7 deals with special provisions applicable to Warehouse Receipts while Part 3 of that Article deals with special provisions applicable to Bills of Lading.

It is the purpose of this article to explain, simply, the subject of warehouse activities under the Uniform Commercial Code. In addition, following the main body of this article, the writer will present a short hypothetical transaction involving bills of lading covered under Part 3 of Article 7.[163]

A. Warehouse; Warehouse Receipts Defined

In your situation with Duke, there may be occasion to harvest oranges and store them pending sale or delivery to a carrier.[164]   In that event, you could store them with Orlando Warehouse or a similar entity.

A *warehouse* is defined under Article 7 as *a person engaged in the business of storing goods for hire.* Section 7-102(a)(13). Upon receipt of the goods to be stored, the warehouse will issue a 'warehouse receipt'.   A *"warehouse receipt"* *means a document of title issued by a person engaged in the business of storing goods for hire.* Section 1-201(b)(42). Any warehouse can issue a warehouse receipt, Section 7-201(1), and upon so doing become an "issuer":

> An *"Issuer"* means a bailee that issues a document of title…. Section 7-102(a)(8).

> *"Bailee"* means a person that by warehouse receipt, bill of lading, or other document of title acknowledges

---

[163] The reader might wish to review the earlier memorandum by Doug at page 96 in which delivery by a bailee to "persons entitled under the documents" is discussed, prior to reading Boola's article.

[164] These oranges would be classified as "goods" per Section 7-102(a)(7):

> *"Goods" means all things that are treated as movable for the purposes of a contract for storage or transportation.*

possession of goods and contracts to deliver them." Section 7-102(a)(1).

Form of Warehouse Receipt

A warehouse receipt need not be in any particular form. Section 7-202(a). In all probability, however, certain terms will be contained in all such documents. The standard terms can be inferred from Section 7-202(b) since the omission of those terms will subject the warehouse to liability for damages caused by such omission. These are common sense in that they identify the goods and other relevant information pertaining to their storage and delivery. Section 7-202(b) states in full as follows:

(b) Unless a warehouse receipt provides for each of the following, the warehouse is liable for damages caused by its omission:

(1) a statement of the location of the warehouse facility where the goods are stored;

(2) the date of issue of the receipt;

(3) the unique identification code of the receipt;

(4) a statement whether the goods received will be delivered to the bearer, to a named person, or to a named person or his order;

(5) the rate of storage and handling charges, unless goods are stored under a field warehousing arrangement in which case a statement of that fact is sufficient on a non-negotiable receipt;

(6) a description of the goods or of the packages containing them;

(7) the signature of the warehouse or its agent;

(8) if the receipt is issued for goods that the warehouse owns, either solely, jointly or in common with others, a statement of the fact of that ownership; and

(9) a statement of the amount of advances made and of liabilities incurred for which the warehouse claims a lien or security interest, unless the precise amount of such advances made or liabilities incurred at the time of the issue of the receipt, is unknown to the warehouse or to its agent that issued the receipt, in which case, a statement of the fact that advances have been made or liabilities incurred and the purpose of the advances and liabilities is sufficient.

B. Duties of a Warehouse

1. Reasonable Care

A warehouse must maintain a certain standard of care with respect to goods which are being stored or it may have to respond in damages. The warehouse must use such

> *'care with regard to the goods that a reasonably careful person would exercise under similar circumstances.'* Section 7-204(1).

That section goes on to state that:

[u]nless otherwise agreed, he is not liable for damages that could not have been avoided by the exercise of that care.

2. Goods to be Kept Separate

Unless the warehouse receipt otherwise provides, the warehouse is required to keep goods covered by a warehouse receipt separate from one another:

Unless the warehouse receipt provides otherwise, a warehouse shall keep separate the goods covered by each receipt so as to permit at all times identification and delivery of those goods... Section 7-207(a).

Section 7-207(a) goes on to state:

However, different lots of fungible goods may be commingled.

***Fungible goods** means:*

(A) goods of which any unit, by nature of usage or trade, is the equivalent of any other like unit. Section 1-201 (b)(18)(A).

Thus, things such as oranges (of the same type), grain and the like may be co-mingled. If goods are so co-mingled, the warehouseman is severally liable to each owner for that owner's share. Section 7-207(b).

C. Selling Goods Stored by a Warehouse

A person storing goods with a warehouse does so with the intention of using or selling those goods at a future time. For one reason or another, presumably the facilities which the warehouse has, the owner of goods has stored them with the warehouse and will sell them at the appropriate time. These goods may be sold in one of a few ways.

First, the seller, holder of the warehouse receipt, may sell the goods covered by that receipt by selling the warehouse receipt. As noted, under Section 7-202(a), no particular form is required for a valid warehouse receipt; however for purposes of this type of sale, the actual wording of the warehouse receipt can be of critical importance, depending on whether the warehouse receipt is negotiable or non negotiable. This is purely a question of the form of the document.

As will be subsequently shown, a purchaser of a negotiable document of title, who takes under certain circumstances, may acquire superior rights to the goods than those of the transferor. Before discussing those rights and the circumstances under which this can occur, the reader is directed to the distinctions in form between a negotiable and non negotiable document.

(a) Except as otherwise provided in subsection (c), a document of title is 'negotiable' if by its terms the goods are to be delivered to bearer or to the order of a named person;

(b) A document of title other than one described in subsection(a) is non-negotiable....

(c) A document of title is nonnegotiable if, at the time it is issued, the document has a conspicuous legend, however expressed, that it is nonnegotiable. Section 7-104(a)(b)(c). [Emphasis added].

As Comment 1 to Section 7-104 notes:

The distinctions between negotiable and nonnegotiable documents in this section makes the most important subclassification employed in the Article, in that the holder of negotiable documents may acquire more rights than its transferor had. (See Section 7-502).

D. Negotiation and Due Negotiation

Before addressing the specifics of 'negotiation and 'due negotiation', it is important to note that the amendments to Article 7 explicitly recognize electronic documents of title as well as standard, tangible documents of title. Both types of documents of title are defined in Section 1-201(b)(16):

*A **tangible document of title** means a document of title evidenced by a record consisting of information that is inscribed on a tangible medium.*

*...An **electronic document of title** means a document of title evidenced by a record consisting of information stored in an electronic medium.*

Section 7-105 provides that both types of documents may be reissued via the alternative medium under the circumstances set forth therein.

There are two categories of rights which can be obtained when a document of title is negotiated. Those acquired by a document of title which has been "duly negotiated" and rights acquired in the absence of due negotiation. A prerequisite to "due negotiation" is negotiation. **Negotiation** of a tangible document of title is governed by Section 7-501(a)(1):

If the document's original terms run to the order of a named person the document is negotiated by the named person's indorsement and delivery. After the named person's indorsement in blank or to bearer, any person may negotiate the document by delivery alone.

Negotiation of an electronic document of title is governed by Section 7-501(b)(1):

If the document's original terms run to the order of a named person or to bearer, the document is negotiated by delivery of the document to another person. Indorsement by the named person is not required to negotiate the document.

As the text clearly indicates, delivery of the document of title is required for negotiation in both situations.

> **Delivery** *with respect to an electronic document of title means voluntary transfer of control and with respect to… a tangible document title…means voluntary transfer of possession.* Section 1-201(b)(15).

Assuming that the negotiation aspects are satisfied, the next question becomes whether or not the document of title has been 'duly negotiated.'

A document of title is 'duly negotiated' if the negotiation satisfies the requirements of Section 7-501(a)(5). That section states as follows:

> *A document of title is duly negotiated if it is negotiated in the manner stated in this subsection to a holder that purchases it in good faith, without notice of any defense against or claim to it on the part of any person, and for value, unless it is established that the negotiation is not in the regular course of business or financing or involves receiving the document in settlement of a monetary obligation.* [Emphasis added.]

The manner of negotiation is covered in Section 7-501(a)(1) noted above. The next requirement for due negotiation is that it be negotiated to a 'holder'. 'Holder' status can be achieved with a tangible document of title or an electronic document of title.

Holder means:

(B) the person in possession of a negotiable tangible document of title if the goods are deliverable either to bearer or to the order of the person in possession;

(C) the person in control of a negotiable electronic document of title. Section 1-201(b)(21)(B)(C).

As noted in Section 7-501(a)(5) the holder, purchasing the document must purchase the document in 'good faith, without notice of any defense against or claim to it by any person, and for value...'

Good faith means honesty in fact and the observance of reasonable commercial standards of fair dealing. Section 7-102(a)(6).

It must be remembered that 'notice' of any defense or claim does not require *knowledge*. If, for example, an individual has 'reason to know' per Section 1-202(a)(3) , he has notice. [See Section 1-202 discussed in footnote 38].

Finally, in order for the negotiation of a document to be a "due negotiation," the negotiation must be in the regular course of business or financing and not in payment or settlement of a monetary obligation. The thrust of Sections 7-501(a)(5) and 7-501(b)(3) [negotiation of electronic documents of title] is that commercially reasonable and honest transactions in the ordinary course of commercial business or financing, involving the sale of documents of title, will be protected. This protection comes from the rights acquired when one takes a document by "due negotiation," which is set forth in Section 7-502(a):

> *Subject to Sections 7-205 and 7-503, a holder to which a negotiable document of title has been duly negotiated acquires thereby:*
>
> 1) *title to the document;*
> 2) *title to the goods;*
> 3) *all rights accruing under the law of agency or estoppel; and*
> 4) *the direct obligation of the issuer to hold or deliver the goods according to the terms of the document free of any defense or claim of the issuer except for those arising under the terms of the document....*
> Section7-502(a)(1)(2)(3)(4).

As can be seen, a person taking a document of title by due negotiation takes title to the goods, as well as the other rights listed in 7-502.

In some situations, this will result is rights superior to those of the transferor in a manner similar to the rights acquired by a holder in due course of commercial paper. Assume for example, seller and buyer agree that Buyer will purchase 50 bicycles stored in Willie's Warehouse through the purchase of the warehouse receipt covering the bicycles. Seller negotiates the warehouse receipt to Buyer who gives Seller a check which bounces. As between Seller and Buyer, Seller will have the right to the bicycles since Buyer did not pay for them. If however, Buyer duly negotiated the warehouse receipt to Tommy Purchaser, Tommy would have the rights to the bicycles, rather than Seller under Section 7-502(a)(2). Seller would have a cause of action against Buyer #1.

In analyzing the foregoing result, it is important to remember that if Tommy Purchaser were not so protected, he would be unlikely to buy the paper. Furthermore, Seller chose to deal with Buyer #1, and made the error of giving up the warehouse receipt without insuring payment.

This is where the importance of the form of the document—i.e.—whether it is negotiable or non negotiable can clearly be seen. In order for there to be a "due negotiation" the document must be negotiable. In that situation [due negotiation] the purchaser receives the rights noted above. In the absence of "due negotiation":

> *A transferee of a document of title, whether negotiable or nonnegotiable, to which the document has been delivered but not duly negotiated, acquires the title and rights that its transferor had or had actual authority to convey.* Section 7-504(a).

In the hypothetical noted above, Buyer #1 had no title, nor did he have actual authority to convey any rights in the bicycles. Hence, in the absence of 'due negotiation', the original seller would prevail over Buyer #2.

There are two notable exceptions to the rights acquired by due negotiation, both of which are referenced in the introductory language to Section 7-502(a).

One is the situation where the document of title involved was procured to cover goods which were stolen. Thus, if X breaks into Willie's Warehouse and steals 50 bicycles, and thereafter procures a document of title upon storage of those bicycles with a warehouse, that document of title confers no rights in good against the owner of the goods. Section 7-503(a)(1).[165]

---

[165] *A document of title confers no right in goods against a person that before issuance of the document had a legal interest or perfected security interest in the goods and that did not:*

(1) deliver or entrust the goods or any document of title covering the goods to the bailor or bailor's nominee with:

(A) actual or apparent authority to ship, store or sell;

(B) power to obtain delivery under Section 7-403;

(C) power of disposition under Section 2-403, 2A-304(2), 2A-305(2), 9-320, or 9-321(c) or other statute or rule of law; or

(2) acquiesce in the procurement by the bailor or its nominee of any document. Section 7-503(a)(1)(A)(B)(C)(2).

The other situation in which the rights of someone to whom a negotiable warehouse receipt had been duly negotiated may be defeated involves a purchase of covered fungible goods by a buyer directly from the warehouseman per Section 7-205. Section 7-205 states in full that:

> *A buyer in the ordinary course of business of fungible goods sold and delivered by a warehouseman who is also in the business of buying and selling such goods takes free of any claim under a warehouse receipt even though it has been duly negotiated.*[166]

E. Delivery Orders

As can be seen from Section 7-502, one method of selling goods covered by the negotiable warehouse receipt is simply to negotiate the warehouse receipt. This method would be most convenient where all of the goods covered under the warehouse receipt were to be sold to one purchaser. A situation could arise, however, where several purchasers were needed in order to sell all of the goods covered by a particular warehouse receipt.

---

[166] Under Section 1-201(b)(9):

A "buyer in the ordinary course of business" means a person that buys goods in good faith, without knowledge that the sale violates the rights of another person in the goods, and in the ordinary course from a person, other than a pawnbroker, in the business selling goods of that kind.

If the purchase is of fungible goods sold and delivered to the warehouseman, and within Section 1-201(9), Section 7-205 requires defeating the holder's claim. The warehouseman will remain liable to the holder of the warehouse receipt.

In such a situation the seller might issue a delivery order to each purchaser:

> *"Delivery order"* means a record that contains an order to deliver goods directed to a warehouse, carrier or other person that in the ordinary course of business issues warehouse receipts or bills of lading. Section 7-102(a)(5).

The seller might, if selling 12 carloads of oranges in a delivery order transaction, sell four carloads of oranges to three different purchasers and issue a delivery order to each for his share. This delivery order, per the above quoted section, orders the warehouseman to deliver the goods to the holder thereof.

It is important to note in connection with the foregoing that until the warehouseman accepts the delivery order, he is not liable under it.[167] Furthermore, if the seller were to "duly negotiate" the warehouse receipt [or a negotiable bill of lading] to someone prior to acceptance of the delivery orders by the warehouse, the party to whom the receipt had been duly negotiated would prevail over the holders of the delivery orders. Section 7-503(b) states in pertinent part:

---

[167] The last sentence to Section 7-502(a)(4) states in part:

...[I]n the case of a delivery order the bailee's obligation accrues only upon the bailee's acceptance of the delivery order....

Title to goods based upon an unaccepted delivery order is subject to the rights of any person to which a negotiable warehouse receipt or bill of lading covering the goods has been duly negotiated. Section 7-503(b).

Of course in such a situation, the seller would probably be acting dishonestly and the holders of the delivery orders would have a cause of action against the seller.

The foregoing discussion deals primarily with the situation where goods are stored by the owner-seller with subsequent transfer of the ownership of those goods accomplished without removal of the goods. Thus, in examples given above, once the seller properly negotiates the warehouse receipt or delivery order to buyer, he, the seller, is out of the transaction.

F. Shipments of Goods: Bills of Lading

Situations often arise which require a seller to ship goods to a buyer locally or non-locally. When a carrier is used to effectuate this transfer, it will issue a document called a "bill of lading" showing the receipt of the goods and a contract to deliver such goods to a named party or destination Section 1-201(b)(6). This article will briefly explore some of the basic mechanics which could be involved in such a situation. The reader is encouraged to integrate the foregoing discussion regarding warehouse receipts in the following hypothetical situation since in many situations a transaction will involve storage of goods with a warehouse prior to their shipment. In addition, a warehouse receipt might be sold once or twice prior to shipment of the goods.

All rules regarding the form necessary to make a document negotiable or non negotiable are identical with respect to warehouse receipts, bills of lading, and all documents of title.

Hypothetical:

Seller is a Miami corporation which has contracted with the ABC carrier to deliver oranges to Buyer in Butte, Montana;

ABC does not traffic west of Chicago;

ABC has contracted with Q-Lines in Chicago to finish the delivery.

Upon receipt of the goods, ABC will issue a bill of lading per the direction of seller. The bill will either be negotiable or non-negotiable depending on the form, in the same manner as warehouse receipts and all documents of title.

The destination stated is for the delivery of the oranges to the buyer in Butte Montana, (as opposed to Q Lines in Chicago) and hence, the bill of lading is a "through bill of lading." As a result, ABC carrier is responsible for Q-Lines' performance as well as its own:

> *The issuer of a through bill of lading or other document embodying an undertaking to be performed in part by persons acting as its agent or by a performing carrier, is liable to any person entitled to recover on the bill or other document for any breach by the other person or the performing carrier of its obligation under the bill or other document....* Section 7-302(a).

If however, Q-Lines, caused injury to goods for which ABC was required to pay, ABC would have a cause of action against Q-Lines:

> *(c) the issuer of a through bill of lading or other document of title described in subsection (a) is entitled to recover from the performing carrier, or other person in possession of the goods when the breach of the obligation under bill or other document occurred:*

> *(1) the amount it may be required to pay to any person entitled to recover on the bill or other document for the breach, as may be evidenced by any receipt, judgment, or transcript of judgment; and*

> *(2) the amount of any expense reasonably incurred by the issuer in defending any action commenced by any person entitled to recover on the bill or other document therefore. Section 7-302(c)(1)(2).*

When the oranges are loaded by the issuer of a bill of lading:

> *(1) the issuer shall count the packages of goods if shipped in packages and ascertain the kind and quantity if shipped in bulk; and*

> *(2) words such as "shipper's weight, load and count," or words of similar import indicating that the description*

> *was made by the shipper are*
> *ineffective except as to goods*
> *concealed in packages.* Section 7-
> 301(b)(1)(2).

If the carrier chooses not to load the goods, but relies on the shipper to do so, a clause in the document such as "shippers weight, load and count" is sufficient to indicate that the description was made by the seller of the goods. If that statement is true, the issuer is not liable for any damages caused by improper loading.

As indicated, the carrier will issue either a negotiable or non negotiable bill of lading depending on the seller's request. There are many potential transactional differences between negotiable and non-negotiable bills. For example, a non-negotiable bill cannot be negotiated and hence, not duly negotiated. This will make sale of the goods by sale of the paper riskier from a buyer's standpoint, for he will not have the certainty of knowing that if he purchases the negotiable document under circumstances giving him the right of due negotiation he will, subject to limited exceptions, get the goods and other valuable rights [per Section 7-502(a)(1)(2)(3)(4) noted earlier].

Another situation which should be noted in this context is the difference in diversion or reconsignment rights. Seller might, for example, be able to get a much better price for the oranges in Kansas City, Kansas, then one agreed upon in Butte. If he decided to sell the Butte designated oranges to Kansas, he would order the carrier to "divert" the oranges to Kansas. Section 7-303(a)(1)(2)(3)(4) deals with diversions and reconsignments and states in full as follows:

(1) Unless the bill of lading otherwise provides, a carrier may deliver the goods to a person or destination other than that stated in the bill or may otherwise dispose of the goods, without liability or misdelivery, on instructions from:

(1) the holder of a negotiable bill; or
(2) the consignor on a non-negotiable bill even if the consignee has given contrary instructions;
(3) the consignee on a non-negotiable bill in the absence of contrary instructions from the consignor, if the goods have arrived at the billed destination or if the consignee is in possession of the tangible bill or in control of the electronic bill; or
(4) the consignee on a non-negotiable bill if the consignee is entitled as against the consignor to dispose of the goods.
[Emphasis added].

Three things are immediately apparent from the text preceding subsections (1) through (4); namely, if the bill provides that the carrier can't divert (a precautionary measure which Butte might have been able to take), the carrier, as a matter of law (not necessarily practice), can't divert. Second, the section states that the carrier "may" divert on certain instructions. It is thus permissive in each instance noted in that section where the bill does not specify otherwise. Examples of how the various subsections to Section 7-303(a) operate are not included as beyond the scope of this article. Finally, when a negotiable bill of lading is involved, only the holder has legal right to diversion or reconsignment.

G. Duty of Care; Carrier's Lien; Enforcement of Lien

1. Duty of Care
Regardless of which type of bill the carrier issues, he must exercise the degree of care with respect to those goods which a reasonably careful person would exercise under similar circumstances. Section 7-309(a). For example, if goods needed refrigeration or would spoil, the carrier should see that they are refrigerated. (Of course the shipper-consignor should be certain the carrier knows this, unless routine shipping procedures of a particular carrier would include finding this out.)

2. Carrier's Lien
A carrier has a lien on the goods covered by a bill of lading or on the proceeds thereof in its possession for charges after the date of carrier's receipt of the goods for storage or transportation. Section 7-307(a).

If the carrier is forced to sell the goods to satisfy the lien he may do so on:

Any terms which are commercially reasonable after notifying all persons known to claim any interest in the goods. Section 7-308(a).

Finally, Section 7-308(h) states in this connection:

The carrier is liable for damages caused by failure to comply with the requirements for sale under this section and in case of willful violation is liable for conversion.

The foregoing has been a brief discussion of warehouse activities and bills of lading under Article 7 of the Uniform Commercial Code. An understanding of the activities discussed, as well as the sale of goods by documentary transfers, is believed by the author to be essential to understanding the sale and movement of goods under the Uniform Commercial Code.

* * *

Stephen read the article and got the general idea. He decided that he would reread it the following week, and call Thomas if he had any questions. While Stephen was reading the article, he didn't know that at the same time, Onus Primo was making the kill. Onus, as he had planned, made out five checks to fictitious payees, endorsed them himself, and mailed the checks to his account at Provo State Bank and Trust Co. in Utah. He planned to make his first stop in Provo, withdraw the cash, and head to Hawaii. He had arranged things so that he would get his two weeks of vacation right after the heist, to give the checks time to clear and make his getaway.

Alan didn't find out what had happened until he went down to the store to meet with Onus on the Monday morning he was to return. He had planned to go over the monthly receipts with Onus. When he entered the store, he asked the clerk where Onus was. The clerk indicated that Onus had not shown up yet. This was highly unusual and Alan knew it, especially since it was the day Onus was supposed to return from his vacation. He immediately telephoned Onus' home.

Needless to say, the phone rang with no answer. Onus Primo had indeed left town. Of course, Alan didn't suspect this until he went in to check the books. As he was going through the books, he saw what had happened to the loan proceeds received from the bank. This really frightened him because he realized that it was possible that Onus had been pulling this type of trick all the way along. His suspicions were confirmed after he went over the books and found out from the bank that the payees of record were non existent suppliers.

Alan, of course, was severely upset by this turn of events. He demanded that the bank recredit his account. The bank refused. Alan immediately went back to his office and told Doug to draft a complaint against the bank to be filed that day. Doug drafted the appropriate complaint which read as follows:

COMES NOW the Plaintiff by and through its undersigned Attorney and alleges as follows:

1) At all times relevant hereto, the Plaintiff was a customer of the Defendant bank.
2) That beginning sometime around January 21, 2007, the Defendant bank

made a series of improper payments and charged the same to the account of Plaintiff. Said items were not properly payable under the Uniform Commercial Code.

3) Plaintiff at all times exercised due care in examining its bank statements to be certain that nothing of this type was happening.

4) Defendant bank was negligent in paying these items.

5) Plaintiff has been damaged in the amount of $125,000 plus attorney's fees.

WHEREFORE, Plaintiff demands judgment against Defendant in the amount of $125,000 plus attorney's fees.

By _____

Alan Lawyer, Esq.
Hopnik, Welscone, Dricus & Smith PA

Section 16

Almost within hours after Alan had filed the lawsuit against the bank, word got out to the business community. Persons who had promised delivery of goods on credit would no longer deliver on credit. Furthermore, the business owed several creditors sums of money ranging from $8,500 to $15,200. These creditors became very frightened when they heard about the filing of the lawsuit. They began consulting their respective attorneys and made demands upon the clothing outlet for money owed to them. Alan was beginning to feel the pinch and the pressure was getting to him. He knew he couldn't pay his debts. He knew that there was little hope of possible salvage and he knew that it would take a long time before his suit against the bank would be resolved. He started thinking about – yes –BANKRUPTCY! As he was thinking about it, Alan received a phone call from one of the creditor's attorneys, a longtime friend. "Looks like you have some trouble, Alan," said his friend Dave.

"I guess you could say that," said Alan. "What should I do?"

"Well, looks to me like if you don't do something soon, they are going to file an involuntary petition against you. Why don't we all get together, that is you and the creditors and attorneys, and see if we can work something out? I think I can round everybody up for an afternoon meeting at my office. These people are pretty anxious to move. Why don't you plan on being at my office at one o'clock unless you hear otherwise from me?"

"Okay," said a half-conscious Alan. "I'll be there."

When Alan snapped out of it he became very nervous and upset. If only I'd stuck to the practice of law instead of trying to be a big shot in business, he thought to himself. Then he realized that Stephen didn't even know about what had happened. Alan hadn't even talked to him since Duke left. And Royal was suing us too. Alan thought. And we're suing the bank! What's going on? And now bankruptcy!

Alan decided to go over to Randy's and have a drink even though it wasn't noon yet. He needed to relax. What was he going to tell Donna? What about all of the others? Alan saw his world crumbling about him.

When he got to Randy's he ordered his usual, Scotch on the rocks. (Alan used to drink other liquors until he found out that he was supposed to drink Scotch.) After downing the first one in a hurry, he ordered another with a shot on the side. By the time he was halfway through the third drink, amazingly, his confidence began to return.

He started thinking that maybe he wasn't out of this one yet. Maybe he could beat the bank. After all, Mr. UCC says he's so good at the Code – damn it, Doug better win this case. Alan knew Doug would kill himself in the bank case – that if Alan played it right (with raises coming up he had some ammunition), he might get Doug to suggest that the research was "on him" (as opposed to billing Alan whatever the cost of the case would be to an outside client.)

And the creditors? He could stall them, let them sue. After all, it wasn't his fault that Onus Primo did what he did. And Royal could be taken care of, he and Doug would handle it – and for whatever would be charged to the firm that would be okay – the business had been much more profitable than Alan ever imagined. He finished his third drink and left for the meeting with the creditors.

Alan went into the meeting ready. He was courteous but firm in stating his desire to fight the bank. The creditors were equally adamant about getting paid or fling a lawsuit. Alan told the creditors to do what they must do and left the meeting, courteously, of course.

When Alan got back to the office, Stephen was waiting.

"Alan, where have you been? I went to the clothing store this morning...."

"I know what happened," Alan interrupted. "We've got some trouble but nothing that can't be handled." He then proceeded to update Stephen on everything that had happened and the lawsuits being undertaken.

Stephen was numb. He couldn't believe it – that would mean he would be involved in *at least* five lawsuits at the same time. He tried to think about what Duke had said – the thing about if you're not getting sued enough, you're not really doing business right. And what Alan had said about no real down side in the outlet case except a suit by Friedman on the note. About how they could stall for a couple of years, etc., and although he knew he would survive it, he again started thinking that it wasn't worth it. Why didn't I just stay on the beach, he thought. Something would have worked out. For now, though, he figured he had no other choice but to stick it out. He and Alan agreed to meet the following week for a strategy meeting, but for now Stephen wanted to try to get his thoughts together. He left Alan's office and went over to Randy's.

Section 17

Before Alan and Stephen even had a chance to have their strategy meeting, an involuntary petition in bankruptcy was filed against the clothing outlet. The trustee, Sol Goldberg, had already been appointed. Sol was well known in the bankruptcy circuit as an extremely successful trustee. Sol liked the cases not only because of the money he made as trustee but also because the attorney for the trustee, Sol's "former" firm, got paid before the rest of the creditors. It was rumored that sometimes Sol would use this fact, subtly, of course, to force a settlement down the creditors' throats when everything was right for Sol. It was rumored that when someone argued with Sol about the law, Sol would say something like "you've raised an interesting point: I think I'll get someone to research it." Of course, the creditors knew that Sol would waste more of their money getting it checked, so they would have a meeting among themselves to discuss it (with Sol out of the room). Rarely was more than one meeting necessary.

As trustee for the outlet, Sol had two hopes of getting sizeable amounts of money for the estate. First, he wanted to win the lawsuit against the bank if possible. Second, he wanted to try to avoid the security interests of West Dade and George Friedman in the inventory. He had counsel working hard on the legal issues in those cases. For now, thought, he had to take care of some of the routine trustee duties which would keep him busy for a couple of months.[168]

---

[168] Footnote 168 is in Appendix II – beginning on page 428.

Section 18

Stephen couldn't believe what was happening to him. He decided to call Duke for some advice. Duke picked up on the first ring, and sounded very excited. In fact, before Stephen could say anything, Duke announced that he had some big news.

"Guess what little brother?"

"I have no idea Duke. Why don't you just tell me?" Stephen replied rather somberly, very disappointed that he was obviously not going to have the discussion he wanted with his brother.

"Little brother, did you ever watch the Beverly Hillbillies?"

"Of course. That was one of Dad's favorites. We watched it all the time."

"Remember the opening?" asked Duke.

Stephen was becoming impatient, and responded "Cut the game Duke and get to the point."

"Easy little brother. Early last week, I had our ranch foreman Randolph Gunston, putting in a septic tank out on west end of the ranch, and as he was digging, he found oil! The early reports are that there is huge potential for a major source of oil."

"That's great!" said Stephen. He was thinking maybe it wasn't so bad being little brother after all. Maybe Duke could bail him out of his current nightmare if he hit it big enough. "Anything I can do to help?"

"As a matter of fact 'yes'. We have a couple of hurdles to get through to get to the oil."

"Like what big brother"?

"Cash. We need money to finance the drilling. We need to have a professional team out here to look this thing over and make some formal recommendations. I figure we need at least $1,000,000 maybe double that."

Stephen was shocked to hear that his brother didn't have enough capital to fund this operation. He always assumed that Duke had millions lying around for anything he wanted. "How can I possibly help with cash? The boat business is doing OK, but doesn't' spin off nearly the kind of cash flow to fund an oil exploration."

"I understand that" replied Duke. "I wasn't looking for you to fund the deal, but I was hoping you might be able to find a bank or some private investors for the project. Someone could hit the long ball for a relatively small investment."

"What about Texas Trust?   You've been doing business with them for years."

"I spoke with Jackson Boulatti yesterday, and he told me that the bank has maxed out its line of credit with me. If we can't get the capital privately, I was hoping that you could talk to Orlando Savings and Loan since they are financing the orange grove operation. Also, I need you to speak to them about borrowing another $500,000."

"For what? Everything is going fine with the orange grove." responded Stephen.

"When's the last time you were out there?" asked Duke.

"About a month ago. Johnny told me everything was running smoothly."

"Things are running smoothly. However, after being in this business for awhile, I see enormous potential for our Florida oranges, particularly since a lot of the Texas crop was destroyed when the hurricane Elvis hit. Right now, the Texas market is up for grabs between Florida and California. I don't want those hippies taking my market. If we can get a quick $500,000 I can make things happen here and we can get that money back in no time. Can you make it happen little brother?"

"OK Duke, I'll see what I can do."

"Thanks. By the way, was there something you wanted to talk about? After all you called me, and I just started rattling my mouth."

"I did have a couple of things on my mind, but we can talk about them some other time. Right now I want to focus on helping you with the funding."

"OK little brother. Don't take too long. I want to feel the Jed Clampett in me soon! I'm working on my own song! *Let me tell you a story 'bout a man named Duke....'* Talk to you soon!" Whereupon, Duke hung up the phone.

Stephen got right to work. He hoped that if he could get the funding for Duke, and the oil hit, Duke would remember his efforts with some commercial love.

The first thing he did was call Alan. He told him about the potential on the oil well, knowing that Alan would literally salivate at the chance to bring in as much money as a good hit with oil would do. He was right. Alan was overjoyed, and told Stephen that he knew of several people who would be interested in such a great opportunity. He told Stephen he would get back to him as soon as he had something.

Once that was in motion, he called Orlando Savings and Loan and scheduled an appointment to meet with Kitty Barnes, the loan officer who was handling "Duke's Orange Express," the name he had given his orange business. He scheduled a meeting with Kitty for the following Monday, November 4, 2007 at 10:00 a.m.

As soon as he got off the phone with Kitty, he sent Doug an Instant Message. He wanted any information he could get, as soon as possible, which would help him understand the transactions. Doug was hooked into his computer, and always answered quickly. He would pay Doug as an independent attorney, rather than try to include this in his arrangement with Alan. He sent the following Instant Message:

STEPHEN: Doug, I hope this finds you doing well. Things here are really active. I just got off the phone with Duke. It looks like they discovered oil on his Texas

Ranch. Also, he wants to jump start his orange business and needs to borrow $500,000 for the business. Duke has asked me to help him with this. I would like you to represent me and help me figure out how best to proceed. Time is of the essence. What do you think? Go Canes!

DOUG: Hi Stephen. Of course I can help. And, thanks for thinking of me! Maybe one of these days I'll get paid what I am worth by this law firm! What can I do for you?

STEPHEN: Obviously, the bank is going to want collateral for the loan. They are already financing the orange inventory. I am not clear on how that works. Can you explain?

DOUG: I haven't seen the documents, but my guess is that they have a security interest in the oranges as 'farm products'. The term is defined under Article 9 of the Uniform Commercial Code:

> ***Farm products*** *means goods, other than standing timber, with respect to which the debtor is engaged in a farming operation and which are: crops grown, growing, or to be grown, including: crops produced on trees, vines and bushes; and....livestock, born or unborn....* Section 9-102(a)(34)(A)(B).

One thing the bank might consider, is using part of the loan proceeds for the purchase of a commodity contract in which the bank could take a security interest. Or it could take a security interest in a commodity account. This would decrease the exposure to the bank.

STEPHEN: Remember, it wasn't too long ago that I was on the beach sipping piña coladas! What is a commodity contract and a commodity account & how would this work.

DOUG: How much time do you have Stephen?

STEPHEN: Whatever it takes! In case you haven't heard, there is an involuntary petition filed against our clothing store. Onus Primo robbed us and my financial outlook is not good right now. I need to be able to help Duke big time so he can maybe help me back! I will send you a retainer in the morning, and if Alan gives you a hard time about this, let me know and I will deal with him.

DOUG: OK. Here goes. I am going to start with the definition and work you through the whole process. I am going to do this in legalese, so bear with me. Also, I am doing this quickly, so before you rely on this, I want some time to review it. Don't want any malpractice possibilities amigo. If you have any questions, just stop me and ask them.

__Commodity Account__ means an account maintained by a commodity intermediary in which a commodity contract is carried for a commodity customer. Section 9-102(a)(14).

In order to understand what a commodity account is, one must define the three terms contained in the foregoing definition:
Commodity intermediary;
Commodity contract;
Commodity customer

"Commodity intermediary" means a person that: (A) is registered as a futures commission merchant under federal commodities law; (B) or in the ordinary course of its business provides clearance or settlement services for a board of trade that has been designated as a contract merchant pursuant to federal commodities law. Section 9-102(a)(17)(A)(B).

"Commodity contract" means a commodity futures contract, an option on a commodities futures contract, a commodity option, or another contract if the contract or option is: (A) traded on or subject to the rules of a board of trade that has been designated as a contract market for such a contract pursuant to federal commodities laws; or (B) traded on a foreign commodity board of trade, exchange, or market, and is carried on the books of a commodity intermediary. Section 9-102(a)(15)(A)(B).

As noted on paragraph 5 to comment 6 to Section 9-102:

The most likely setting in which a person would want to take a security interest in a commodity contract is where a lender who is advancing funds to finance an inventory of a physical commodity requires the borrower to enter into a commodity contract as a hedge against the risk of decline in the value of the commodity.

"Commodity Customer" means a person for which a commodity intermediary carries a commodity contract on its books. Section 9-102(a)(16).

Example: Assume that Orlando Savings and Loan agrees to loan Duke the $500,000 to increase the national marketing of his orange business. Further assume that Orlando Savings and Loan has a security interest in the oranges, as 'farm products' and takes all steps necessary to have an enforceable perfected security interest in the oranges.

In order to further protect its capital, Orlando Savings and Loan may require Duke to enter a futures contract on oranges which will guarantee a receivable of $350,000 for the bank, which in the bank's opinion is a sufficient hedge against a decline in the price of oranges. Duke would be the 'customer' under Section 9-102(a)(16).

If the futures contract cost $250,000, Duke will still have $250,000 to promote the business, and Orlando Savings and Loan will be satisfactorily protected.

If the commodities contract complies with Section 9-102(a)(15)(A) or (B); the commodity intermediary complies with the requirements of Section 9-102(a)(17)(A) or (B), and Duke's contract is carried by such an intermediary, the transaction would be within Article 9.

The security interest itself could be in the 'commodity account', or the 'commodity contract'.

Where multiple contracts are being secured, it would probably be in the overall account, rather than each individual contract. In either event, it would be designated as "investment property" under Article 9:

"Investment property" means a security, whether certificated or uncertificated, security entitlement, securities account, commodity contract, or commodity account. Section 9-102(a)(49).

The rules governing enforceability and perfection have certain similarities and some important distinctions with other types of collateral. **Enforceability:** Once again, the basic rules of Section 9-203(b) apply.

> *Except as otherwise provided in subsection (c) through (i), a security interest is enforceable against the debtor and third parties with respect to the collateral only if:*
>   *(1) value has been given;*
>   *(2) the debtor has rights in the collateral or the power to transfer rights in the collateral to a secured party; and*
>   *(3) one of the following conditions has been met:.....*
> *(A) the debtor has authenticated a security agreement that provides a description of the collateral and, if the security interest covers timber to be cut, a description of the land concerned;*
> *(B)....*
> *(C)....or;*
> *(D) the collateral is deposit accounts, electronic chattel paper, "**investment property**", or letter of credit rights, and the secured party has "**control**" under Section 9-104, 9-105, 9-106, or 9-107 pursuant to the debtor's security agreement.*
> Section 9-203(b)(1)(2)(3)(A)(D). [Emphasis added]

STEPHEN: I think I understand so far. In many ways this is similar to my Security Agreement with South Dade Bank. One of the things that confuses me is under subsection (A), you need a security agreement, and from my reading of subsection (D) you also need a security agreement. It looks like subsection (D) requires control and a security agreement whereas subsection (A) only requires a security agreement. Am I missing something?

DOUG: The security agreement referred to in Section 9-203(b)(3)(D) is not an authenticated security agreement of the type required under Section 9-203(b)(3)(A). As comment 4 to Section 9-203 notes:

That phrase [pursuant to the debtor's security agreement as used in Section 9-203(b)(3)(D)] refers to the debtor's agreement to the secured party's possession for the purpose of creating a security interest.   The phrase should not be confused with the phrase "debtor has authenticated a security agreement" used in paragraph (3)(A), which contemplates the debtor's authentication of a record.

STEPHEN: I still don't understand why a secured party would do whatever it takes to get control, when a simple signed security agreement would make the security interest enforceable.

DOUG: Although an authenticated security agreement can be used as the third element for enforceability, it will not give the secured party the highest protection available. That will be accomplished by *control* which is why that is the route that Orlando Savings and Loan is most likely to take. Let me explain.

As noted, a commodity contract or commodity account fits within the definition of 'investment property'. Section 9-106 deals with control of investment property. Subsection (b) deals with control of a commodities contract, while subsection (c) deals with control of a commodities account. Under subsection (b):

A secured party has control of a commodity contract if:

….

(1) the secured party is the commodity intermediary with which the commodity contract is carried; or
(2) the commodity customer, secured party, and commodity intermediary have agreed that the commodity intermediary will apply any value distributed on account of the commodity contract as directed by the secured party without further consent by the commodity customer.   Section 9-106(b)(1)(2).

The matter with Orlando Savings and Loan would fall under subsection (b)(2). If Duke [the commodity customer], Orlando Savings and Loan [the secured party] and the commodity intermediary have agreed that the commodity intermediary will *'apply any value distributed on account of the commodity contract'* as directed by Orlando Savings and Loan, without further consent by Duke, control is established under Section 9-106(b)(2). Furthermore, if more than one futures contract is entered into by Duke, and placed in the account that is being secured, Orlando Savings and Loan will have a security interest in those contracts as well:

A secured party having control of all security entitlements or commodity contracts carried in a securities account or a commodity account has control over the securities account or commodities account. Section 9-106(a)(3).

STEPHEN: Sorry to interrupt again, but you still haven't explained to me why this is better than simply signing the security agreement.

DOUG: I was just about to do that. It all boils down to the two ways in which a security interest can be perfected in investment property and the relative protection each affords the secured party.

There are two methods in which a security interest In investment property can be perfected. One is by filing a financing statement:

A security interest in chattel paper, negotiable documents, instruments, or investment property may be perfected by filing. Section 9-312(a).

The second way in which a security interest investment property can be perfected is by *control*:

A security interest in investment property, deposit accounts, letter-of-credit rights, or electronic chattel paper may be perfected by control of the collateral under Section 9-104, 9-105, 9-106, or 9-107. Section 9-314(a).

Therefore, assuming that value has been given [Section 9-203(b)(1)], and the debtor has rights in the collateral or the power to transfer rights [Section 9-203(b)(2)], the security interest will become enforceable and perfected simultaneously upon the secured party establishing control of the investment property under Section 9-106.

The matter of critical importance to the secured party once enforceability is out of the way is priority. Section 9-328 states specific rules for priority with respect to investment property.

The following rule governs priority among conflicting security interests in investment property:

(1) A security interest held by a secured party having control of investment property under

Section 9-106 has priority over a security interest held by a secured party that does not have control of the investment property.

There are some more detailed rules under Section 9-328, dealing with specific situations, but for purposes of this discussion, the main point is that control of investment property creates a priority for the secured party having control.

STEPHEN: Alan told me that the first to file *always* had priority. Even if the other party lent the money first!

DOUG: I probably shouldn't put this in writing, but since it is you, and I trust you, I will. Alan *thinks* he knows the UCC. The reality is, he knows *part* of it pretty well, but I'm the one who *really* knows it.

Even though I shouldn't have put that in writing, I sure feel better!

Now, let me finish up with this priority matter, so we can address anything else you need. I have been up since 3:00 a.m. and I need some sleep soon.

The rule of Section 9-328, bears some similarity to certain priority rules with respect to deposit accounts. Like deposit accounts, these unique rules are a product of the commercial setting in which they occur. This result is explained in Comment 3 to Section 9-328:

The rule that a security interest perfected by filing can be primed by a control security interest, without regard to awareness, is a consequence of the system of perfection and priority rules for investment property. These rules are designed to take account the circumstances of the securities markets, where filing is not given the same effect as for some other forms of property.

That pretty well does if as far as the commodity situation. Anything else you need?

STEPHEN: Actually, there is, but you've done enough for today. How does tomorrow morning look for you?

DOUG: Anytime after 10:00 a.m. will work. However, I have to be in court at 1:30 p.m. and then we have a firm meeting at 4:00 p.m. Why don't we just schedule a call for 11:00 a.m. and send me an email by 9:00 a.m. so I can have a heads up on what you want to discuss.

STEPHEN: Sounds great! Thanks for your help. Would you like to go to the Miami game next week? I have some great seats, and I will treat. I will pick you up in my XGT and we can head over to Dolphin stadium for the tailgate party.

DOUG: I'm in. Talk to you tomorrow. Glad I could help. DON'T TELL ALAN WHAT I SAID!

***

After he finished with Doug, Stephen felt much better. With what he had just learned, he was confident that he could make a very good pitch to Kitty on Monday and if could get the funding, he knew that would make Duke very happy. He was surprised at how his mind was working—all of a sudden seeing Duke as a possible escape route from the financial mess he had gotten himself into—and he realized that the mind is quite an adaptive mechanism. He started to visualize that in a few months, everything would be back on track. Alan had as much or more to lose than Stephen, and he figured Alan would come up with something—he always did.

So, Stephen decided it was time to create a positive perspective on everything. In fact, he thought it would be a good idea to head over to the mall and purchase a beautiful $10,000 entertainment center he had been looking at. That would definitely make him feel better. So, off he went to Outlandish Mall to make the purchase.

Stephen went directly to The Music Emporium. He had originally planned to buy a DVDSEW#345, a free standing entertainment center which would look perfect in his study, but when he got there he was blown away by the REDQED#2098 Raptor Entertainment Center. Unlike the DVDSEW, which was designed to be a free standing unit, the Raptor was to be installed in his house. It was a much larger unit that he had planned, but the sound system was incredible, and it had a large computer monitor which could be used with a voice activated Internet keyboard.

Although he had some concerns about the cost of the Rapor B costing $8,500, it was on sale, down from $10,445, and he had been working so hard! Maybe the entertainment center would help him cut down on his drinking, which he realized had become a very costly and detrimental habit. In fact, he thought that if the entertainment center delivered what he hoped, he might be able to pay for it with the money he saved from not drinking! He made his decision: he and the Raptor were going to become one.

He was able to get the Raptor for $2,500 down and a monthly payment of $200 for 36 months. He signed a conditional sales contract and scheduled delivery for Monday, November 4th, 2007 at 4:00 p.m. He would meet with Kitty at 10:00 a.m., head over to the business for a few hours, and come home. He could hardly wait.

As he was getting into the car to leave the Mall, he got a text message from Alan:

ALAN: "Stephen, Great news! I got five of my law partners to invest in Duke's drilling. Each of us will put up $250,000. Need to speak to Duke ASAP to discuss terms. Call me as soon as you get this!"

Stephen's first reaction as he read the text was stress! He did not want to have to deal with Alan right now. However, this was replaced with a new sense of euphoria as he realized that if he could put this deal together, and the well hit, Duke would definitely take care of him. So, he called Alan immediately.

"Hi buddy. That's the kind of news I like to hear!"

"Stephen, if we hit on this one, our financial troubles are over!"

Stephen got excited. He liked the "we" word, but he couldn't imagine that Alan would cut him in out of the goodness of his heart.

"Not that I am complaining Alan, but how exactly did I get included in all of this?" asked Stephen.

"Well, as you know I am having the same cash problems that you are. So, I don't have the $250,000 handy. In order to get it, I need to mortgage something. I have already taken all of the equity out of our house. I never should have let Donna talk me into buying that condominium in Vail, but it's too late now. The only thing left is the land and building where the boat business is located. It has appreciated over $300,000 since we bought it."

Stephen got a sick feeling in his stomach. "Are you telling me we have to refinance our business for this oil venture?"

"Stephen, we don't have to do anything. We can sit here and get beaten up by creditors and lawsuits, or we can make a move. Did you read the paper today?" Alan asked.

"No, as a matter of fact. I have been working all day trying to get Duke some money for the Orange Express. By the way, Doug was a great help to me."

"Doug?"

"Yes, Doug. I contacted him and needed some information. I am aware of the fact that Doug does a lot of the UCC work for our business, and I decided to go directly to him, since I had no time to go through the usual contacting you and the rest of the game we usually play."

Alan was furious. He did not like Stephen's tone of voice, and Doug should have contacted Alan before doing anything. He was ready to say something really nasty to Stephen, but he realized that if Stephen didn't sign off on the refinance, he would not be able to get the $250,000 and he knew his partners would like nothing better than to cut him out of the deal.

"Stephen, buddy, Doug is part of our team. My only concern in having matters run through myself is in your best interests. I must point out however, that while Doug is very much a part of our UCC analysis, I am the one who teaches Secured Transactions at the University of Miami." Who cares, anyway Alan thought.

Alan continued, "The only thing that matters to me is that Stephen's Boats gets the best counsel available."

"I need to know if you are "in" or "out" on the oil deal. If you want to jump in, you and I will be 50-50 partners. As for today's paper, the front page had a story about an oil find in North Dakota that looks like it will yield $50,000,000-$100,000,000 over the next ten years. How does that sound?"

Stephen liked the sound of that very much.

"I like it very much. But I am not keen on losing all our equity in the land."

"What difference does it make? We still have the business operating the same as before, and this gives us an opportunity to be set for life!"

Stephen thought about that for a moment, and decided that as much as didn't want to add any new debt, he was so far over his head now, that it made sense to try the oil deal.

"Alright Alan. I'm in. What now?"

"I'll take care of the refinance matter tomorrow morning and have the paperwork by tomorrow afternoon. I already talked to Johan at South Dade, and it's all good with them."

"Anything else?" Stephen asked.

"Yes. My partners want collateral for the money they are investing, as well as a percentage of the yield. They have requested a conference call for next Tuesday with Duke and his attorney to iron out the details. In the meantime they are drafting some documents which I will send to you, and which you should forward to Duke."

"O.K. Alan. I will talk to Duke later today, and try to schedule this for Tuesday afternoon. I will let you know as soon as I have an answer."

"Awesome, Stephen! This is it my friend. I can feel it."

When Stephen got off the phone, he knew that he was either going to come out of all of this in great financial shape, or he was in deep trouble. Having come to that conclusion, he got out of the car and went back to the Mall. This time he went to Electronics World, and purchased a $7,000 plasma television. He had an empty space on the Raptor Entertainment Center in which the plasma set would fit perfectly. He was able to get the plasma television on terms similar to the Raptor B, $1400 down, and an installment sales contract of $200 per month for 36 months. The set was to be delivered on Tuesday at 5:00 p.m.

When he returned home, Stephen was drained, but excited. He believed that the well was going to make him a very wealthy man. He began to think about retirement and going back to the beach! However, there was a lot to do before that happened.

He called Duke and was able to arrange the conference call for Tuesday afternoon as Alan had requested.

With all of this behind him, Stephen was ready for a drink. He poured himself a triple and sat in front of the spot where the new entertainment center was going to be installed. He liked the way it felt. After about an hour, and two more drinks, Stephen ordered a pizza, had dinner and went to sleep.

Section 19

On Monday, November 4, 2007, Stephen drove to Orlando to meet with Kitty Barnes. Kitty was in her early thirties, and had joined the bank when she graduated from the University of Central Florida. She was very bright, and Stephen's dealings with her had always been pleasant. He was confident she would give him the $500,000 and take the security interest in the commodities account as Doug had predicted. Stephen was feeling pretty good about himself as he walked into the bank wearing his Stephen's Boats embroidered polo shirt, and dress slacks with a nice pair of deck shoes.

After waiting a few minutes, Kitty came out to meet him and take him back to her office.

"Hi Kitty. It's been awhile. How's everything going?"

"Things are great Stephen. How about you?"

"You know how it is Kitty. One day things are smooth, next day it's a war zone. But overall, I am pleased with everything. Did you hear about the flood damage to the orange crop in Texas?"

"Of course. Hurricane Elvis did some real damage to whole region. Why do you ask?"

"Well as you know, Duke lives near Houston and has a lot of contacts in Texas. Naturally, he was as upset as anyone about what Elvis did to Texas, but he realized that there is going to be a huge need for oranges in that part of the country, and he would like some extra capital from the bank to promote the sales of Orange Express and for shipment direct to the stores that he contracts with."

"Has he made any contacts?" Kitty asked with what Stephen sensed was a lack of enthusiasm.

"Absolutely. He has the full reach of Duke's Enterprises out there making things happen."

"Stephen, as you know, we are already financing his inventory. We also have the uncertainty of our own weather here in Florida. So we are going to need some security before we can loan the Orange Express anything. Plus, there is this little matter to deal with."

At which point, Kitty handed Stephen about eight pages held together with a binder clip. On the top of the first page was a notation stating:

NOTICE OF AGRICULTURAL LIEN ON ALL ORANGES OF ORANGE GROVE EXPRESS

AMOUNT OF LIEN: Twenty thousand dollars [$20,000] plus interest as it accrues.

LIEN HOLDER: Orlando Farming Supplies

BASIS OF LIEN : From August 3, 2007-September 8, 2007 Orlando Farming Supplies did furnish to Orange Grove Express, in the ordinary course of its business fertilizer, insect repellant, and five Protant Orange Pickers for which Orlando Farming Supplies has not been paid. Several attempts to collect the outstanding balance of $20,000 have been unsuccessful.

Stephen turned to page two, and saw that a financing statement had been filed against Orange Grove Express with the Florida Secured Transactions Registry on October 21, 2007, claiming a security interest in, among other things *'all oranges and other farm products of the Orange Express'*.

"I had no idea that Orange Express owed anybody anything! Why wasn't I aware of this?" Stephen asked almost rhetorically.

Kitty replied, "That is a good question. But that is not my concern. My concern, or I should say, the bank's concern, is that with this lien on the property, there is no way we can loan you anything."

"Kitty, you know Duke. He is going to be furious about this. I guess I have been too busy with my own businesses to pay this the kind of attention it needs. I need to raise the money and pay this off, or I am going to have some serious problems. Before I undertake that, would you please explain how this works?" Stephen said.

"Sure. It isn't very complicated, and we deal with this on a regular basis. Are you familiar with the Uniform Commercial Code?"

Stephen couldn't believe it. It seemed that everywhere he went, the UCC was there. "More so than I ever imagined I would. Since I opened the boat business, I have had so much contact with the UCC that I almost feel like a lawyer."

"I know what you mean," said Kitty. "We deal with it everyday at the bank."

"How can you understand it Kitty? Whenever I try to read it, I get a headache and need to take a nap! If it wasn't for my attorneys, I wouldn't have a clue."

"I agree with you on the difficulty of reading and understanding the Code. For years, every time we had a UCC question we called our attorney. That got expensive, but we felt so uncertain about even the most basic issues, that the Board of Directors told us to make the call. Fortunately, we don't have to do that anymore."

"Why not?"

Kitty reached to the right corner of her desk and picked up a book, and said "Because we have this."

"What is it?"

"It is a new book called **The Uniform Commercial Code Made Easy** written by Robert LeVine. Our bank president heard him speak at a banking seminar and he was introduced to the book. It's written in the form of a short story, and makes the UCC easy to understand."

"I think I know who you mean, replied Stephen. "Is this the same guy that does the late night infomercials?

Where he is being interviewed by five women about 'navigating' the UCC?"

"That's him. Can you believe that guy? Anyway, if you read the book, you can get a good understanding of the Uniform Commercial Code, and the book is actually enjoyable to read. Let's take a look at what he says about agricultural liens."

Kitty opened *The Uniform Commercial Code Made Easy*, and turned to the Appendix:

Agricultural lien:

Definition: Agricultural lien *means an interest in farm products:*

(A) which secures payment or performance of an obligation for:

> *(i) goods or services furnished in connection with a debtor's farming operations; . . .*

(B) which is created by statute in favor of a person that:

> *(i) in the ordinary course of business furnished goods or services to a debtor in connection with a debtor's farming operation; ... and*
>
> *….*

(C) whose effectiveness does not depend on the person's possession of the personal property. Section 9-102(a)(5).

"As you can see from the NOTICE OF LIEN, Orlando Farming Supplies is taking a security interest in *'all oranges and other farm products of the Orange Express'*. This would includes the oranges on the tree and to be grown, as well as the oranges which have been harvested."

> ***Farm products*** *means goods, other than standing timber, with respect to which the debtor is engaged in a farming operation and which are:*
>
> *(A) crops grown, growing, or to be grown, including: (i) crops produced on trees, vines and bushes; and ...*
>
> *(B) livestock, born or unborn....*
>
> *(C) Supplies used or produced in a farming operation; or*
>
> *(D) products of crops or livestock in their manufactured state.*
> Section 9-102(a)(34)(A)(B)(C)(D).

"So, it is clear that the oranges fit the definition of 'farm products'. The fertilizer, farming tools, and insect repellant were all furnished in connection with the farming operations of Orange Grove Express, in the ordinary course of Orlando Farming Supplies business.

Furthermore, Florida Statute § 679.3021 expressly provides for the creation of this lien, and the effectiveness of the lien does not depend on the lien holder having possession. The lien becomes enforceable when it becomes effective, but here, not only is it effective and enforceable, it is perfected. Do you know what 'perfected' means?"

Stephen nodded.

Kitty continued, "perfection of the agricultural lien occurred when Orlando Farming Supplies filed its financing statement with the Florida Secured Transaction Registry."

Perfection: An agricultural lien is perfected if it has become effective and all of the applicable requirements for perfection in Section 9-310 have been satisfied….. Section 9-308(b).

"The agricultural lien would become effective once the statutory requirements noted above have been fulfilled. It would be perfected upon the filing of a financing statement:"

Except as provided in subsection (b) and Section 9-312(b), a financing statement must be filed to perfect all security interests and agricultural liens. Section 9-310(a).

"The exceptions noted do not apply to agricultural liens, and therefore, a financing statement must be filed to perfect."

"If we were to lend money to the Orange Express at this time, our security interest would be subordinate to the agricultural lien of Orlando Farming Supplies, even if our security interest was perfected."

Priority: A security interest or agricultural lien is subordinate to a person entitled to priority under Section 9-322. Section 9-317(a)(1).

Section 9-322(a)(1) states as follows:

Except as otherwise provided in this section, priority among conflicting security interests and agricultural liens in the same collateral is determined according to the following rules:

(1) Conflicting perfected security interests and agricultural liens rank according to priority in time of filing or perfection....

"What do I need to do?" asked Stephen.

"You need to pay off Orlando Farming Supplies before we can even consider this loan. Once that is done, we have something to talk about."

Kitty could see that Stephen was visibly upset. She felt bad for him, but her feelings were irrelevant. She saw this kind of situation regularly, and was amazed how sloppy people were with their financial affairs.

"Thanks Kitty. I need to get that taken care of right away. I'll get back to you as soon as it's done, and hopefully, we can get the loan. If Duke happens to call, please avoid telling him about the lien if at all possible. I would really appreciate it."

When Stephen left the bank, he felt like he had just come out of a dark movie theatre into the bright sunlight. He was hot, tired, and drained, but he knew there was no time to rest. He called Alan.

Alan picked up on the first ring as soon as he saw Stephen's number pop up.

"Hola amigo" said Alan, sounding as cheerful as could be.

"Hi Alan," replied Stephen. "I need $21,233.45 wired to our Orange Express account at Orlando Savings and Loan immediately."

"Why are you asking me?" Alan remarked.

"Does the word 'oil' ring a bell?"

"A loud one. But I still don't see what that has to do with me."

Stephen proceeded to explain the whole situation to Alan. He concluded by telling Alan: "If Duke thinks that I screwed up on this farming lien, he won't have anything to do with us on the oil deal. You are my business partner. He found out about the involuntary petition against the outlet and somehow about Onus Primo. If, on top of that, he thinks I can't even handle routine bills on the Orange Grove, there is no way he will do business with us."

Alan knew he had no choice.

Stephen gave him the wiring instructions, and within the hour, the money was wired to Orlando Savings and Loan. By the end of the day, Orlando Farming Supplies was paid in full, and the lien was removed.

Stephen needed a drink and a nap. He called Stephen's Boats and told them he wouldn't be in that day.

Section 20

Stephen's alarm went off at 3:00 p.m. He felt much better, as he made some strong coffee and awaited the arrival of his entertainment center at 4:00 PM. He could hardly wait to have it installed and play some of his favorite music. Stephen liked all different kinds of music, but lately he was really interested in Salsa. He hadn't told anyone, but he was taking Salsa dancing lessons at a studio near his boat dealership every Tuesday and Thursday after work. He even had some special 'Salsa shirts' that he wore for his lessons. He was going to a wedding in July of 2008, and he was going to unveil 'Salsa Steve' as he called himself.

Just as he was beginning to fantasize about his entrance to the dance floor, the doorbell rang. The delivery and installation team from The Music Emporium had arrived right on time. He let them in, offered them cold water, and watched them install the Raptor in less than a half an hour.

As soon as they left, he put on his favorite Salsa album and cranked up the volume. He poured himself a drink and began doing some of the moves he would use tomorrow at class. He kept checking himself out in the mirror, imagining that he was at the wedding and everyone was watching him in amazement. Just as he saw everyone standing and clapping for his brilliant performance, the door bell rang again. The plasma television had arrived.

He was snapped back into reality, and hoped that the delivery/installation team hadn't looked in while he was dancing.

As he opened the door, he identified Clyde and Jorge by the name tags on their shirts. "Hi guys" said Stephen as he invited them in and offered them something to drink.

As they entered the house, Clyde said slowly, in his deep Southern accent, "If I ever did the kind of moves I just seen you do, they would never let me back on the farm."

"That's your problem Clyde" Jorge interrupted with his thick Cuban accent. He smiled, looked at Stephen, made a quick Salsa move with his hips and said "Home boy has some moves!"

Stephen wished he was invisible.

The installation took less than fifteen minutes, as the plasma television was hooked onto the entertainment center with eight brackets.

Clyde and Jorge left, and Stephen was left alone with his beautiful entertainment center. It looked even better than he thought it would. He spent the next three hours dancing and watching television.[169]

---

[169] Footnote 169 is in Appendix I on page 403.

Section 21

Stephen had arranged the conference call for 2:00 p.m. Tuesday. He went in early to the office and had a productive morning. He was excited about the call, and had done some online research about the oil find in North Dakota. "Why not us" he thought to himself.

He called in on the conference line at 1:55 p.m. He liked being the first one on the line, and as each person joined the call, he felt in control.

"Hello. This is Duke. Anyone there?"

"Hi Duke."

"Little brother, is that you?"

"It sure is."

Just then everyone from Alan's firm joined in. They were placing the call from the conference room at the law firm.

"Hi Duke." said Alan. "Before we get started, let's have everyone say 'hello'.

"Hi Duke, Dimit Welscone here. Managing partner at Hompik, Welscone, Dricus and Smith."

"Hi Duke. Tinsley Mannix here."

"Hi Duke. Bruce Babcock. Nice to meet you."

"Hi Duke. Brenda Seals. We are all excited about this oil! I can tell you that."

"Hello to all of you. It's great to meet all of you. I'd like to introduce you to my attorney, Vincent John Thomas III. Say hello Vinny."

Vincent hated to be called Vinny and Duke knew it. But for $450,000 a year, a luxury automobile, and four weeks vacation a year, he could call him whatever he wanted.

"Hello everybody" said Vincent.

Duke began. "As you know, we got some exciting news last week. Texas style. We have no way of knowing exactly what the yield on the oil well can be, but I have been told we are looking at one of the biggest finds in twenty-five years — maybe a billion barrels."

"I don't know how up to speed y'all are on oil, but that's a whole bunch which could make us all very wealthy."

Alan interrupted: "We are all excited to be a part of this Duke. There are five of us, all willing to pitch in $250,000. Will that get you going?"

"It certainly will get me started. We may need more down the road, but I think that will definitely be enough for testing, evaluating and some drilling." Duke said.

"Great," said Dimit. "Let's talk business for a moment Duke. I know there is huge potential in your find, but I also know that it could turn out to be nothing. So we need two things. First, we need to lock down just how much of a percentage of the yield we are going to get for our investment. Second, we need some collateral to secure the loan."

"Gentlemen, I completely understand. I am willing to split 50-50 on the wells. However, all of my assets are tied up with Texas Trust. Unless of course, you want security which is subordinate to theirs" said Duke.

"Actually," replied Dimit, "we were thinking about taking a security interest in the oil itself."

Vincent John Thomas III quickly interrupted, in his slow Texas drawl, "Why Dimit, y'all know that oil in the ground is not 'goods' under the UCC. You can't get a security interest in oil in the ground" finished Vincent, very proud of himself for putting those Florida lawyers on check.

"Well now Vincent John, y'all [sarcastically delivered by Dimit] don't understand the UCC very well if you make that statement. Under Section 9-102(a)(44), **Goods** *means all things that are movable when a security interest attaches....The term...does not include...oil, gas, or other minerals **before** extraction.*" As he concluded this statement he raised his arms high in the air, like a football referee does after the extra point is kicked. All of the partners in the room gave Dimit the thumbs up.

Duke looked at Vincent with an expression which said "Why am I paying you $450,000 a year?"

Vincent was not going to give up. "Just because there can't be a security interest in oil *before* extraction, doesn't mean that there can be a security interest in oil *after* extraction. I would never advise my client to take collateral based upon some inference from a UCC section." Vincent was feeling very good about that response.

Brenda said, "neither would I Vincent. In fact, in this precise case, I would have my client take a look at Section 9-102(a)(6)."

Vincent John Thomas was perspiring profusely.

"Do you have your UCC handy, Vinny?" Brenda continued.

"No. But I am sure you do. What does Section 9-102(a)(6) say?"

"Section 9-106 discusses something called '*As-extracted collateral,*'" responded Brenda.

Vincent John Thomas was dripping in sweat at this point. Duke was staring holes in him. Meanwhile, back at the conference room, everyone was laughing, quietly of course.

"Under section 9-102(a)(6),

As extracted collateral means:

    (A) oil, gas or other minerals that are subject to a security interest that:

        (i) is created by a debtor having an interest in the minerals before extraction;

        (ii) and attaches to the minerals as extracted; or

(B) accounts arising out of the sale at the wellhead or minehead of oil, gas, or other minerals in which the debtor had an interest before extraction.
Section 9-102(a)(6)(A)(i)(ii)(B).

"Would you like me to explain how this works Vinny?"
Vincent was as furious as he was embarrassed.
"No thank you Brenda"
Duke interjected, "I would."
As Brenda began her explanation, Vincent John Thomas slipped a note to Duke which said:

"All of this is new since I went to law school. I told you I needed some time for continuing legal education. I can figure this out. We don't need them."

"Go ahead Brenda. I am sure that both of us will find this informative," continued Duke.
"Thank you Duke. As you can see, under Section 9-102(a)(6), the security interest in the oil is created 'before extraction'. You would be a debtor that has an interest in the oil prior to extraction, since you own the land. The security interest being created will attach when the oil is extracted under Section 9-102(a)(6)(ii).
Being nice to Vincent, Brenda continued, "as Vincent noted "Goods" are defined under Section 9-102(a)(44) in a manner which explicitly excludes oil, gas and timber before extraction. However, once extracted, they become goods and at that moment, the security interest in the oil will attach.
"From your perspective, it is important to note that even though we will have a security agreement executed prior to advancing the $1,250,000, it will not be enforceable until we actually loan you the money, as required by Section 9-203(b)(1), i.e., that value has been given. The standard rules of Section 9-203(b)(1)(2)(3) will apply to the whole transaction. We have already

established that you have rights in the collateral, and therefore, once the security agreement is executed and the money has been given to you, there is an enforceable security interest."

Trying to recover from his earlier damage, Vincent John Thomas III added, "but you still need more in order to have the highest protection. Also, you need to be certain that you don't list any extra collateral we haven't agreed upon. I need to be certain that my client is not over encumbered."

"You are right Vinny," replied Brenda. Several of the attorneys were making faces as Vincent made this statement.

"Would you like to explain, or should I?" asked Brenda.

"Go ahead Brenda. After all, this is your money."

"First of all, we have no interest or any intent of seeking collateral other than in the oil produced from the well. We realize this is a risky venture, no matter how the original projections look. But, we do want to be certain that we have perfected our security interest in the oil as it is produced, and we want to be equally certain that we are first in line for that oil.

"The starting point for analysis, as in all perfection situations, is the general rule contained in Section 9-310(a):

Except as otherwise provided in subsection (b) and Section 9-312(b), a financing statement must be filed to perfect all security interests and agricultural liens.

Most financing statements will either be filed with the Secretary of State, or with a privatized agency, like the Florida Secured Transactions Registry, as it is in Florida. This is the basic rule of Section 9-501(a)(2).

However, when the collateral is 'as extracted collateral' such as the oil, the place for filing becomes the office where a mortgage would be recorded or flied:

> ...[T]he office in which to file a financing statement to perfect the security interest or agricultural lien is:
>   1) the office designated for the filing or recording or a record of mortgage on the related real property, if:
>   (A) the collateral is as-extracted collateral or timber to be cut.

Furthermore, the law governing the transaction will be Texas law:

> The local law of the jurisdiction in which the wellhead or minehead is located governs perfection, the effect of perfection or non perfection, and the priority of a security interest in as-extracted collateral. Section 9-301(4).

"Regarding priority, the general priority rules of Section 9-322(a)(1)(2)(3) apply to 'as-extracted collateral'. So as long as there are no other financing statements on file when we file ours, we are good to go."

"Do you have any questions Duke?"

"Yes. I want to move as quickly as possible. Like NOW. What do I need to do to move this along?"

Once again, Vincent interrupted "We can sign a financing statement and overnight it to you. You will have it by tomorrow", he said with supreme confidence.

"Actually, Vinny, there is no need for a debtor to sign the financing statement. The amended version of Article 9 eliminated that requirement, but of course, there is a requirement to authenticate the security agreement" responded Brenda.

Vincent John Thomas III needed a drink, badly.

Duke just looked at him, then said "Brenda, I want the money wired to me as soon as possible. I have given Stephen a power of attorney. He can sign the security agreement on my behalf."

Dimit stepped in "Sounds great Duke. We'll have the documents drawn up and have emailed to you within the hour. If everything is in order, we will have the funds wired first thing in the morning. And Duke...?"

"Yes."

"May the power of the drill be with you!"

Section 22

After the initial shock of everything, life sort of returned to normal. For a couple of months, Alan went back to being a lawyer and Stephen went back to the boat business. The pain was about to begin, though, as interrogatories were about to be dropped on Stephen and Alan. In addition, both received notices that their depositions were going to be taken.

When Stephen got the interrogatories he started to feel physically ill. He had, it seemed, been answering these things from the day he started in the business. And why, for God's sake, he thought himself, did they want to know every address he had lived at since he was 19 years old!

As time wore on, Stephen was becoming more and more miserable. Rumor had it that he had become an extremely heavy drinker and had been seen with women *other* than his wife — and openly! He was missing work, as well, because he had developed stomach troubles over all of the lawsuits in which he was involved.

During one of his drinking sessions he realized that something had to be done. He didn't want to go on. He just didn't know what to do. Then it dawned on him. Maybe, he thought, he didn't have to go on with it. He could leave everything. Perhaps, he thought, he could be happy again. That was it. He decided he would quit all the businesses and go back to the beach to be with his old friends and get his head back together. That afternoon he went to see Alan who, of course, tried to talk him out of it. Stephen, however, had listened enough. He was through.

With that, Stephen left the office, went home as fast as his XGT could take him, changed into his swim suit and went to the beach.

THREE MONTHS LATER

It was different now. None of the old crew was there and Stephen felt uncomfortable. Fortunately for Stephen, however, after a few weeks at the beach he was able to find a new group of friends who felt just like the old crew. In fact, it was a source of amazement to him that in each member of his new group he could see something almost identical to those departed. From this, Stephen learned something about life.

Alan saw to it that things worked out well for him. Doug had done all the research for free in the hopes Alan would get him a good raise. Unfortunately for Doug, as Alan told it—at the partnership meeting, he (Alan) led the drive to get the associates more money and give the partners less; but, alas, he was voted down. He told Doug he knew how Doug felt, for when Alan was an associate he felt cheated too. He and the then associates swore that when they became partners, things would be different. He told Doug to wait because everybody at the firm always got what he or she deserved.

The lawsuit with Royal had proved a major victory to Alan (now the sole owner of Stephen's Boats, Inc.)[170] He suffered no damages, and, as indicated, didn't even have to pay for any legal fees. In addition, he had worked out a settlement with the bank on the Onus Primo heist and the creditors dropped the lawsuit on Alan's agreement to pay them back over an extended period. He was back in business now and *knew* he'd never make the same mistake again.

The only immediate winner in the whole mess was Stephen's father. He had watched his son suffer tremendously, knowing all the time that he was

---

[170] Footnote 169 is in Appendix I on page 403.

powerless to help. He knew that Stephen had gotten caught up in something that he didn't want in the first place, which had then taken him over. It was as though Stephen had fallen into a fast moving river with no beginning and no end. He hoped that Stephen would be able to work things out.

He had also seen a big change in Alan over the last few years. He remembered him when he was still in college and how Alan had wanted to become a lawyer. What a nice kid Alan was, he thought to himself. He shook his head in disbelief when he reflected on what Alan had become.

He was determined to somehow incorporate all of this into his life. So, about a month after Stephen returned to the beach, his father hired a junior partner in the liquor business whom he had known and trusted for a long time. Stephen Seller II gave Ralph (the junior partner) a good salary -- fair by both persons' standards in exchange for Ralph being solely responsible for the store in Mr. Seller's absence, as well as helping him run the store.

Mr. Seller was able to spend more time with his family and became involved in a group which met twice a month. The group was primarily composed of young people just starting out in business as well as business students from the university. He was able to offer them some practical insights about business and share some of his own thoughts with them.

In addition, he was able to travel and enjoy himself much more. He quickly confirmed his suspicions that he didn't need as much money as he thought. Sure, he had to watch his spending a little bit, but being able to travel and be with his family made him a much happier person, and the group — maybe, he thought, just maybe one or two of those kids will make it without making the major mistake. He knew he was going to try to help, and from his efforts he quickly understood how much satisfaction one can derive from really trying to help somebody. When he balanced all of this against the money he was paying Ralph...he only wished he'd found out sooner.

THREE YEARS LATER

After several months of deep reflection and soul searching during his time on the beach, Stephen came to the realization that he needed more purpose in his life. He understood the reality that he needed to pay his way, but was not prepared to accept a life in which the relentless pursuit of money took priority over the values that gave his life meaning. During his time in the boat business Stephen had seen so much misery among those whose life was totally focused on work and money that he was determined to maintain a more balanced perspective.

As he approached the South Florida Children's Academy, Stephen found himself immediately surrounded by five excited young children of the twenty with whom he worked. It was like that every day when he arrived, and Stephen was happier than he had ever been. Prior to going to work at the Academy, Stephen had no idea that there were children in such desperate need, and his commitment to put these children on a pathway to a meaningful, productive, and happy life was total and complete.

Alan's life went in a different direction. After enjoying success in the boat business, and a thriving law practice, Alan was convinced that he was on his way to great wealth. He doubled the space of Alan's Boats [he changed the name once Stephen was gone], and purchased a sizable inventory of large boats. Unfortunately for Alan, he did not factor in the collapse of the economy, and the growing number of clientele who could no longer afford to purchase his boats or make their payments. Alan filed for Chapter 7 bankruptcy on May 27, 2010, listing assets of $3,764,894.00 and liabilities of $12,563,936.

Doug and Stephen became close friends. In fact, for the past two years, Doug was a weekly visitor at the Academy and mentored those who wanted to learn about life and how to realize their goals for a better life. Doug was extremely impressed with what the children had survived, and how well he and Stephen could connect with them. He saw tremendous potential and felt a strong desire to do more.

After spending several weeks trying to figure out how to become more involved with the children and have a greater impact, it occurred to Doug that if he could enlist the support of the law firm, life could get better for everyone at the South Florida Children's Academy.

Doug scheduled a meeting with Dimit Wellscone, the managing partner, after deciding to just go the top, rather than try to systematically garner support among the members of the firm. If Dimit would support this type of involvement, everyone would be immediately on board. Doug anticipated much resistance when he walked into Dimit's office on June 11, 2010.

Much to his utter amazement, Dimit was very excited about the idea. In fact, he shared with Doug that he had spent several years in foster care and knew how tough it was for the kids. Dimit assured Doug that he would have his full support in helping with funding and mentoring.

And so began a wonderful relationship between Hompkins, Wellscone, Dricus & Smith and the South Florida Children's Academy. Three years later there were five new facilities and a college scholarship fund which was sending the fund's first recipient to Emory University in the fall of 2011. Members of the firm were put in touch with a life altering experience, and were uplifted and proud to be part of something so positive and productive.

Word of the Hompkins Welscone's involvement spread throughout the community, and ultimately caught the attention of a well known documentary film maker who did a short film on the firm's involvement with the Children's Academy. The film, entitled *'Everyone Can Make a Difference',* was posted on YouTube and was quickly viewed by millions of people in America and throughout the world. The film inspired law firms across the United States to follow the lead of Homkins Welscone, literally changing the lives of hundreds of thousands of children and attorneys in the process.

Appendix I

FOOTNOTE: 38

Section 9-403 deals specifically with this type of agreement made by purchasers of goods whose chattel paper is assigned;

(b). Except as otherwise provided in this section, an agreement between an account debtor [Stephen's purchaser] and an assignor [Stephen] not to assert defenses against an assignee [South Dade Bank] any claim or defense that the account debtor may have against the assignor is enforceable by an assignee that takes the assignment:

1) for value;

2) in good faith;

3) without notice of claim of a property or possessory right to property assigned;

4) without notice of a defense or claim in recoupment of the type that may be asserted against the person entitled to enforce a negotiable instrument under Section 3-305(a).

Thus, someone purchasing a boat from Stephen on the facts as hypothesized, who signed a conditional sales contract which contained an agreement not to assert claims or defenses against an assignee of the paper, would not be able thereafter to assert defenses against South Dade Bank to whom the chattel paper was assigned or sold.

There are several very important code sections which bear directly on the assignment of chattel paper under the circumstances described above.

First, Section 9-403(d) references the Federal Trade Commission rule which requires that in the case of consumer transactions, i.e., goods used for 'personal, family or household purposes' *'the record include a statement to the effect that the rights of an assignee are subject to claims or defenses that the account debtor could assert against the original obligee.'* In such a consumer transaction, therefore, the account debtor cannot be forced to waive the right to assert any such defenses.

In the event the contract under consideration does not have the language required by the Federal Trade Commission which is referred to in Section 9-403, Section 9-403(d)(1) states that *'the record has the same effect as if the record included such a statement'.* Consistent with this rule, subsection 9-403(d)(2) states that: *the account debtor may assert against an assignee those claims and defenses that would have been available if the record included such a statement.* Thus, to the extent the purchaser of the boat is purchasing the boat as consumer goods [for personal, family or household purposes], the assignee [South Dade Bank] takes the chattel paper subject to the claims or defenses that could have been asserted against Stephen's Boats [the assignor].

Second, it is important to note the circumstances under which South Dade, as assignee, would have to take the chattel paper to be protected from these defenses. First of all, the chattel paper must be taken for value. [In this section *value* has the meaning provided in Section 3-303(a). Section 9-403(a). Section 3-303 is reproduced in the statutory supplement.] Second, the paper must be taken in **good faith** and hence there must be honesty in fact and the observance of reasonable commercial standards of fair dealing in the transaction [Section 9-102(a)(43)] Where amended Article 1 has been enacted, Section 9-102(a)(43) has been deleted since the new Article 1 definition of good faith is the same, and would apply throughout the Code] third, South Dade must take the assignment of the paper without notice of conflicting claims to the property assigned; and finally, it must be taken without notice of the type of claim referred to in Section 9-403(b)(4). [That type of claim referred to will be discussed later in this book.]

Notice is a very important term under the Uniform Commercial Code, for what is says as well as the frequency with which the term is used throughout the text. Section 1-202(a)(1)(2)(3) reads as follows:

> *Subject to subsection (f), a person has "**notice**" of a fact if the person:*
> 1) *has actual knowledge of it;*
> 2) *has received a notice or notification of it; or*
> 3) *from all the facts and circumstances known to the person at the time in question, has reason to know it exists.*

Leaving aside the consumer transaction in which the defenses can be asserted, many of the purchases would be classified as 'equipment' and thus a business expense. In that situation, the defenses against the assignee would be cut off if the contract so specified. At first, the reason behind this rule of Section 9-403 might not be apparent. You might be asking yourself why is it fair to allow for someone to be deprived of recourse against someone like South Dade Bank. In connection with making such an agreement not to assert these defenses, it is obvious that the purchaser has no bargaining power, and therefore must either sign the agreement as presented, or not purchase the boat.

There are a couple of answers to the question. First of all, South Dade Bank is financing the business in part by purchasing the chattel paper. If South Dade Bank were to be subject to claims for breach of warranty and defective goods, the cost of such financing would rise. The cost would be passed along to the purchasers and the purchasers would thereafter be bearing the burden of the claims which would be asserted against an assignee like South Dade Bank.

Second, it must be remembered that the buyer of the goods will still have a cause of action against the seller of the goods for any problems with respect to the goods under Article 2. Thus, the buyer still has recourse if the goods prove to be defective. It should be noted that if a buyer of goods does not enter an agreement not to assert defenses against the assignee, the rights against the assignee would be the same as those against the assignor. Section 9-404(a) states as follows:

Unless an account debtor has made an enforceable agreement not to assert defenses or claims...the rights of an assignee are subject to:
(1) all terms of the agreement between an account debtor and assignor and any defenses or claims in recoupment arising from the transaction that gave rise to the contract;
(2) any other defense or claim of the account debtor against the assignor which accrues before the account debtor receives a notification of the assignment authenticated by the assignor or assignee.

FOOTNOTE 45. (continued)

Section 9-309 states when a security interest is perfected upon attachment, and therefore, for which a filing is not required. Of particular relevance here is Section 9-309(1) which states:

The following security interests are perfected when they attach [i.e. become enforceable]:

(1) a purchase money security interest in consumer goods, except as otherwise provided in Section 9 311(b) with respect to consumer goods that are subject to statute or treaty described in Section 9-311(a).

As noted previously, the conditional sales contacts generated by Stephen's Boats, would result in purchase-money security interests. Many typical purchase money security interests in consumer goods would be within 9-309 (1) and automatically perfected. Examples would include such things as televisions, appliances and the like. However, purchases from Stephens boats would not be automatically perfected by reason of the *'except as otherwise provided'* references in subsection (1) of 9-309, which are noted in 9-311(a)(b).

Section 9-311(a)(2) states:

Except as otherwise provided in subsection (d), the filing of a financing statement is not necessary or effective to perfect a security interest in property subject to:

...
(2) [list any certificate of title statute covering automobiles, trailers, mobile homes, boats,

farm tractors, or the like, which provides for a security interest to be indicated on the certificate as a condition or result of perfection...]

Accordingly, no financing statement is required [*or effective*] to perfect Stephen's security interest in boats which he sells; however, upon compliance with the Certificate of Title requirements, Stephen would be fully protected:

Compliance with the requirements of a statute, regulation, or treaty described in subsection (a) for obtaining priority over the rights of a lien creditor is equivalent to the filing of a financing statement under this article.... Section 9-311(b).

Certificate of Title regulations in Florida, require the security interest to be noted on the title. Section 9-102(a)(10) which defines Certificate of Title incorporates this requirement in the definition:

"Certificate of Title" means a certificate of title with respect to which a statute provides for the security interest in question to be indicated on the certificate as a condition or result of the security interest's obtaining priority over the rights of a lien creditor with respect to the collateral.

Therefore, for Stephen to have a perfected security interest in the boat, such interest must be noted on the certificate of title. Once this is done, and the chattel paper is assigned to South Dade, it will have the same perfected status in the boat that Stephen had prior to the assignment (Section 9-310(c)). In this connection, it should perhaps be pointed out that in certain situations (generally when the value of the vessel is considered substantial enough by the lender to warrant it, or perhaps the lender prefers to proceed under federal rather than state jurisdiction), the vessel will be documented (i.e., registered) under the laws of the United States and subject to the Ship Mortgage Act 46 USC SS911 Et. Seq., rather than the Uniform Commercial Code.

The other situations in which a security interest is perfected upon attachment are generally outside the mainstream of secured transactions, or involve a security interest arising outside of Article 9. They are contained in Sections 9-309(2) through 9-309(14). The reader should probably wait to review these exceptions until completion of this book, and a basic understanding is achieved.

One very important point should be noted before leaving this section; namely, during the time the boats are held as inventory for sale, South Dade would perfect its interest in inventory by filing the financing statement. This is governed by Section 9-311(d) which states:

> *During any period in which collateral is subject to a statute specified in subsection (a)(2) is inventory held for sale or lease by a person or leased by that person as lessor and that person is in the business of selling goods of that kind, this section does not apply to a security interest in that collateral created by that person.*

During this time frame, the general rule of Section 9-501(a)(2) would apply. Hence the filing would be with the Florida Secured Transactions Registry.

FOOTNOTE 52:

As noted, section 9-104(a)(2)(3) sets forth two other situations in which a secured party has control. Under 9-104(a)(2):

A secured party has control of a deposit account if:

the debtor, secured party, and the bank have agreed in an authenticated record that the bank will comply with instructions originated by the secured party directing disposition of the funds in the deposit account without further consent by the debtor. Section 9-104(a)(2).

Assume that Stephen's Boats maintains an account exactly like the one discussed between Alan and Stephen. Stephen subsequently borrows money from Joe Lender. Stephen, Joe and South Dade have executed a security agreement, signed by all parties that the bank will have the disposition rights stated in Section 9-104(a)(2). The security agreement is a **'record'** under Section 9-102(a)(69) since it is *"information that is inscribed on a tangible medium or which is stored in an electronic or other medium and is retrievable in perceivable form, which has been authenticated because it has been signed by the parties."* [Section 9-102(a)(7)(A)].Therefore, control would be established under Section 9-104(a)(2).

The other example, as noted, is found in Section 9-104(a)(3):

A secured party has control of a deposit account if: *the secured party becomes the bank's customer with respect to the deposit account.* Section 9-104(a)(3).

Assume the same facts as noted above. If Joe Lender became 'the bank's customer' with respect to the deposit account' control would be established under Section 9-104(a)(3).

As noted in Section 9-104(b), the fact that Stephen has the right to direct the disposition of the funds in the account, does not affect the control of the secured party established under Section 9-104(a)(1)(2)(3).

In addition to the unique method of perfection required in a deposit account situation, there are equally unique priority rules for this collateral. Section 9-327 contains specific provisions for priority with respect to deposit accounts. That section is states as follows:

The following rules govern priority among conflicting security interests in the same deposit account:

> *(1) A security interest held by a secured party having control of the deposit account under Section 9-104 has priority over a conflicting security interest held by a secured party that does not have control;*
>
> *(2) Except as otherwise provided in paragraphs (3) and (4), security interests perfected by control under Section 9-314 rank according to priority in time of obtaining control;*
>
> *(3) Except as otherwise provided in paragraph (4), a security interest held by the bank with which the deposit account is maintained has priority over a conflicting security interest held by another secured party;*
>
> *(4) A security interest perfected by control under Section 9-104(a)(3) has priority*

> *over a security interest held by a bank*
> *with which the deposit account is*
> *maintained.*

Section 9-327(1) speaks of a security interest in which one secured party has control, and another secured party 'that does not have control'. Of course, without control, there could be no perfected security interest in the account as direct collateral. However, if the second secured party had a perfected security interest in underlying collateral, it would also have a perfected security interest in proceeds received from the original collateral per Section 9-315(c). If those proceeds were deposited in the deposit account, there would be competing perfected security interests in certain monies in the deposit account. Subsection (1) gives priority to the secured party with control of the deposit account, even if the security interest in the collateral which gave rise to the perfected security interest was perfected prior to the bank's.

Comment 4 to Section 9-327 explains this result as follows:

> A rule of this kind enables banks to extend
> credit to their depositors without the need to
> examine either the public record or their own
> records to determine whether another party
> might have a security interest in the deposit
> account.

If however, the other secured party perfects the interest in the deposit account by taking control of that account under Section 9-104(a)(3), i.e., *if the secured party becomes the bank's customer with respect to the deposit account* the other secured party will take priority over the bank's interest per Section 9-327(4).

FOOTNOTE 82

Section 9-320(a) states in relevant part as follows:

> ...[A] buyer in the ordinary course of business [Section 1-201(b)(9)]...takes free of a security interest created by the buyer's seller, even though the security interest is perfected and the buyer knows of its existence.

In the instant situation, Stephen would be a buyer in the ordinary course of business [from 'his seller' i.e. the car dealership]. Buyer in the ordinary course of business is defined under Section 1-201(a)(9) which states in relevant part:

> **"Buyer in the ordinary course of business"** means a person who in good faith and without knowledge that the sale to him is in violation of the ownership rights or security interest of a third party in the goods buys in the ordinary course from a person in the business of selling goods of that kind....

Stephen would be purchasing the car in good faith which is defined under Section 9-102(a)(43) [or 1-201(b)(20)] as honesty in fact and the observance of reasonable commercial standards of fair dealing'. On the facts presented, Stephen was clearly acting in "good faith." Furthermore, Stephen had no knowledge that the sale to him was violation of the ownership rights or security interest of whomever was financing the dealership's inventory, and of course, the sale to him was precisely the type of transaction contemplated by whomever was financing the car dealership in exactly the same manner as South Dade contemplates boat sales by Stephen. Finally, the purchase would be in the ordinary course from a person whose business was selling the goods involved, i.e., the cars.

At first, the policy of Section 9-320(a) might not be apparent. It might seem "wrong" to allow the secured party's interest to be cut off when the purchaser has knowledge of its existence. Several comments should be made in this connection. First, it must be remembered that the secured party contemplates precisely the type of sale under which Stephen, or the boat purchasers, buy the goods. In fact, the secured party wants these sales since it wants a viable business which can repay monies advanced, as well as creating a stream of chattel paper which the lender probably seeks to purchase. Second the secured party would still have a proceeds interest after the sale. The third most important point to most of us comes from the perspective of the consumer purchasing goods subject to a security interest.

If goods purchased in the ordinary course were subject to claims of secured parties, people would be extremely hesitant to purchase goods, for the obvious reason that they would not know if a secured party would come along and take the goods involved.

It is important to distinguish between **knowledge of** a perfected security interest under Section 9-320(a), which does not preclude one from being a buyer in the ordinary course of business, and the **knowledge that the purchase of goods involved was *in violation*** of the security interest of which one has knowledge. Thus, if Stephen were to purchase 10 cars from the dealership and knew, for example, of a provision in the contract between the dealership and its inventory financer that precluded such large purchases without prior written consent of the financer, Stephen would have taken with knowledge that the sale to him was in violation of the security interest of the third party and hence would not be a buyer in the ordinary course of business. By purchasing one car, however, he would not be in violation of the hypothesized agreement.

Another section which should be noted at this time is Section 9-320(b), for it, too, contemplates a situation in which goods subject to a security interest are purchased, although not in the ordinary course contemplated above. Section 9-320(b) states as follows:

> *Except as otherwise provided in subsection (e), a buyer of goods from a person who used or bought the goods for use primarily for personal, family or household purposes takes free of a security interest even if perfected, if the buyer buys:*
>> *(1) without knowledge of the security interest;*
>> *(2) for value;*
>> *(3) primarily for the buyer's personal family, or household purposes; and*
>> *(4) before the filing of a financing statement covering the goods.*

In this situation, purchaser is not buying from one engaged in the business of selling the subject goods; rather, he is buying from a person who is a debtor with respect to an item not being sold from inventory, and probably not in a business setting. An example would be as follows:

- Buyer #1 purchases a plasma TV from Department Store for his home;
- Buyer #1 signs a conditional sales contract for the TV;
- Buyer #1 sells the TV to his neighbor, Buyer #2

The first thing to note is that the purchase by Buyer #1 is a purchase money security interest [*see* footnote 17]. As such, the security interest becomes perfected when it attaches:

The following security interests are perfected when they attach: a purchase money security interest in consumer goods... Section 9-309(1).

Therefore, Department Store would have an automatically perfected security interest in the TV. At this point, it would need to decide whether to take a further step and file a financing statement. If Department Store chooses not to file, however, and Buyer #1 sells the TV to Buyer #2 who *buys without knowledge of the security interest, for value, and primarily for ...[Buyer #2's] personal, family or household purposes* Buyer #2 *takes free of a security interest even though perfected* per section 9-320(b). As noted in subsection (b)(4) to section 9-320, the buyer would not take free of the security interest if a financing statement had been filed prior to the sale to Buyer #2.

The decision to file or not to file in this situation is clearly a business/economic one. It costs money to file financing statements and most approved consumers will not sell their financed goods. For smaller items, the increased costs would severely cut profits. However, in the case of an item as expensive as a plasma TV, particularly one of the more expensive ones, it makes good sense to file the financing statement, as the cost is minimal in comparison to the item being sold.

FOOTNOTE 83 (Continued)

Express Warranties

Under Section 2-313(1) a seller may create an express warranty in several ways. That section states in full as follows:

> (1) '***Express warranties***' by the seller are created as follows:
>
> (a) Any affirmation of fact or promise made by the seller to the buyer which relates to the goods and becomes part of the basis of the bargain creates an express warranty that the goods shall conform to the affirmation or promise.
> (b) Any description of the goods which is made part of the basis of the bargain creates an express warranty that the goods shall conform to the description.
> (c) Any sample or model which is made part of the basis of the bargain creates an express warranty that the whole of the goods shall conform to the sample or model.

Thus, a seller will create an express warranty by an affirmation of fact or promise (which relates to the goods), description of the goods, or by sample or model if, in each instance, the affirmation or promise, description, etc., becomes part of the "basis of the bargain." Basis of the bargain is not a defined term under the Code, but official comment 4 to Section 2-313 and the change made by the Code in this regard from prior law gives guidance as to what the drafters intended.

[T]he whole purpose of the law of warranty is to determine what it is that the seller has in essence agreed to sell...

From this perspective and the basis of the bargain test it is clear that Stephen would not have had to read the express warranty attending the sale of the XGT and affirmatively rely thereon in order to sue for breach of the express warranty. By making the warranty, the seller has agreed to furnish goods of particular quality and this will be reflected in the price. Accordingly, the warranty should be treated as part of the basis of the bargain.

It is important to note that the seller need not have an intention to create such a warranty in order for one to arise, nor need to use "words such as 'warrant' or 'guarantee'" Section 2-313(2); however, *an affirmation of the value of the goods or a statement purporting to be merely the seller's opinion or commendation of the goods does not create a warranty* Section 2-313(2), (e.g., when the seller says, "This is one great car!")

Implied Warranty of Fitness for a Particular Purpose

This warranty is contained in Section 2-315 which states in full:

Where the seller at the time of contracting has reason to know any particular purpose for which the goods are required and that the buyer is relying on the seller's skill or judgment to select or furnish suitable goods there is unless excluded or modified under the next section an implied warranty that the goods shall be fit for such purpose.

In the case under consideration this type of warranty would probably not have arisen. Stephen wanted to use the car for ordinary purposes, not a particular purpose within Section2-315. An example of the latter in a car purchase situation might be when the buyer sought to use the car for rugged back road or mountain travel, and an ordinary car (as opposed, for example, to a four-wheel-drive heavy-duty jeep) wouldn't suffice. In this regard comment 2 to section 2-315 states:

> A "particular purpose" differs from the ordinary purpose for which the goods are used in that it envisages a specific use by the buyer which is peculiar to the nature of his business whereas the ordinary purpose for which goods are used are those envisaged in the concept of merchantability and go to uses which are customarily made of the goods in question. For example, shoes are generally used for the purpose of walking upon ordinary ground, but a seller may know that a particular pair was selected be used for climbing mountains.

It should be pointed out that a buyer claiming an implied warranty of fitness for a particular purpose would have to *rely on* the seller within the language of Section 2-315 and, or course, the seller would need "reason to know" as set forth in that section.

Under Section 2-315, as with Section 2-313, there is no requirement that the seller be a merchant [as is the case under Section 2-314].   Unlike Section 2-313 requiring the basis of the bargain test, the buyer, under the fitness warranty, must show the required reliance. Under the merchantability warranty, *neither* basis of the bargain nor reliance must be shown. The reason for these differences is easily accounted for by the circumstances surrounding the various sales transactions being undertaken. In the merchantability situation, for example, you have a merchant making the sale. When a consumer buys from someone in the business of selling particular goods, the consumer properly expects to have a threshold quality of product. Hence, there is no need for either reliance by the buyer or of the basis of the bargain test.

In the express warranty situation, the seller has engaged in conduct which he should be called upon to back up; hence, he need not be a merchant. Finally, in the particular purpose warranty the seller's reason to know and the buyer's reliance furnish suitable circumstances for the special warranty. The different natures of these warranties is also reflected in the provisions of the Code which deal with the exclusion or modification of these warranties.

Exclusion or Modification of Implied Warranties

Section 2-316(2) sets forth the basic rules for excluding or modifying the warranty of merchantability and fitness for a particular purpose.

> *(2) Subject to subsection (3), to exclude or modify the implied warranty of merchantability or any part of it the language must mention merchantability and in case of a writing must be conspicuous, and to exclude or modify any implied warranty of fitness the exclusion must be by a writing and conspicuous. Language to exclude all implied warranties of fitness is sufficient if it states for example, that "There are no warranties which extend beyond the description on the face hereof."*

Thus, in the merchant sale situation in which the warranty of merchantability arises automatically, any disclaimer language must mention merchantability and if a writing in involved, the disclaimer language must be conspicuous:

Conspicuous *with reference to a term, means so written, displayed, or presented that a reasonable person against which it is to operate ought to have noticed it. Whether or not a term is "conspicuous" or not is a decision for the court. Conspicuous terms include the following:*

(A) a heading in capitals equal to or greater in size that the surrounding text, or in contrasting type, font, or color to the surrounding text of the same or lesser size; and

(B) language in the body of a record or display in larger type than the surrounding text, or in contrasting type, font, or color of the same size, or set off from the surrounding text of the same size by symbols or other marks that call attention to the language.
Section 1-201(b)(10)(A)(B).

This requirement of conspicuousness also applies for exclusions or modifications of the fitness warranty; however, there is no need to mention the fitness warranty when disclaiming it.

There are three ways in which the warranty of merchantability and fitness for a particular purpose warranty may be disclaimed without complying with the requirements noted above. Section 2-316(3)(a)(b)(c) which deals with those disclaimers states in full as follows:

Notwithstanding subsection (2)

> *(a) unless the circumstances indicate otherwise, all implied warranties are excluded by expressions like "as is", "with all faults" or other language which in common understanding calls for the buyer's attention to the exclusion of warranties and makes plain that there is no implied warranty; and*
>
> *(b) when the buyer before entering into the contract has examined the goods or the sample or model as fully as he desired or has refused to examine the goods there is no implied warranty with regard to defects which an examination ought in the circumstances to have revealed to him; and*
>
> *(c) an implied warranty can also be excluded or modified by course of dealing or course of performance or usage of trade.*

As regards the disclaimer by trade usage, course of dealing or course of performance, the reader might wish to refer to the warranty discussion contained in Doug's memo to Alan on the Royal Boats contract.

Limitation of Express Warranties

The limitation of express warranties is covered by Section 2-316(1) which states as follows:

Words or conduct relevant to the creation of an express warranty and words or conduct tending to negate or limit warranty shall be construed wherever reasonable as consistent with each other; but subject to the provisions of this Article on parol or extrinsic evidence (Section 2-202) negation or limitation is inoperative to the extent that such construction is unreasonable.

In connection with the Section 2-316(1), reference to Comment 4 of Section 2-313 is useful:

In view of the principle that the whole purpose of the law of warranty is to determine what it is that the seller has in essence agreed to sell, the policy is adopted of those cases which refuse to except in unusual circumstances to recognize a material deletion of the seller's obligation. Thus a contract is normally a contract for a sale of something describable and described. A clause generally disclaiming "all warranties, express or implied" cannot reduce the seller's obligation with respect to such description and therefore cannot be given literal effect under Section 2-316.

This is not intended to mean that the parties, if they consciously desire, cannot make their own bargain as they wish. But in determining what they have agreed upon good faith is a factor and consideration should be given to the fact that the probability is small that a real price is intended to be exchanged for a pseudo-obligation.

Cumulation and Conflict of Warranties

Before leaving the area of warranties the reader should be alerted to two other provisions of the Code which deal with warranties. Section 2-317 deals with Cumulation and Conflict of Warranties. It sets forth the basic rule that *[w]arranties whether express or implied shall be construed as consistent with each other and as cumulative...* If, however, *such construction is unreasonable the intention of the parties shall determine which warranty is dominant.* This Section then goes on to state rules for determining that intention:

(a) *Exact or technical specifications displace an inconsistent sample or model or general language of description.*
(b) *A sample from an existing bulk displaces inconsistent general language of description.*
(c) *Express warranties displace inconsistent implied warranties other than an implied warranty of fitness for a particular purpose.*

Third Party Beneficiaries

The final section to be noted in connection with warranties is Section 2-318, Third Party Beneficiaries of Warranties Express or Implied. As the caption to the section indicates, it discusses which parties other than the buyer are protected by a seller's warranty. Section 2-318 gives the states three alternatives to choose from.

The three Alternatives are as follows:

1) Alternative A

A seller's warranty whether express or implied extends to any natural person who is in the family or household, of his buyer or who is a guest in his home if it is reasonable to expect that such person may use, consume or be affected by the goods and who is injured in person by breach of the warranty. A seller may not exclude or limit the operation of this section.

2) Alternative B
A seller's warranty whether express or implied extends to any natural person who may reasonably be expected to use, consume or be affected by the goods and who is injured in person by breach of the warranty. A seller may not exclude or limit the operation of this section.

3) Alternative C
A seller's warranty whether express or implied extends to any person who may reasonably be expected to use, consume or be affected by the goods and who is injured by breach of the warranty. A seller may not exclude or limit the operation of this section with respect to injury to the person or an individual to whom the warranty extends.

It is clear from reading the above that depending on which jurisdiction one is in, and the Alternative enacted, the law can vary drastically. In this connection, one drafting documents should check this out *prior* to drafting, and, of course, execution; and in the context of maximizing his client's interest and in good faith, he might wish to avail himself of the right to choose the applicable law set forth in Section 1-301. (Section 1-301 is discussed later in the Appendix).

FOOTNOTE 116

Section 3-302(a)(1)(2) states that '...a *holder in due course* means the holder of an instrument if:

> *(1) the instrument when issued or negotiated to the holder does not bear such apparent evidence of forgery or alteration or is not otherwise so irregular or incomplete as to call into question its authenticity; and*
> *(2) the holder took the instrument*
>> *(i) for value,*
>> *(ii) in good faith,*
>> *(iii) without notice that the instrument is overdue or has been dishonored or that there is an uncured default with respect to payment of another instrument issued as part of the same series, (v) without notice of any claim to the instrument described in Section 3-306, and (iv) without notice that the instrument contains an authorized signature or has been altered, and (vi) without notice that any party has a defense or claim in recoupment in Section 3-305(a).*

The essence of Section 3-302 [discussed below] is that when a instrument [which is defined as a *negotiable instrument* under Section 3-104(b)], is purchased under a certain set of commercial circumstances, the purchaser of the note will be given the legal status of a 'holder in due course' with various attendant rights. As Alan will explain to Stephen in the subsequent discussion, if the writing is not negotiable, there can be no holder in due course.

The circumstances of the protected purchase basically amount to a good faith 'normal' commercial transaction which is of a type which should be protected. Since the transaction contemplated is one undertaken in **good faith**, there will be *'honesty in fact and the observance of reasonable commercial standards'* Section 3-103(a)(6). In either event, the first part of the standard for the protected transaction is an honesty, part two requires a commercially reasonable transaction.

Specific examples of commercial reasonableness are stated in Section 3-302. Subsection 3-302(a)(1), states for example, that the instrument involved has to appear, on its face, to be proper—i.e., 'no evidence of forgery or alteration…'. Secondly, the holder must give value for the note, and finally, that there is no notice of certain problems with respect to the instrument involved such as are listed in Section 3-302(a)(2)(iii)(iv)(v)(vi). **Notice** is defined under Section 1-202(a) as follows:

> *…[A] person has notice of a fact if the person:*
>   *(1) has actual knowledge of it;*
>   *(2) has received notice or notification of it;*
>   *(3) from all the facts and circumstances known to the person at the time in question, has reason to know that it exists.*

The value requirement is expanded upon in Section 3-303(a)(1)(2)(3)(4)(5). Section 3-303(a)(1) would govern in the case being discussed between Alan and Stephen:

> *(a) An instrument is issued or transferred for **value** if:*
>   *(1) the instrument is issued or transferred for a promise of performance, to the extent the promise has been performed*

In the hypothetical which Alan was discussing with Stephen, George would have transferred the note for the bank's promise to pay George $680,000. Once George has been paid, that 'promise has been performed', and hence, value would have been given. As stated, the next requirement for holder in due course status, is that the holder take the instrument in "good faith."

The honest purchase of the note within ordinary banking transactions would satisfy Section 3-103(a)(4). Assuming that the instrument was not overdue [Section 3-304] reproduced in the statutory supplement or within any of the other matters delineated, the bank would become a holder in due course of the instrument.

The *rights of a holder in due course* are found within the text of Section 3-305(b).

*The right of a holder in due course to enforce the obligation of a party to pay the instrument is subject to defenses of the obligor stated in (a)(1) [real defenses, such as infancy or duress], **but is not** subject to defenses of the obligor stated in subsection (a)(2) [certain Article 3 defenses and simple contract defenses] or claims in recoupment stated in subsection (a)(3) against a person other than the holder.* [Emphasis added]

The essence of these rights is that the holder in due course will take the instrument free and clear of personal defenses which may exist between the original obligor and the payee. That section makes exception for certain 'real defenses' such as infancy. If for example, an instrument were signed by an eight year old, and later transferred to a holder in due course, the latter could not enforce the instrument since the eight year old lacked the legal capacity to sign. On the other hand, if the original payee/obligee had failed to perform an obligation for which the instrument was issued, a subsequent holder in due course would not be subject to the defense of failure of consideration by the person obligated on the instrument. This will be discussed in greater detail in the discussion between Alan and Stephen.

In the Outlet situation, the person obligated to pay the note would be the maker of the note. The **maker** of the note *'means a person who signs or is identified in a note as a person undertaking to pay'*, Section 3-103(a)(7), in this case, Alan & Stephen [as co-maker's]. The payee is George Friedman. As Alan stated in his discussion with Stephen, if George made a mistake in assessing the value of the inventory, Alan and Stephen could assert that defense against George, but not against a subsequent holder in due course. Failure of consideration is a personal defense, which is cut off by a holder in due course.

FOOTNOTE 143 (Continued)

As noted, the basic rule of Section 5-108(a) requires an issuer to honor a presentation that appears, on its face, to strictly comply with the letter of credit. If, however, there is fraud in the transaction or the documents are forged, the bank may (it need not) refuse honor unless payment is being demanded by certain parties noted in Section 5-109(a)(1):

(a) If a presentation is made that appears on its face strictly to comply with the terms and conditions of the letter of credit, but a required document is forged or materially fraudulent, or honor of the presentation would facilitate material fraud by the beneficiary on the issuer or applicant:

*(1) the issuer **shall honor** the presentation, **if** honor is demanded by (i) a nominated person* who has given value in good faith** and without notice of forgery or material fraud, (ii) a confirmer who has honored its confirmation in good faith, (iii) a holder in due course of a draft drawn under the letter of credit which was taken after acceptance by the issuer or nominated person,(iv) an assignee of the issuer's or nominated person's deferred obligation that was taken for value and without notice of the forgery or material fraud after the obligation was incurred by the issuer or nominated person, and*

(2) the issuer acting in good faith, may honor or dishonor the presentation in any other case. Section 5-109(a)(2). [Emphasis added]

Where fraud or forgery is alleged, an applicant can petition an appropriate court for an injunction under Section 5-109(b), which will be granted if the court makes the specific findings required by Section 5-109(b)(1)(2)(3)(4).

******Nominated person*** *means a person whom the issuer (i) designates or authorizes to pay, accept, negotiate, or otherwise give value under a letter of credit and (ii) undertakes by agreement or custom and practice to reimburse.* Section 5-102(a)(11).

*** **Good faith** under Article 5 is defined as "honesty in fact in the conduct or transaction concerned."* Section 5-102(a)(7). [See footnote 58.]

FOOTNOTE 160

This case raises several sections already discussed in the book as well as some new material. Several general points can be noted at the outset. First, a postdated check is considered to be an instrument *'payable at a definite time'* within Section 3-108(b). As the facts indicate, the check was signed in a corporate capacity by Alvin Thomas as treasurer of Burger Czar, and as such, would be a signature by representative governed by Section 3-402.

Subsection (a) to Section 3-402 states the basic rule under which a represented person is bound [here, Burger Czar]:

> *If a person acting, or purporting to act, as a representative signs an instrument by signing either the name of the represented person or the name of the signer, the represented person would be bound to the same extent the represented person would be bound if the signature were on a simple contract.*

Comment 1 to Section 3-402 explains this by saying 'If under the law of agency the represented person would be bound' by the representative's signature, 'the signature is the authorized signature of the represented person.' In the present case, Thomas was acting in his corporate capacity as treasurer. He clearly was acting within the scope of his authority, and therefore, the corporation would be bound by his representative signature. As the second sentence to Section 3-402(a) states:

If the represented person is bound, the signature of the representative is the "authorized signature of the represented person" and the represented person is liable on the instrument...

It is important to note that the form in which the representative's signature is made is extremely important for a few reasons. First, if the representative signature is in the proper form, and is in fact authorized, the representative is not liable on the instrument:

If the form of the signature shows unambiguously that the signature is made on behalf of the represented person who is identified in the instrument, the representative is not liable. Section 3-402(b)(1).

The corollary to that rule is stated in Section 3-402(b)(2):

Subject to subsection (c), if (i) the form of the signature does not show unambiguously that the signature is made in a representative capacity or (ii) the represented person is not identified in the instrument, the representative is liable to a holder in due course that took the instrument without notice that the representative was not intended to be liable....

Finally, Section 3-402(c) referred to in 3-402(b)(1) states:

If a representative signs the name of the representative as drawer of the check without indication of the representative status and the check is payable from an account of the represented person who is identified on the check, the signer is not liable on the check if the signature is an authorized signature of the represented person.

When the beef patties in the present case were received by Burger Czar, it made payment by check. The check which was delivered was stolen, and the endorsement was forged. The thieves endorsed the check as Brad Garcia and were given cash. Brad's forged endorsement was:

...an unauthorized signature [and] is ineffective cxccpt as the signature of the unauthorized signer [the thief who cashed the check] in favor of a person who in good faith pays the instrument or takes it for value. Section 3-304(a).

Therefore, the thief was not a 'holder' nor a 'person entitled to enforce the instrument' [Section 3-301], and, as a result the check was not properly payable. Absent some culpable conduct by Burger Czar, it would be entitled to have its account recredited.

FOOTNOTE 161

As indicated, George took a security interest in inventory, equipment and accounts receivable. An *account* is defined under Section 9-102(a)(2) in part as:

...[R]ight to payment of a monetary obligation, whether or not earned by performance, (i) for property that has been or is to be sold, leased, licensed, assigned or otherwise disposed of....

It was unnecessary for George to specifically claim the interest in accounts inasmuch as he would automatically have a security interest in such accounts as proceeds. Analysis begins with Section 9-203(f) which states as follows:

> *The attachment of a security interest in collateral gives the secured party the rights to proceeds provided by Section 9-315 ....*

The basic rule regarding the security interest in proceeds is found in Section 9-315(a)(2):

> *Except as otherwise provided in this article and in Section 2-403(2):*
>
> *....*
>
> *(2) a security interest attaches to any identifiable proceeds of collateral.*

The accounts would be clearly identifiable as proceeds from the sale of specific inventory. Therefore, George would have a security interest in those accounts.
The next question is whether or not the security interest which George has in the accounts is perfected. That question is answered by Sections 9-315(c) initially and Section 9-315(d) subsequently. Section 9-315(c) states as follows:

> *A security interest in proceeds is a perfected security interest if the security interest in the original collateral was perfected.*

Therefore, if George perfected his security interest in inventory by appropriately filing a financing statement, his security interest in the accounts would be perfected. However, unless Section 9-315(d) is complied with, that perfected status would lapse after 21 days:

'A perfected security interest in proceeds becomes unperfected on the 21st day after the security interest attaches to the proceeds unless:

(1) the following conditions are satisfied:
(A) a filed financing statement covers the original collateral;
(B) the proceeds are collateral in which a security interest may be perfected by filing in the office in which the financing statement has been filed; and
(C) the proceeds are not acquired with cash proceeds;
(2) the proceeds are identifiable cash proceeds; or
(3) the security interest in the proceeds is perfected other than under subsection (c) when the security interest attaches to the proceeds or within 20 days thereafter.

George's security interest in the proceeds would remain perfected under subsection (1)(A)(B)(C). Subsection (A) would be satisfied since a financing statement covering the 'original collateral', [inventory], was covered by a 'filed financing statement'. The security interest in the proceeds [accounts] can be perfected in the same office as the security interest in the inventory, [subsection (B)] and are not acquired with cash proceeds [subsection (C)].

The policy reason for this result is simple: anyone checking the files who sees a security interest in inventory, and who has the requisite knowledge of this type of financing, will be aware that accounts will be produced from inventory sales and that the first lender's interest in these accounts is protected.

Moreover, the security interest in these proceeds would have the same priority as the priority with regard to inventory. The basic rule of priority for collateral is stated in Section 9-322(a)(1):

> *Except as otherwise provided in this section, priority among conflicting security interests and agricultural liens rank according to priority in time of filing or perfection. Priority dates from the earlier of the time of filing covering the collateral is first made or the security interest or agricultural line is first perfected, if there is not period when there is neither filing for perfection.*

Section 9-322(b)(1) states the rule with respect to priority for proceeds in relation to the underlying collateral:

> *[T]he time of filing or perfection as to a security interest in collateral is also the time of filing or perfection as to a security interest in proceeds.*

Thus, someone lending against accounts (resulting from the sale of inventory on open account) after George had properly perfected his interest in inventory, would take subject to George's interest in the accounts. This would be true for the first twenty-one days without further action by the secured lender, and if Section 9-315(d) is satisfied, as long as the original filing remains valid.

As noted in Jerry's letter, the bank can obtain priority with respect to purchase money security interests in equipment and inventory if it complies with the guidelines stated in the UCC for those priorities. Jerry also discussed ways in which the bank can insure that funds provided are used for the intended purchase of the equipment or inventory. While the bank can control how the funs are disbursed, it must, of course, relinquish control of the goods so that the outlet can use the equipment and sell the inventory.

If the bank requested and receives a negotiable bill of lading as part of the required documentation, it will release the bill of lading to Jerry or someone on behalf of the outlet to obtain possession of the equipment and inventory. In that event, the bank will have a perfected purchase-money security interest in the collateral which will be perfected by possession of the document. Section 9-312(c)(1).

Possession of the document by the bank will also result in perfection of the security interest in the document per Section 9-313(a). [Perfection of a document can also be obtained by filing a financing statement per Section 9-312(a).] If the bank endorses the bill of lading to the outlet for the purpose of allowing it to pick up the equipment or inventory, and the document has been perfected by possession, the interest will remain perfected for 20 days per Section 9-312(f)(2). In such a situation, however, should Stephen or Alan become dishonest and sell the bill of lading under circumstances amounting to a "due negotiation" (a concept to be discussed shortly in the book), the bank's interest would be defeated.

FOOTNOTE 162

TO: Jeremy Alconte
FROM: Lemont Burnsgrass
RERERENCE: Electronic Funds Transfers &
                     Transaction With Duke's
                     Enterprises

Jeremy:

I worked up the following per our discussion. I am assuming that Duke will be wiring $850,000 to you at Orange Grove Savings & Loan. When I spoke with Bamford Pusar, Duke's comptroller, he advised that they banked with Texas Trust.

I will basically run you through the transaction, and some of the things to watch for. If you have any questions when you are finished, give me a call.

                                      Regards,
                                      Lemont

Basic Fact Pattern [1-4]

Step #1: You and Duke agree that he will pay you $850,000 for the orange grove, and that payment will be made by wire transfer;

Step #2: You further agree that the wire transfer will be deposited to your designated account: #203837636 at Orange Grove Bank;

Step #3: You and Orange Grove Bank agree that the money is to be received at least three days prior to the formal closing on the orange grove;

Step #4: Duke's Enterprises instructs Texas Trust to initiate a wire transfer from Duke's Enterprise to your designated account at Orange Grove Bank, which is stated as follows:

Jeremy Alaconte
Account: #203837636;

Identification of Parties & Basic Terms

The instruction by Duke's Enterprises, to Texas Trust to make payment to you is a **Payment order**, *since it is an instruction of a sender [Duke's], to a receiving bank [Texas Trust] ... to pay a fixed or determinable amount of money to a beneficiary' [Jeremy]. The order can be transmitted 'orally, electronically, or in writing'. Section 4A-103(a)(1).*

The following three conditions must exist for the order to be a valid 'payment order':

    i.   *the instruction does not state a condition to payment to the beneficiary other than the time of payment;*

    ii.   *the receiving bank is to be reimbursed by debiting an account of, or otherwise receiving payment from, the sender, and*

    iii. *the instruction is transmitted by the sender directly to the receiving bank or to an agent, funds transfer system, or communication system for transmittal to the receiving bank.*
        Section 4A-103(1)(i)(ii)(iii).

1. *Duke is the* **sender** *as 'the person giving the instruction to the receiving bank;'* Section 4A-103(a)(5).

2. *Texas Trust is the* **receiving bank** *as 'the bank to which the sender's instruction is addressed;'* Section 4A-103(a)(4).

3. *Jeremy is the* **beneficiary** *as 'the person to be paid by the beneficiary's bank;'* Section 4A-103(a)(2).

4. *Orange Grove Bank is the* **beneficiary's bank** *as 'the bank identified in a payment order in which an account of the beneficiary is to be credited pursuant to the order....';* Section 4A-103(a)(3).

5. *Duke would also be the* **originator**, *as 'the sender of the first payment order in a funds transfer;'* Section 4A-104(c).

6. *Texas Trust, correspondingly, would be 'the* **originator's bank** *as 'the receiving bank to which the payment order of the originator is issued.'* Section 4A-104(d).

In some situations, the wire transfer may involve a bank or banks in addition to the originator's bank and beneficiary's bank. One situation in which this will occur is where the originating bank and the beneficiary's bank do not have a direct banking relationship. A Federal Reserve Bank which has accounts with both, may be used to facilitate the transaction. Such a bank or banks are classified as **intermediary banks** since they are *'a receiving bank other than the originator's bank or the beneficiary's bank'*. Section 4A-104(b).

The account designated by Duke as the source of payment for the payment order is classified as an 'authorized account';

> **Authorized account** *means a deposit account of a customer in a bank designated by the customer as a source of payment of payment orders issued by the customer to the bank….* Section 4A-105(a)(1).

The totality of the foregoing transactions among Duke's Enterprises, Texas Trust, Orange Grove Savings & Loan and yourself, is called a 'funds transfer'.

> **Funds transfer** *means the series of transactions, beginning with the originator's payment order, made for the purpose of making payment to the beneficiary of that order….'* Section 4A-104(a).

Rules governing time considerations for payment orders are governed by Section 4A-106:

> *The time of receipt of a payment order or communication canceling or amending a payment order is determined by the rules applicable to receipt of a notice stated in Section 1-202….*

Basic Fact Pattern Continued [5-7]

Step #5: Texas Trust reviews the payment order received in accordance with security measures in place regarding those payment orders;

Step #6: If everything is in order, Texas Trust issues a payment order to Orange Grove Bank for $850,000 to be deposited in Account: #203837636;

Step #7: Orange Grove Savings and Loan credits Account: #203837636.

Security Procedures by Texas Trust

This is an extremely important step in the process, because it is here that the bank makes its determination as to the validity of the payment order, and consequently whether or not to initiate the wire transfer.

The security measures will be worked out in advance between Texas Trust and Duke and may include special authorization for payment orders over a certain amount; for calling a certain party before issuing a payment order, or algorithms or various codes which insure the validity of the transactions. This type of validation process is called a *'security procedure':*

Security procedure means a procedure established by   agreement of a customer and a receiving bank for the purpose of

(i) *verifying that a payment order is that of the customer, or*

(ii) *detecting error in the transmission or the content of the payment order or communication.*

A security procedure may require the use of algorithms or other codes, identifying words or numbers, encryption, callback procedures, or similar security devices.... Section 4A-201(i)(ii).

Once the appropriate procedures have been followed Texas Trust will make a decision whether to accept or reject the payment order. If something is wrong in the established protocol, Texas Trust should reject the payment order. The manner of rejection is stated in Section 4A-210(a):

> *A payment order is rejected by a notice of rejection transmitted to the sender orally, electronically, or in writing. A notice of rejection need not use any particular form....*

If all procedures check out properly, thc payment order will be accepted, and Step #6 will be undertaken. Once there has been an acceptance of a payment order, the opportunity to reject is gone:

> *Acceptance of a payment order precludes a later rejection of the order. Rejection of a payment order precludes a later acceptance of the order.* Subsection 4A-210(d).

> Step #6: Texas Trust issues a payment order to Orange Grove Savings and Loan to be deposited in Account: #203837636;

If everything is in order, Texas Trust will initiate the wire transfer process by issuing the payment order as directed by Duke's Enterprises. If Texas Trust does not accept the payment order, it will be liable to Duke's Enterprise to the extent stated in its agreement with Duke's or as provided in Article 4A:

> *If a receiving bank fails to accept a payment order that it is obliged by express agreement to accept, the bank is liable for breach of the agreement to the extent provided in the*

agreement or in this Article, but does not otherwise have any duty to accept a payment order.... Section 4A-212.

Responsibilities for Accepted Payment Orders

1. Receiving Bank

Once Texas Trust decides to accept the payment order, certain obligations are imposed upon it. The essence of the undertaking is that Texas Trust, as a receiving bank is:

'obligated to issue, on the execution date, a payment order complying with the sender's order and to follow the sender's instructions...' Section 4A-302(a)(1).

Once Texas Trust issues the payment order as directed by Duke's Enterprises, Texas Trust will have '***accepted***' and '***executed***' the payment order:

*...[A] receiving bank other than the beneficiary's bank, **accepts** a payment order when it executes the order.* Section 4A-210(a).

*A payment order is **executed** by the receiving bank when it issues a payment order intended to carry out the payment order received by the bank.* Section 4A-301(a).

2. Sender's Responsibility

At the moment of acceptance of the payment order by Texas Trust, Duke's Enterprises, is required to make payment to Texas Trust in the amount of $850,000:

> ....*With respect to a payment order issued to a receiving bank other than the beneficiary's bank, acceptance of the order by the receiving bank obliges the sender to pay the amount of the sender's order.* Section 4A-402(c).

> Step #7: Orange Grove Savings and Loan accepts thc payment order by crediting Account: #203837636;

Acceptance of Payment Order by Beneficiary's Bank

The moment Orange Grove Bank credits your account and notifies you of your right to withdraw funds, it will have accepted that payment order:

> '...*[A] beneficiary's bank accepts a payment order at the earliest of the following times:*

> *(1) when the bank (i) pays the beneficiary as stated in Section 4A-405(a) or 4A-405(b); or (ii) notifies the beneficiary of receipt of the order or that the account of the beneficiary has been credited with respect to the order....;* Section 4A-209(b)(1)(i)(ii):

Upon acceptance of the payment order, Orange Grove Trust will be required to pay you:

> ....[I]f a beneficiary's bank accepts a payment order, the bank is obligated to pay the amount of the order to the beneficiary of the order. Section 4A-404(a).

Payment & Effect of Payment to Beneficiary

Orange Grove can satisfy the obligation to pay noted above as follows:

> If the beneficiary's bank credits an account of the beneficiary of a payment order, payment of the bank's obligation under Section 4A-404(a) occurs when and to the extent.
>
> (i)   the beneficiary is notified of the right to withdraw the credit,
> (ii) the bank lawfully applies the credit to a debt of the beneficiary, or
> (iii) funds with respect to the order are otherwise made available to the beneficiary. Section 4A-405(a)(i)ii)(iii).

Orange Grove Savings & Loan will also be deemed to have accepted the payment order if it is paid for the order by Texas Trust.

> ...[A] beneficiary's bank... accepts a payment order.... when the bank receives payment of the entire amount of the sender's order pursuant to Section 4A-403(a)(1) or 4A-403(a)(2). Section 4A-209(b)(2).

As noted in Section 4A-209, whichever contingency occurs first will be considered the time of payment.

If Texas Trust has not made payment to Orange Grove prior to Orange Grove's acceptance of the payment order, it will be required to do so once that acceptance has occurred:

> *With respect to a payment order issued to the beneficiary's bank, acceptance of the order by the bank obliges the sender to pay the bank, but payment is not due until the payment date of the order.* Section 4A-402(b).

Once Orange Grove Savings & Loan accepts the payment order, Duke will be deemed to have paid you for the orange grove:

> *Subject to Sections 4A-211(e), 4A-405(d), and 4A-405(e) the **originator of a funds transfer pays the beneficiary** of the originator's payment order at the time a payment order for the benefit of the beneficiary is accepted by the beneficiary's bank in the funds transfer and in an amount equal to the amount of the order accepted by the beneficiary's bank, but not more than the amount of the originator's order.* Section 4A-406(a). [Emphasis added.]

The effect of payment would be to discharge Duke under his contract of purchase with you:

> *If payment under subsection (a) is made to satisfy an obligation, the obligation is discharged to the same extent discharge would result from payment to the beneficiary of the same amount in money….* Section 4A-406(b).

If for some reason, Orange Grove fails to make timely payment to you after you have demanded the same, it could be liable for special damages under Article 4A:

> *If the bank refuses to pay after demand by the beneficiary and receipt of notice of particular circumstances that will give rise to* **consequential damages** *as a result of non payment, the beneficiary may recover damages resulting from the refusal to pay to the extent the bank had notice of the damages, unless the bank proves that it did not pay because of a reasonable doubt concerning the right of the beneficiary to payment. (Emphasis added).* Section 4A-404(a).

Part II: Potential Problems

Jeremy:

The foregoing scenario is an example of how things will proceed if there are no problems. We've both been around long enough to know that sometimes problems arise, and sometimes the consequences are serious. For the most part, the greatest areas of exposure fall on the sender of the wire transfer; however, as beneficiary, there are some things that can happen as well.

I am not going to attempt to detail all possible problems which can occur with a wire transfer, but I will explain some of the more important issues which can arise. If you have any questions about these, you can either call or email me and I will get right back with you.

Unauthorized Payment Order
1. *When Unauthorized Payment Order Effective*
2. *When Unauthorized Payment Order Not Effective*

1. When Unauthorized Payment Order Effective

The importance of the bank following properly established security procedures is dramatically illustrated by section 4A-202(b) which describes a situation in which an unauthorized payment order will be considered effective. Section 4A-202(b)(i)(ii) reads as follows:

> *If a bank and its customer have agreed that the authenticity of payment orders issued to the bank in the name of the customer as sender will be verified pursuant to a security procedure, a payment order received by the receiving bank is effective as the order of the customer,* **whether or not authorized, if**
>
> *(i) the security procedure is a commercially reasonable method of providing security against unauthorized payment orders;*[171]

---

[171] Section 4A-202(c) states that *'[c]ommercial reasonableness of a security procedure is a question of law....'* Therefore, this issue will be decided by the court.

In making its determination, the court is instructed by Section 4A-202(c) to consider the *'wishes of the customer as expressed to the bank, the circumstances of the customer known to the bank, including the size, type, and frequency of orders normally issued by the customer to the bank, alternative security procedures offered to the customer, and security procedures in general use by customers and receiving banks similarly situated.*

(ii) the bank proves that it accepted the payment order in good faith and in compliance with the security procedure and any written agreement or instruction of the customer restricting acceptance of payment orders issued in the name of the customer. [Emphasis added].

An example of an unauthorized payment order for which Duke would be liable might involve a scam whereby Bamford Jones made the payment order to an accomplice of his so that they could pocket the $250,000, rather than paying you, the intended beneficiary. If Texas Trust, the receiving bank, follows the commercially reasonable security procedures in place, and the bank accepted the payment order in good faith   and in compliance with the security procedures, and followed any instructions of the type noted in (ii) which may have existed, Duke's Enterprises will be responsible for the amount involved.

2. When Unauthorized Payment Order Not Effective

There is one major exception to the bank's right to payment under Section 4A-202(a), even when all criteria of that section have been met. That exception is contained in Section 4A-203(a)(2):

If an accepted payment order is not, under Section 4A-202(a), an authorized order of the customer identified as sender, but is effective as an order of the customer pursuant to Section 4A-202(b), the following rules apply:

....

> *(2) The receiving bank is not entitled to enforce or retain payment of the payment order **if** the customer proves that the order was **not caused**, directly or indirectly, by a person*
>> *(1) entrusted at any time with the duties to act for the customer with respect to payment orders or the security procedure, or*
>> *(2) who obtained access to transmitting facilities of the customer, or who obtained from a source controlled by the customer…information facilitating breach of the security procedure….* [Emphasis added].

As stated at the beginning of Section 4A-203(a)(2), for that section to be activated the payment order must be 'unauthorized'. Section 4A-202(a) states when a payment order is an authorized order:

> *A payment order received by the receiving bank is the **authorized order** of the person identified as sender if that person authorized the order or is otherwise bound by the order under the law of agency.*

Even though Bam had no authority to write a fraudulent payment order, as Treasurer of Duke's Enterprises with authority to issue payment orders generally, he certainly may be held to have had the apparent authority to execute the payment order, hence binding his principal, Duke. In that event, the payment order would be considered authorized and the exceptions of Section 4A-203(a)(2) would not apply.

If, on the other hand, the order was considered unauthorized, Section 4A-203(a)(2) would be activated.

Under subsection (2)(i), on the hypothetical posed, Duke's Enterprises would be liable since Bam was 'entrusted' to act for Duke in the execution of payment orders. The policy is very clear. As the entrusting party, Duke selected the individual involved and furthermore empowered him to undertake the transaction. In that case the loss should logically fall on Duke.

On the other hand, if a hacker was able to access the banks records and figure out how to transmit a payment order which passed through the security procedure established between Duke and the bank, Duke would not be liable per Section 4A-203(a)(2)(i)(ii).

1. Erroneous Payment Orders

Erroneous payment orders are governed by Section 4A-205. The three situations contemplated by Section 4A-205 are delineated in subsection (a)(1)(2)(3), as well as applicable rules to that situation:

> *If an accepted payment order was transmitted pursuant to a security procedure for the detection of error and the payment order (i) erroneously instructed payment to a beneficiary not intended by the sender,(ii) erroneously instructed payment in an amount greater than the amount intended by the sender, or (iii) was an erroneously transmitted duplicate of a payment order previously sent by the sender, the following rules apply:*

If the sender proves that the sender or a person acting on behalf of the sender pursuant to Section 4A-206 complied with the security procedure and that the error would have been detected if the receiving bank had also complied, the sender is not obligated to pay the order to the extent stated in paragraphs (2) and (3).

If the funds transfer is completed on the basis of an erroneous payment order described in clause (i) or (iii) of subsection (a), the sender is not obligated to pay the order and the receiving bank is entitled to recover from the beneficiary any amount paid to the beneficiary to the extent allowed by law governing mistake and restitution;

If the funds transfer is completed on the basis of a payment order described in clause (ii) of subsection (a), the sender is not obligated to pay the order to the extent the amount received by the beneficiary is greater than the amount intended by the sender.

If for example, Texas Trust directed payment to someone other than yourself, (a)(i) would apply; if it was directed to you in an amount greater than $850,000, subsection (a)(ii); and if a duplicate payment order was sent to you by Texas Trust, (a)(iii) would apply.

In the event Duke can prove that Duke's Enterprises complied with the security procedures in place, and that the error would have been detected if the bank had also complied, Duke would not be required to pay an erroneous payment order under

Section 4A-205(a)(i) or (iii). If the erroneous order was covered by Section 4A-205(a)(ii), Duke would not have to pay the amount in excess of $850,000.

Subsection (b) to 4A-205 places a duty of 'ordinary care' on the sender if that person is to avoid liability on the erroneous payment order. That section states as follows:

> *If the sender of an erroneous payment order described in subsection (a) is not obliged to pay all or part of the order, and the sender receives notification from the receiving bank that the order was accepted by the bank or that the sender's account was debited by the bank with respect to the order, the sender has a duty to exercise ordinary care, on the basis of information available to the sender, to discover the error with respect to the order and to advise the bank of the relevant facts within a reasonable time, not exceeding 90 days after the bank's notification is received by the sender....*

The final sentence to Section 4A-205(b) states the effect of the sender's failure to perform the foregoing duties:

> *If the bank proves that the sender failed to perform that duty, the sender is liable to the bank for the loss the bank proves it incurred as a result of the failure, but the liability of the sender may not exceed the amount of the sender's order.*

2. Misdescription of Beneficiary

Misdescription of a beneficiary is governed by Section 4A-207. Two situations are contemplated by that section: first, is where the beneficiary refers to a non existent or unidentifiable person or account; the second is where there is a conflict between the named beneficiary and a designated account number. The case of the nonexistent, or unidentifiable beneficiary is governed by Section 4A-207(a) which states as follows:

> *Subject to subsection (b), if, in a payment order received by the beneficiary's bank, the name, bank account number, or other identification of the beneficiary refers to a non existent or unidentifiable person or account,* ***no person has rights as a beneficiary of the order, and acceptance of the order cannot occur.*** [Emphasis added]

In such a situation, 'each sender in the funds transfer that has paid its payment order is entitled to get its money back.' [Comment 1 to Section 4A-207(a)].

The second situation, where there is a conflict between the person described in the payment order and an identifying or bank account number, is governed Sections 4A-207(b)(c). Under subsection(b)(1):

> *...if the beneficiary's bank does not know that the name and number refer to different persons, it may rely on the number as the proper identification of the beneficiary of the order.'*

The last sentence of Section 4A-207(b)(1) states:

The beneficiary's bank need not determine whether the name and number refer to the same person.

The rules regarding acceptance and payment of the payment orders described in subsection (b) are found in Section 4A-207(c)(1)(2):

If (i) a payment order described in subsection (b) is accepted, (ii)   the originator's payment order described the beneficiary inconsistently by name and number, and (iii) the beneficiary's bank pays the person identified by number as permitted by subsection (b)(1), the following rules apply:

(1) If the originator is a bank, the originator is obliged to pay its order;

*(2) If the originator is not a bank and proves that the person identified by number was not entitled to receive payment from the originator, the originator is not obliged to pay its order **unless** the originator's bank proves that the originator, before acceptance of the originator's order, had notice that payment of a payment order issued by the originator might be made by the beneficiary's bank on the basis of an identifying or bank account number even if it identifies a person different from the named beneficiary. Proof of notice may be made by any*

> *admissible evidence.* ***The originator's bank satisfies the burden of proof if it proves that the originator, before the payment order was accepted, signed a writing stating the information to which the notice relates.*** Section 4A-207(c)(1)(2). [Emphasis added.]

The rule of Section 4-207(c)(1) is very clear: the liability for erroneous payment for a payment order described in Section 4A-207(b) rests with the originator, if the orIginator is a bank.

Upon reading Section 4A-207(c)(2), which applies when the originator is not a bank, it appears initially as though the originator would not have to pay for the order; however, as the last sentence indicates, notice by the originator will be presumed if he or she signed a writing 'stating the information to which the notice relates'. Therefore, if a bank customer signs a writing showing notice [reason to know per Section 1-202(a)(3)] that there may be a payment to a beneficiary via account or bank number, the customer will be required to make payment within the circumstances described in the first paragraph of Section 4A-207.

3. Misdescription of Intermediary or Beneficiary Bank

The final contingency to be looked at is Misdescription of Intermediary Bank or Beneficiary's Bank, which is covered by Section 4A-208. There are two different situations contemplated by Section 4A-208.

Section 4A-208(a):

> *applies to a payment order identifying an intermediary bank or the beneficiary bank **only** by an identifying number*

In such a situation:

> *The receiving bank may rely on the number as the proper identification and need not determine whether the number identifies a bank.* Section 4A-208(a)(1).

Under Section 4A-208(a)(2):

> *The sender is obligated to compensate the receiving bank for any loss and expenses incurred as a result of its reliance on the number in executing or attempting to execute its order.*

The other situation, contemplated by Section 4A-208(b):

> *applies to a payment order identifying an intermediary bank or the beneficiary bank **both by name and an identifying number if the name and number identify different persons.*** [Emphasis added.]

If the payment order from Texas Trust identified Orange Grove by name and the identifying number was for a different bank, subsection (b) would apply.

Section 4A-208(b)(1) deals with the situation where the sender of the payment order is a bank:

If the sender is a bank, the receiving bank may rely on the number as the proper identification of the intermediary or beneficiary's bank, if the receiving bank, when it executes the sender's order, does not know that the name and number identify different persons....

Under Section 4A-208(b)(1), there is no duty to 'determine whether the name and number refer to the same person or whether the number refers to a bank....'

In such a situation:

The sender is obligated to compensate the receiving bank for any loss and expenses incurred by the receiving bank as a result of its reliance on the number in executing or attempting to execute the order. Section 4A-208(b)(1).

Section 4A-208(b)(2) deals with the situation where the sender is not a bank:

If the sender is not a bank and the receiving bank proves that the sender, before the payment order was accepted, had notice that the receiving bank might rely on the number as the proper identification of the intermediary or beneficiary's bank even if it identifies a person different from the bank identified by name, the rights and obligations of the sender and the receiving bank are governed by subsection (b)(1), as though the sender were a bank.

*Proof of notice may be made by any admissible evidence. **The receiving bank satisfies the burden of proof if it proves that the originator, before the payment order was accepted, signed a writing stating the information to which the notice relates.*** [Emphasis added].

FOOTNOTE 169

Fixtures & Accessions
1. Fixtures defined
2. Security Interests in Fixtures

Fixtures are defined under Article 9 as follows:

***Fixtures** means goods that have become so related to particular real property that an interest in them arises under real property law.* Section 9-102(a)(41).

Therefore, if the Raptor Entertainment Center was installed into the wall in Stephen's home in such a manner that an interest in the entertainment center would arise under Florida real estate law, it would become a 'fixture' in which a security interest could be created.

Statutory authority to create a security interest in fixtures is found under Section 9-334(a):

A security interest under this article may be created in goods that are fixtures or may become fixtures....

Some of the rules regarding security interests in fixtures are the same as with other types of collateral, and others are unique to fixtures. The following list covers the basics and will be reviewed in their listed order:

1. Enforceability
2. Perfection
3. "Fixture Filing"
4. Contents of Financing Statement.
5. Place of Filing

1. Enforceability

The basic rules regarding the enforceability of a security interest in fixtures contained in Sections 9-203(b)(1)(2)(3)(A)(B)(C)(D) apply.

2. Perfection

The basic rule requiring the filing of a financing statement to perfect the security interest also applies:

> *Except as otherwise provided in subsection (b) and Section 9-312(b), a financing statement must be filed to perfect all security interests and agricultural liens.* Section 9-310(a).

Fixtures are not within either exception noted, and therefore, a financing statement must be filed to perfect a security interest in fixtures.

3. "Fixture Filing"

A financing statement covering fixtures is called a 'fixture filing':

> **Fixture filing** *means the filing of a financing statement covering goods that are or are to become fixtures and satisfying Section 9-502(a)(b)... [contents of financing statement discussed immediately below].* Section 9-102(a)(40).

4. Contents of Financing Statement

Section 9-502(a), referred to in Section 9-102(a)(41) above, states basic requirements as to the sufficiency of *all* financing statements and reads as follows:

> *Subject to subsection (b), a financing statement is sufficient only if it:*
> *(1) Provides the name of the debtor;*
> *(2) Provides the name of the secured party or a representative of the secured party;*
> *(3) Indicates the collateral covered by the financing statement.*

When fixtures are involved, the financing statement must also contain the information required by Section 9-502(b):

> *... [T]o be sufficient, a financing statement ...* **which is filed as a fixture filing** *and covers goods that are or are to become fixtures, must satisfy subsection (a) and also:*
>
> *(1) indicate that it covers this type of collateral;*
> *(2) indicate that it is to be filed in the real property records;*
> *(3) provide a description of the real property to which the collateral is related; and*
> *(4) if the debtor does not have an interest of record in the real property, provide the name of the record owner.*
> Section 9-502(b)(1)(2)(3)(4). [Emphasis added.]

5. Place of Filing

Under Section 9-502(b)(2)(3), in order to perfect a security interest in fixtures, the financing statement must be filed in the office where a mortgage on real estate would be filed. This rule is contained in Section 9-501:

> *(a)...[T]he office in which to file a financing statement to perfect...[a] security interest or agricultural lien is:*
>
> *(1) the office designated for the filing or recording of a record of a mortgage on the related real property, if:*
>
> *....*
>
> *(B) the financing statement is filed as a fixture filing and the collateral is goods that are or are to become fixtures. Section 9-501(a)(1)(B).*

It should also be noted with regard to filing, that under Section 9-502(c) *'a record of mortgage is effective, from the date of recording, as a financing statement filed as a fixture filing...* if the mortgage has the contents contained in Section 9-502(c)(1)(2)(3)(4).

> ***Priority:*** As a general rule, *"...a security interest in fixtures is subordinate to a conflicting security interest of an encumbrancer or owner of the related real property other than the debtor."* Section 9-334(c).

Under this general rule, the person who holds the mortgage on the real estate would prevail over someone who held a security interest in fixtures. However, the general rule is subject to several major exceptions which are listed in Sections 9-334(d) through (h). Most relevant here are the exceptions contained in subsections (d) & (e).

The exception under subsection (d) deals with purchase money security interests:

> *Except as otherwise provided in subsection (h), a perfected security interest in fixtures has priority over a conflicting security interest of an encumbrancer or owner of the real property if the debtor has an interest of record or is in possession of the real property and;*
>
> *(1) the security interest is a purchase-money security interest;*
> *(2) the interest of the encumbrancer or owner arises before the goods become fixtures; and*
> *(3) the security interest is perfected by a fixture filing before the goods become fixtures or within twenty days thereafter.*

Stephen was in possession of his mortgaged home, so attention can be turned to subsections (1)(2)(3). Music Emporium, had a purchase-money security interest in the Raptor Entertainment Center, so subsection (1) is satisfied. That security interest clearly arose before the Raptor became a fixture. The remaining question whether the security interest is perfected by a fixture filing within the 20 day time limit.

The confusion arises with respect to the third requirement, for on its face it requires 'perfection by a fixture filing'. As a consumer good, purchased under a typical installment sales contract, Music Emporium would have a purchase-money security interest in consumer goods with automatic perfection under Section 9-309(1).

Therefore, on its face subsection (d) would not appear to apply, since the security interest is not *perfected* by a fixture filing. However, the policy of requiring the fixture filing would apply with equal force to the automatically perfected purchase-money security interests in consumer goods—i.e.—to put subsequent parties on notice that a security interest is claimed in certain goods which are fixtures. Without the fixture filing, even in the automatically perfected consumer goods, this would not be accomplished. This reasoning seems to be borne out in comment 7 which speaks of the purchase-money priority *'provided the security interest is filed as a fixture filing in the real property records'* within the twenty days. The comment does not use the term 'perfection'.

If the entertainment center were classified as equipment, which it would be if it were being installed for example, in the waiting room of Stephen's Boats, a financing statement would be required to perfect the security interest. As long as the financing statement was filed 'before the goods become fixtures or within twenty days thereafter', Music Emporium would have priority in the entertainment center over South Dade Bank who holds the mortgage on the land where Stephen's Boats is located.

Other priorities of security interests in fixtures over interests in real property are contained in Section 9-334(e). Of particular interest here is Section 9-334(e)(2):

> *A perfected security interest in fixtures has priority over a conflicting security interest of an encumbrancer or owner of the real property if:*
>
> *....*
>
> *(2) before the goods become fixtures, the security interest is perfected by any method permitted by this article and the fixtures are readily removable:*
>
> *(A) factory or office machines;*

> *(B) equipment that is not primarily used or leased for use in the operation of real property; or*
> *(C) replacements of domestic appliances that are consumer goods;*
> *....*

There are also special rules regarding fixtures when there is a construction mortgage. A *'construction mortgage'* is defined in the first sentence of Section 9-344(h):

> *A mortgage is a* **construction mortgage** *to the extent that is secures an obligation incurred for the construction of an improvement on land, including the acquisition cost of the land, if a recorded record of the mortgage so indicates.*

That section goes on to state:

> *Except as otherwise provided in subsections (e) and (f), a security interest in fixtures is subordinate to a construction mortgage if a record of the mortgage is recorded before the goods become fixtures and the goods become fixtures before the completion of the construction.*

6. Accession

Definition: "Accession" *means goods that are physically united with other goods in such a manner that the identity of the original goods is not lost.* Section 9-102(a)(1).

The plasma television set became an accession when Clyde and Jorge attached it to the entertainment center.

Enforceability: As with all types of collateral, the basic rules of Section 9-203(a) & Sections 9-203(b)(1)(2)(3)(A)(B)(C)(D) apply.

Therefore, if value has been given to the debtor by the secured party, and the debtor has rights in the collateral or is legally entitled to transfer rights to a secured party, the first two steps for enforceability have been met. The remaining requirement is satisfied if any of the conditions stated in Section 9-203(3) are satisfied. Subsection (A) would be satisfied since the conditional sales contract will also be an authenticated security agreement with a description of the collateral.

Perfection: Specific authority to create a security interest in an accession, is provided by Section 9-335(a) which states:

> *A security interest may be created in an accession and continues in collateral that becomes an accession.*

Section 9-335(b) goes on to state:

> *If a security interest is perfected when the collateral becomes an accession, the security interest remains perfected.*

In the case under consideration, the security interest in the plasma television would be automatically perfected as a purchase money security interest in consumer goods under Section 9-309(1). Therefore, it would be perfected at the time it became an accession.

> ***Priority:*** *Except as otherwise provided in subsection (d), the other provisions of this part determine the priority of a security interest in an accession.* Section 9-335(c).

The exception referred to [for certificate of title situations] does not apply here, and therefore 'other provisions' of part 3 determine priority. Section 9-324(a) governs this situation:

> ....*[A] perfected purchase-money security interest in goods... has priority over a conflicting security interest in the same goods....*

Therefore, Electronics World, the seller of the plasma television would take priority over Music Emporium's security interest in the entertainment center, which could be enforced by removing the plasma television set from the entertainment center.

> *After default, subject to Part 6, a secured party may remove an accession from other goods if the security interest in the accession has priority over the claims of every person having an interest in the whole.* Section 9-335(e).

If however, Electronics World damages the entertainment center in any way, it will be required to reimburse Music Emporium for the cost of repair:

> *A secured party that removes an accession from other goods under subsection (e) shall promptly reimburse any holder of a security interest or other lien on, or owner of, the whole or of the other goods, other than the debtor, for the cost of repair or any physical injury to the whole or the other goods.....* Section 9-335(f).

The result would be different if the plasma television had been mounted on the wall of the master bedroom of one of Stephen's boat purchasers, for this would place the transaction within the exception of Section 9-335(d) referred to in Section 9-335(c):

> *A security interest in an accession is subordinate to a security interest in the whole which is perfected by compliance with the requirements of a certificate-of-title statute under Section 9-311(b).* Section 9-335(d).

Depending on the classification of the goods involved, and the structure of the transaction, a financing statement may or may not need to be filed in order to perfect the security interest in the goods which are to become accessions. If the goods involved are equipment, e.g. machines used in connection with a business, a financing statement will need to be filed under the general rule of Section 9-310. If the goods are consumer goods, and the transaction is a purchase-money security interest, perfection will occur automatically under Section 9-309(1) except as provided in Section 9-311(b).

FOOTNOTE 159

Appendix II
LEASES: DEFAULT

Part 5 of Article 2A deals with default. It is broken down into three parts, and like the rest of Article 2A, it closely resembles Article 2. Part A is comprised of general default provisions which apply to both the lessor and the lessee; Part B provides remedies to the lessee where a lessor is in default; Part C provides remedies to the lessor when the lessee is in default. Some of these provisions have already been discussed.

Part A

IN GENERAL

The basic rule regarding default is stated in Section 2A-501(1):

> *Whether the lessor or the lessee is in default under a lease contract is determined by the lease agreement and this Article.*

Consistent with this rule is the basic remedial provision contained in Section 2A-501(2):

> *If the lessor or lessee is in default under the lease contract, the party seeking enforcement has rights and remedies as provided in this Article and, except as limited by this Article, as provided in the lease agreement.*

As noted in the discussion with Alan and OLR, rights and remedies may be modified per Section 2A-503(1). However:

> *Resort to a remedy provided under this Article or in the lease agreement is optional unless the remedy is expressly agreed to be exclusive. If circumstances cause an exclusive remedy to fail of its essential purpose, or provision for an exclusive remedy is unconscionable, remedy may be had as provided in this Article.* Section 2A-503(2).

The limitations on modification of rights for personal injury where consumer goods are involved were discussed in the conversation between Alan and OLR.

As also noted in the discussion between Alan and OLR, damages may be liquidated per Section 2A-504(1).

The liquidated damages must *"be reasonable in light of the then anticipated harm caused by the default or other act or omission"*.

In connection with all of these provisions, it is very important to note the rule of Section 2A-505(4):

> *Rights and remedies for material representation or fraud include all rights and remedies available under this Article for default.*

This is a critically important statutory provision, for it opens up the full litany of remedies to the non breaching party when fraud or misrepresentation is proven. The Article 2 counterpart is found is Section 2-721.

The rules regarding 'cancellation' and 'termination' of the lease contract are virtually identical to the Sales counterparts. Thus, Section 2A-505(1) states:

> *On cancellation of the lease contract, all obligations that are still executory on both sides are discharged, but any right based on prior default or performance survives, and the canceling party also retains any remedy for default of the whole lease contract or any unperformed balance.*

If for example, Babylon Medical Group cancelled the lease contract because the copy machines were defective, all obligations for future performance by either party would be discharged; however, Babylon would retain rights to bring an action for the default resulting from defective goods, and may sue for default of the whole lease contract or any unperformed balance.

Where a lease contract is terminated, the non breaching party has rights against the defaulting party for breach, but unlike cancellation, the remedies do not include default for breach of the whole contract:

> *On termination of the lease contract, all obligations that are still executory on both sides are discharged but any right based on prior default or performance survives.* Section 2A-505(2).

The Statute of Limitations for bringing an action under Article 2A is covered in Section 2A-506. Subsection (1) states as follows:

> *An action for default under a lease contract, including breach of warranty or indemnity must be commenced within 4 years after the cause*

*of action accrued. By the original lease
contract the parties may reduce the period of
limitation to not less than one year.*

PART B
DEFAULT BY LESSOR

The structure and content of the default provisions of Article 2A are very similar to the breach provisions of Article 2. Section 2A-508(1) states the general remedies available to a lessee in a manner similar to which Section 2-711 states the general remedies available to the buyer. Section 2A-508 states in full as follows:

If a lessor fails to deliver the goods in conformity to the lease contract, [Section 2A-509] or repudiates the lease contract, [Section 2A-402] or a lessee rightfully rejects the goods, [Section 2A-509] or justifiably revokes acceptance of the goods, [Section 2A-517]

> *and with respect to all the goods if under and installment lease contract the value of the lease contract is substantially impaired [Section 2A-510] the lessor is in default under the lease contract, and the lessee may:*
>
> > *(a) cancel the lease contract (Section 2A-505(1);*
> > *(b) recover so much of the rent and security as has been paid and is just under the circumstances;*
> > *(c) cover and recover damages as to all goods affected whether or not they have been identified to the lease contract (Sections 2A-518 and 2A-520) or recover damages for nondelivery (Sections 2A-519 and 2A-520);*

> *(d) exercise any other rights or pursue any other remedies provided in the lease contract.*
> *(2) If a lessor fails to deliver the goods in conformity to the lease contract or repudiates the lease contract, the lessee may also;*
> *(a) if the goods have been identified, recover them (Section 2A-522); or*
> *(b) in a proper case, obtain specific performance or replevy the goods (Section 2A-511).*
> *(3) If a lessor is otherwise in default under a lease contract, the lessee may exercise the rights and pursue the remedies provided in the lease contract, which may include a right to cancel the lease.*

An example will illustrate the application of Section 2A-508(1): Assume that Stephen's Boats decided to lease 10 plasma televisions, with 28" screens, from Plasma World to be mounted in each office of his showroom, and several in the main showroom, for continuous video promotions of his boats at $150 per month.

When the plasma televisions arrived, four of them had 21" screens.

Stephen's Boats would have certain options regarding how to proceed under the foregoing scenario. In addition to any general remedies applicable under 2A-508(1), Section 2A-509 would be activated.

> *Subject to the provisions of Sections 2A-510; on default on installment lease contracts, if the goods or the tender of delivery fail in any respect to conform to the lease contract, the lessee may reject or accept the goods or*

accept any commercial unit or units and reject the rest of the goods. Section 2A-509(1).

If Stephen chooses to reject some or all of the televisions, he would have certain statutory responsibilities. First, rejection must be within a reasonable time; second, Stephen would have to notify Plasma World within a reasonable time.

Rejection of goods must be within a reasonable time after their delivery or tender. It is ineffective unless the lessee seasonably notifies the lessor. Section 2A-509(2).

If the Stephen rejects the goods he shall:

(1)...after rejection of the goods in his [or her] possession or control, shall follow any reasonable instructions received from the lessor or supplier with respect to the goods....

Furthermore:

In the absence of those instructions, a merchant lessee shall make reasonable efforts to sell, lease, or otherwise dispose of the goods for the lessor's account if they threaten to decline in value speedily. Instructions are not reasonable if on demand indemnity for expenses ins not forthcoming. Section 2A-511(1)

In addition, Stephen would need to state any defect *'which is ascertainable by reasonable inspection'* or risk serious consequences:

> (1) *In rejecting goods, a lessee's failure to state in a particular defect that is ascertainable by reasonable inspection precludes the lessee from relying on the defect to justify rejection or to establish default:*
>
>> (a) *if, stated seasonably, the lessor or the supplier could have cured (Section 2A-513); or;*
>>
>> (b) *between merchants if the lessor or the supplier after rejection has made a request in writing for a full and final written statement of all defects on which the lessee proposes to rely.*
>
> (2) *A lessee's failure to reserve rights when paying rent or other consideration against documents precludes recovery of the payment for defects apparent in the documents.* Section 2A-514(1)(a)(b)(2).

As noted in Section 2A-514(1)(a) one of the reasons it is important to state what the particular defects are is that the lessor may have a right to **cure** under Section 2A-513. These have been discussed in the Online instruction.

The cure provisions of Article 2A and Article 2 are very similar. Policies and construction of the cure provisions between sales and leases are virtually identical. These provisions are discussed in detail by

Doug and Alan following Doug's Article 2 memorandum in Part 2, Section 1, and apply with full force here.

In addition to the remedies provided by Section 2A-508(1)(a)(b), Section 2-508(1)(c) provides that Stephen may: *cover and obtain damages under Section 2A-518.*

As with its Sales counterpart under Section 2-712, cover allows the lessee to procure substitute goods to replace the goods upon which the lessor defaulted:

> *After a default by a lessor under the lease contract of the type described in Section 2A-508(1), or, if agreed, after other default by the lessor, the lessee may* **cover** *by making any purchase or lease of or contract to purchase or lease goods in substitution for those due from the lessor.* Section 2A-518(1). [Emphasis added].

Under that provision, Stephen would be entitled to lease or purchase, or contract to lease or purchase other plasma televisions. Damages in such a situation are governed by Section 2A-518(2):

> *...[I]f a lessee's cover is by a lease agreement substantially similar to the original lease agreement and the new lease agreement is made in good faith and in a commercially reasonable manner, the lessee may recover from the lessor as damages*
>
> > *(i) the present value, as of the date of the commencement of the term of the new lease agreement, of the rent under the new lease agreement applicable to that period of the new lease term which is comparable to the then remaining term*

> *of the original lease agreement minus
> the present value as of the same date of
> the total rent for the then remaining
> lease term of the original lease
> agreement, and*
>
> *(ii) any incidental or consequential
> damages, less expenses saved in
> consequence of the lessor's default.*
>
> ...

Let's assume that Stephen rejected the four non conforming televisions. Further assume that one month after rejecting the four televisions Stephen covered by leasing four replacement plasma televisions from Equity Plasma at a rental price of $175 per month, and that the lease between Stephen and Equity was made in good faith and in a commercially reasonable manner as required by Section 2A-518(2). Under 2A-518(2) Stephen would recover for damages for each plasma television as follows:

The time period for which computations would be made under Section 2A-518(2)(i) would be 23 months [the then remaining term of the original lease.] The new rent of $175 is multiplied by that number to yield an amount of $4025. As Section 2A-518(2)(i) states, the 'present value' of that amount must be ascertained as part of the formula for determining damages:

> ***"Present value"*** *means the amount as of a
> date certain of one or more sums payable in
> the future, discounted to the date certain....*
> Section 2A-103(1)(u).

Once the present value of the new lease is determined from that time block, the present value of the same time frame is determined under the original lease. That would be the present value of $3450 [23 x $150].

The present value of $3450 would be subtracted from the present value of $4025 in computing the damages per Section 2-518(2)(i). In addition, any additional incidental damages, and where appropriate consequential damages. [highly unlikely on the facts given]. The amount of these damages would then be multiplied by four, the number of units in breach.

If the breach had been for nondelivery of the televisions, Stephen would have the option to recover damages for nondelivery Section 2A-519(1).

PART C
DEFAULT BY LESSEE

The layout of Part C of Article 2A, default by lessee, mirrors the Sales provisions for default by the buyer under Article 2. Thus Section 2A-523 and Section 2-703 begin with stating the general remedies of the lessor and seller:

> If the lessee wrongfully rejects or attempts to revoke acceptance of goods or fails to make a payment when due or repudiates with respect to a part or the whole, then, with respect to any goods involved, and with respect to all of the goods if under an installment lease contract the value of the whole lease is substantially impaired (Section 2A-510), the lessee is in default under the lease contract and the lessor may:
>> (a) cancel the lease contract (Section 2A-505(1));

(b) proceed respecting goods not identified to the lease contract (Section 2A-524) ;

(c) withhold delivery of the goods and take possession of goods previously delivered (Section 2A-525);

(d) stop delivery of the goods by any bailee (Section 2A-526);

(e) dispose of the goods and recover damages under (Section 2A-527) or retain the goods and recover damages (Section 2A-528); or in a proper case recover rent;

(f) exercise any other rights or pursue any other remedies provided in the lease contract

Section 2A-523(1)(a)(b)(c)(d)(e)(f)

Upon the occurrence of any of the foregoing contingencies, 'the lessor has the right to take possession of the goods. Section 2A-525(2). Furthermore Section 2A-525(2) provides that '[w]ithout removal, the lessor may render unusable any goods employed in trade or business, and may dispose of goods on the lessee's premises (Section 2A-527).

Action taken under Section 2A-525(2) without judicial process, must be done without breach of the peace:

The lessor may proceed under subsection (2) without judicial process if it can be done without breach of the peace or the lessor may proceed by action. Section 2A-525(3).

In addition to these specific remedial provisions, Section 2A-523(2) provides a "catch all" remedy:

If a lessor does not fully exercise a right or obtain a remedy to which the lessor is entitled

*under subsection (1), the lessor may recover
the loss resulting in the ordinary course of
events from the lessee's default as determined
in any reasonable manner, together with
incidental damages, less expenses saved in
consequence of the default.*

Section 2A-523(1)(a) allows the lessor to cancel the
lease upon the occurrence of any of the contingencies
stated.

Under Section 2A-524(1)(a)(b), upon default by the
lessee, the lessor may:

*(a) identify to the lease contract conforming
goods not already identified if at the time
the lessor learned of the default they
were in the lessor's or supplier's
possession or control; and*

*(b) dispose of goods (Section 2A-527(1))
that demonstrably have been intended
for the particular lease contract even
though those goods are unfinished.*

Like its Article 2 counterpart, Section 2A-524(2)
requires a lessor, or supplier to use reasonable
commercial judgment if a decision is made to complete
manufacture or otherwise dispose of the goods.

There may be situations where a lessor learns that a
lessee with whom he has contracted has become
insolvent. In that situation, Section 2A-525(1) gives the
lessor the right to refuse to deliver the goods. It must be
pointed out that a debtor can have assets and still be
insolvent under the UCC. Section 1-201(b)(23) defines
insolvent:

"Insolvent" *means:*

(A) *having generally ceased to pay debts in the ordinary course of business other than as a result of bona fide dispute;*
(B) *being unable to pay debts as they become due;*
(C) *being insolvent within the meaning of federal bankruptcy law.*

In addition to refusing delivery under Section 2A-525 upon discovery of the lessee's insolvency:

A lessor may stop delivery of goods in the possession of a carrier or other bailee.... Section 2A-526(1).

The lessor's right to dispose of goods upon default by the lessee is covered by Section 2A-527. Lessor can dispose of the goods per Section 2A-527(1) *'by lease, sale or otherwise'.* The damages available to the lessor mirror the damages available to the lessee where the lessor enters into a subsequent lease of the goods involved:

...[I]f the disposition is by lease agreement substantially similar to the original lease agreement and the new lease agreement is made in good faith and in a commercially reasonable manner, the lessor may recover from the lessee as damages
   i.   accrued and unpaid rent as of the date of the commencement of the term of the new lease agreement,
   ii. the present value, as of the same date, of the total rent for the then remaining lease term of the original lease

agreement minus the present value, as of the same date, of the rent under the new lease agreement applicable to that period of the new lease term which is comparable to the then remaining term of the original lease agreement, and

iii. *any incidental damages allowed under Section 2A-530, less expenses saved in consequence of the lessee's default.* Section 2A-527(2)(i)(ii)(iii).

The final default provision to be noted is Section 2A-528. It covers Lessor's Damages for Non-acceptance, Failure to pay, Repudiation and Other Default.

Footnote 168

BANKRUPTCY DISCUSSION

In a pure analytical sense all areas of law are relevant to the main subject matter of this book; some, of course, more relevant than others: Contract law, and the Convention on Contracts for the International Sale of Goods, for example, in connection with Article 2; or banking law, the Federal Reserve System, and usury in connection with Articles 3, 4, 5 & 9, Although discussions of these areas would enhance any book dealing with the Uniform Commercial Code, they are not essential to an adequate treatment of the subject. On the other hand, any Commercial Law book would be seriously deficient absent some discussion of certain Bankruptcy Act provisions and their interrelationship with various Article 9 provisions, for one of the major concerns of secured creditors is protection of their collateral in the event their debtor does go into bankruptcy. Indeed, unless a secured creditor is confident that his position is adequately protected in the debtor bankruptcy situation, he would be foolish to lend (absent of course, an economic adjustment to reflect the incurred risk).

Commencement of Case

Chapter 3 of the Bankruptcy Act, contained in Title 11 of the United States Code, deals with the commencement of a case in bankruptcy.   Cases may be either voluntary, in which the debtor files the petition; or they may be involuntarily filed against a debtor, as was the case with the clothing outlet. In the voluntary situation the mere filing of a petition constitutes an "order for relief." 11 U.S.C. Section 301.

After the order for relief is issued, an "interim trustee" is appointed. (The role of the trustee will be discussed shortly.) In either situation (voluntary or involuntary) a secured party will be automatically stayed from enforcing its security interest. Section 362(a). The secured party may, however, seek adequate protection of its interests under Section 361.

The Involuntary Petition

In the involuntarily filed petition, certain requirements must be met before a case can be validly filed, and hence before an order for relief can be granted. If there are 12 or more creditors, a valid petition requires three or more must be "*a holder of a claim against such person* [the debtor] *that is not contingent as to liability or amount...if such noncontingent, undisputed claims aggregate at least $12,300 more than the value of any lien on property of the debtor securing such claims held by the holders of such claims.* 11 U.S.C. Section 303(b)(1). If there are less than 12 creditors only one must file, but the $12,300 requirement remains the same. 11 U.S.C. Section 303(b)(2) .

Since the outlet case was involuntary in nature, the order for relief would not issue at the mere filing of the petition; rather the court will not order relief unless the petition is timely controverted (11 U.S.C. Section 303(h), or after trial in the circumstances set forth in 11 U.S.C.

Section 303(h) . As noted, after the order for relief is entered, the court will appoint one disinterested person to act as "interim trustee." 11 U.S.C. Section 701. However, *if necessary to preserve the property of the estate or prevent loss to the estate* the court may, upon the request of a party in interest and after proper notice and hearing, appoint an interim trustee prior to the order for relief. 11 U.S.C. Section 303(g). This can be done *'after notice to the debtor and a hearing. . . .'*

The Trustee

The trustee is the *representative of the estate and has the capacity to sue and be sued.* 11 U.S.C. Section 323.   Only certain persons or corporations may serve as trustee (11 U.S.C. Section 321), and such trustees must qualify (e.g., by filing the requisite bond under Section 322 prior to assuming their duties). The duties of the trustee are set forth in 11 U.S.C. Section 704. Primary among these duties is the obligation of the trustee to *'collect and reduce to money the property of the estate for which such trustee serves, and close the estate as expeditiously as is compatible with the best interests of parties in interest'.* 11 U.S.C. Section 704(a)(1). (The balance of section 704 is reproduced at the end of this discussion.)

The interim trustee will serve until a permanent trustee is selected by the procedures and per the requirements set forth in 11 U.S.C. Section 702(a)(b)(c). If no trustee is selected as provided in 11 U.S.C. Section 702, the interim trustee will serve as the trustee in the case. 11 U.S.C. Section 702(d).

As an officer on the court, the trustee will be entitled to *reasonable compensation for actual, necessary services rendered...*11 U.S.C. Section 330(a), subject to certain limitations stated in 11 U.S.C. Section 326. The trustee is given the power to employ professional persons (for example, attorneys or accountants) to *represent or assist* [him] *in carrying out* [his] *duties. .* 11 U.S.C. Section 327(a). Compensation for persons so employed may, with the court's approval, be on *a retainer, an hourly basis, or on a contingent fee basis.* 11 U.S.C. Section 726(a)(1), 507(a)(1)(C), 503(b). Hence, the point alluded to the outlet case: the more expensive the bankruptcy proceedings (i.e. the administrative expenses), the less money for creditors.

The Trustee and Property of the Estate

When the involuntary petition was filed against the clothing outlet, an "estate" was created. 11 U.S.C. Section 541(a). Section 541 discusses this in some detail. For present purposes, however, it may be briefly stated that the property of the estate is, with limited exception, comprised of *all legal or equitable interest of the debtor in property as of the commencement of the case.* 11 U.S.C. Section 541(a). In the outlet case it would include, for example, the outlet interest in the inventory, equipment and any accounts receivable.

One of the main goals of the trustee is to create as large an estate as possible in each situation, for the greater the estate, the larger amount available for creditors. One of the methods the trustee might use to enlarge the estate will be to attack the validity of various security interests in the debtor's property, and it is in this context that the interrelationship between the Bankruptcy Act and Article 9 is most appropriately viewed. If the trustee is successful in his attack, the would-be secured creditor will be an unsecured creditor, and hence will be forced to share his claim with the unsecured creditors, rather than being able to realize the value of his would-be secured collateral.

Preferences

Section 547 deals with preferences and provides the trustee with his main vehicle for attacking the various security interests of parties claiming secured status under Article 9. Section 547(b) sets forth the elements of a preference and confers upon the trustee the power to *avoid any transfer of property* within the circumstances set forth therein. Section 547(b) deals with transfers to non insiders and states in full as follows:

> *(b) Except as provided in subsection (c) and (i) of this section, the trustee may avoid any transfer of an interest of the debtor in property—*
>
>> *(1) to or for the benefit of a creditor;*
>> *(2) for or on account of antecedent debt owed by the debtor before such transfer was made;*
>> *(3) made while the debtor was insolvent;*
>> *(4) made—*
>>
>>> *(A) on or within 90 days before the date of the filing of the petition; or*
>>> *(B) between 90 days and one year before the date of the filing of the petition, if such creditor, at the time of such transfer was an insider; and*
>>
>> *(5) that enables such creditor to receive more than such creditor would receive if—*
>>
>>> *(A) the case were under chapter 7 of this title;*
>>> *(B) the transfer had not been made, and*

> (C) such creditor received payment of such debt to the extent provided by the provisions of this title.

In the non-insider situation the following must thus be present:

1. A transfer of an interest of a debtor in property;
2. To or for a creditor;
3. On account of an antecedent debt;
4. The debtor must be insolvent at the time of the transfer;
5. The transfer must be made on or within 90 days of the filing of the petition; [in the non insider situation]
6. The creditor must, because of the transfer, receive more than he would have in a liquidation case under Chapter 7 (and two other noted requirements of Section 547(b)(5).

Although the elements appear to be straightforward and easily understandable, further analysis, especially as to various definitions is necessary in order to understand the section. Two of these sections, dealing with the definition of 'transfer' and "antecedent debt" will be looked at prior to analyzing Section 547.

Transfer

"*Transfer*" is defined in 11 U.S.C. Section 101(54) as:

> (A) the creation of a lien;
> (B) the retention of title as a security interest;
> (C) the foreclosure of a debtor's equity of redemption;

> (D) each mode, direct or indirect, absolute or
> conditional, voluntary or involuntary, or
> disposing of or parting with
> (i) property; or
> (ii) an interest in property

When the outlet gave George Friedman a security interest in inventory, equipment and accounts, a lien was created within subsection (A) noted above:

> *The term lien means charge against or interest*
> *in property to secure payment of a debt or*
> *performance of an obligation.* 11 U.S.C.
> Section 101(37).

Antecedent Debt

Analytically, of course, any time there is a property transfer *after* the debt is created, the transfer of property being made for the debt, there is a transfer of property on account of antecedent debt. By reason of several Bankruptcy Act provisions, however, all such transfers are not treated as being on account of antecedent debt.

The first provision to be noted in this context is 11 U.S.C. Section 547(e)(2), which discusses when a transfer is made for purposes of Section 547.

Sections 547(e)(2)(A)(B) state as follows:

> *(2) For the purposes of this section, except as*
> *provided in paragraph (3) of this*
> *subsection, a transfer is made*
>
> *(A) at the time such transfer takes effect*
> *between the transferor and transferee, if*
> *such transfer is perfected at, or within*

30 days after such time except as provided in subsection (c)(3)(B);
(B) at the time such transfer is perfected, if such transfer is perfected after such 30 days.

Thus, when the Outlet created the security interest in favor of George, the transfer would be deemed to have taken place at that time if George had immediately perfected his interest or if he had perfected it within 30 days of such transfer.

If he waited beyond the thirty days to perfect, the time the transfer would take effect is the time of perfection [per 11 U.S.C. Section 547(e)(2)(B)]. For purposes of the Bankruptcy law, perfection occurs as follows:

A transfer of a fixture or property under other than real property is perfected when a creditor on a simple contract cannot acquire a judicial lien that is superior to the transferee. 11 U.S.C. 547(e)(1)(B).

The Bankruptcy Act will refer to state law to ascertain when that level has been reached. For this purpose, the primary place the court will look is Article 9 of whatever state is involved. A prior perfected security interest under Article 9 would not be subject to defeat by the lien described above, and such an interest would therefore be perfected for Section 547 purposes.

11 U.S.C. 547(c) contains six exceptions to the rule of Section 547(b)   The first of the three to be briefly discussed herein is (c)(1) which states in full as follows:

(c)The trustee may not avoid under this section a transfer

(1) To the extent that such transfer was

(A)   intended by the debtor and the creditor to or for whose benefit the transfer   was   made   to   be   a contemporaneous exchange for new value to the debtor; and

(B)   in   fact   a   substantially contemporaneous exchange.

Thus, if a creditor lent money to the outlet and took a perfected security interest in inventory, both parties intending *a substantially contemporaneous exchange, which, in fact, occurred,* the trustee may not avoid such transfer. This rule, of course, would serve to encourage lenders to put capital even into a weak debtor without fear of lending and taking its interest within 90 days of the petition, assuming that it could adequately secure the loan.

The second exception to the trustee's general avoidance powers of Section 547(b) to be noted is like the purchase money security interest of Section 9-103. It is contained in 11 U.S.C. 547(c)(3) and states that:

The trustee may not avoid under this section a transfer –that creates a security interest in property acquired by the debtor – to the extent that such security interest secures a new value that was- given at or after the signing of a security agreement that contains a description of such property as collateral; given by or on behalf of the secured party under such agreement; given to enable the debtor to acquire such property; and that is perfected on or before 20 days after the debtor receives possession of the property.

As with the exception noted in Section 547 (c)(1), this provision will allow for funds to be put into a weak debtor within the 90-day period with the creditor knowing that if adequate steps are taken he will be protected even if the filing for bankruptcy occurs within 90 days. A seller of equipment, for example, would be able to sell to a weak debtor on credit and under the circumstances of Section 547(c)(3), knowing that even if the debtor goes bankrupt within 90 days, his security interest will not be avoided as a preference. In some situations, credit willingness to step into a weak debtor situation under either (c)(3) or (c)(3) might be the difference between a bankruptcy or a turnaround. Absent the provisions protecting creditors in such situations, such transactions would rarely occur.

The final exception to be noted herein is Section 547(c)(5) . That section states in full as follows:

(c) The trustee may not avoid under this section a transfer-

(5) that creates a perfected security interest in inventory or a receivable or the proceeds of either, except to the extent that the aggregate of all such transfers to the transferee caused a reduction, as of the date of the filing of the petition and to the prejudice of other creditors holding unsecured claims, of any amount by which the debt secured by such security interest exceeded the value of all security interest for such debt on the latter of-

(A)

(i) with respect to a transfer of which subsection (b)(4)(A) of this section applies, 90 days before the date of the filing of the petition; or
(ii) with respect to a transfer to which subsection (b)(4)(B) of this subsection applies, one year before the date of the filing of the petition; and

(B) the date on which new value was first given under the security agreement creating such security interest.

Under the foregoing, George's or South Dade's interest in the noted collateral would be protected even as to inventory which came into the outlet during the 90-day period, except to the extent either *improved its position* during the 90-day period, and to the prejudice of the unsecured creditors within the circumstances noted in the text. If, for example, South Dade's position with respect to the noted collateral was 25% secured 90 days prior to the filing of the petition and 28% secured when the petition was filed, a preference would be created as to the 3% increase. The trustee could avoid this as preferential, and the 3% would become part of the estate.

Distribution

11 U.S.C. Section 726 sets forth detailed rules for distributing the property (liquidated) of the estate. For our purposes, the critical point is that a properly perfected security interest, that is not voidable, protects the property rights of the secured creditor in that collateral, and keeps such collateral from becoming part of the debtor's estate, which is distributed pro rata to the general creditors. This distribution will be after administrative expenses under Section 507(a)(2) , as

well as other expenses listed in Section 507. This rule of distribution is set forth in Section 726(a)(1).

After all of these expenses, there is usually very little remaining for general creditors; hence, the importance of timely perfection and maintaining that status is clearly seen.

Duties of the Trustee

704. Duties of trustee:

(a) The trustee shall-

(1) *collect and reduce to money the property of the estate for which such trustee serves, and close up such estate as expeditiously as is compatible with the best interests of parties in interest;*

(2) *be accountable for all property received;*

(3) *ensure that the debtor shall perform his intention as specified in section 521(2)(B) of*

(4) *investigate the financial affairs of the debtor;*

(5) *if a purpose would be served, examine proofs of claims and object to the allowance of any claim that is improper;*

(6) *if advisable, oppose the discharge of the debtor;*

(7) *unless the court orders otherwise, furnish such information concerning the estate and the estate's administration as is requested by a party in interest;*

(8) *if the business of the debtor is authorized to be operated, file with the court, with the United States trustee, and with any governmental unit charged with responsibility for collection or determination of any tax arising out of such operation,*

periodic reports and summaries of the operation of such business, including a statement of receipts and disbursements, and such other information as the court requires; and

(9) make a final report and file a final account of the administration of the estate with the court

(10) if with respect to the debtor there is a domestic support obligation, provide the applicable notice specified in subsection (c);

(11) if, at the time of the commencement of the case, the debtor (or any entity designated by the debtor) served as the administrator (as defined in section 3 of the Employee Retirement Income Security Act of 1974) of an employee benefit plan, continue to perform the obligations required of the administrator;

(12) Use all reasonable and best efforts to transfer patients from a health care business that is in the process of being closed to an appropriate health care business that-

(A) is in the vicinity of the health care business that is closing;

(B) provides the patient with services that are substantially similar to those provided by the health care business that is in the process of being closed; and

(C) maintains a reasonable quality of care.

One final point in this connection and in connection with secured status under Article 9 is that a security interest will remain perfected a maximum of five yeas under Section 9-515(a) unless a continuation statement is timely filed pursuant to Section 9-515(c). As that sections states, at the end of that period, absent the continuation statement, the security interest becomes unperfected.

> *The effectiveness of a filed financing statement lapses on the expiration of the period of its effectiveness unless before the lapse a continuation statement is filed pursuant to subsection (d). Upon lapse, a financing statement ceases to be effective and any security interest or agricultural lien that was perfected by the financing statement becomes unperfected, unless the security interest is otherwise perfected.* Section 9-515(a).

The result in such a situation is that a would-be secured creditor would, in fact, be unsecured, *even though* he may have been secured at one time. If, for example, George had sold the outlet on 12/5/99 and taken a valid security interest in inventory, etc., which was perfected, absent the noted continuation statement, the security interest would have lapsed 12/5/04 and George would have been unsecured in the outlet bankruptcy.

My own experience has revealed a general lack of awareness of the lapse provisions. The potential damage is enormous and it is imperative to create internal systems which flag security interests which are nearing the end of the five year [or shorter stated] time limit so appropriate action can be taken.

Outlet v. South Dade

As indicated, the trustee has the ability *to sue and be sued* under 11 U.S.C. Section 323. He could thus bring this suit even if Alan hadn't filed against the bank. Since, however, Alan had filed, the trustee would not need to independently bring the suit inasmuch as he would succeed to the debtor's interest in the suit under 11 U.S.C. Section 541. In the latter situation the trustee would be free to discontinue the lawsuit if he decided that it was not in the best interests of the estate to pursue it.

The outlet case was set up as it was to create a factual setting in which to discuss Section 3-404 which deals with Imposters & Fictitious Payees. The situation under discussion deals with a fictitious payee since the payees on the checks involved did not exist. Therefore, subsection (b) to 3-404 applies. That section reads as follows:

> (b) If (i) a person whose intent determines to whom an instrument is payable (Section 3-110(a) or (b)) does not intend the person identified as payee to have any interest in the instrument, or (ii) the person identified as payee of an instrument is a fictitious person, the following rules apply until the instrument is negotiated by special indorsement:
>
> (1) Any person in possession of the instrument is its holder.

(2) An indorsement by any person in the name of the payee stated in the instrument is effective as the indorsement of the payee in favor of a person who, in good faith, pays the instrument or takes it for value. Section 3-404(b)(i)(ii).

The present situation falls within 3-404(b)(ii) since 'the person identified as payee of [the] instrument is a fictitious person', i.e., the person does not exist. Therefore, Onus Primo was the 'holder' of the instrument, and his endorsement would be 'effective' under (b)(2). Furthermore, the Outlet would be bound by Onus' signature under Section 3-402. South Dade would prevail against the Outlet.

Section 3-404(a) deals with the 'Imposter' situation, and reaches a similar result to the one noted above. That section states as follows:

If an imposter, by use of the mails or otherwise, induces the issuer of an instrument to issue the instrument to the imposter, or to a person acting in concert with the imposter, by impersonating the payee of the instrument or a person authorized to act for the payee, an indorsement of the instrument by any person in the name of the payee is effective as the indorsement of the payee in favor of a person who, in good faith, pays the instrument or takes it for value.

Two things should be pointed out prior to leaving this case. First, under Section 3-404(b)(a), it states that an *indorsement by any person* will be effective under the circumstances noted in that section. Thus, if Onus had lost the checks prior to depositing them and they were found by a stranger who proceeded to cash them, the endorsement *(by any person)* would be effective. Second, is the rule of Section 3-404(d) which states that:

> *With respect to an instrument to which subsection (a) or (b) applies, if a person paying the instrument or taking it for value or for collection fails to exercise ordinary care in paying or taking the instrument and that failure substantially contributes to loss resulting from payment of the instrument, the person bearing the loss may recover form the person failing to exercise ordinary care to the extent the failure to exercise ordinary care contributed to the loss.*

Absent some defense however, the check would be considered 'effectively endorsed' and the account would be properly charged under Section 4-401.

FOOTNOTE 170

ROYAL BOATS, INC. V. STEPHEN'S BOATS, INC.
Case # 139284
Superior Court, for Dade County, Florida
Honorable Ripley Marquette, Presiding

Opinion of the Court

Plaintiff, Royal Boats, Inc., a corporation organized under the laws of the State of Georgia, brings this action against the defendant, Stephen's Boats, Inc., a Florida corporation, for alleged breach of a "Distributorship and Sales Agreement" entered into between these parties on October 17, 2007. A copy of said agreement is attached hereto and made a part hereof as an appendix to this opinion.

It is plaintiff's contention that under clause numbered five of the above-mentioned agreement, the defendant was prohibited from selling the boats of any manufacturer other than Royal without the express written consent of Royal; and that in contravention of said clause defendant, without the written consent of plaintiff, unlawfully engaged inn the sale of the boats of Crown Boats, Inc., beginning sometime prior to March 5, 2007. Plaintiff further states that repeated demands for the removal of the Crown boats were ignored by Stephen's Boats. Plaintiff has refused further shipments to defendant and seeks, *inter alia*, judicial recognition from this court of the validity of its cancellation of said contract.

Defendant does not dispute the validity of clause numbered five nor does it deny selling the boats of Crown, but states as an affirmative defense that the permission required by clause numbered five was in fact given. Defendant bases this contention on a letter written on February 8, 2007, wherein it requested permission to sell the boats of Crown. It is essentially defendant's contention that plaintiff's action amounted to a modification of the contract, or in the alternative, serves to estop the plaintiff from bringing this present action. Defendant has also counterclaimed for damages in excess of the jurisdictional amount due to the refusal of Royal to ship any other boats to it.[172]

Article 1: Mandate to the Courts

At the outset it should be pointed out that this Court is guided in construing the various applicable provisions of the Uniform Commercial Code in this case by certain provisions in Article 1 of the Code. Article 1 applies to each substantive article of the Code, and an application of Article 1 in each UCC case is essential:

This article applies to a transaction to the extent that it is governed by another article of the Uniform Commercial Code. Section 1-102.

The first mandate given to the courts by the legislature in the enactment of the Uniform Commercial Code, was designed to direct the courts in the interpretation and application of the Code. Thus, we are directed to 'liberally construe' the UCC. We are also given the reason to do so:

[The Uniform Commercial Code] must be liberally construed and applied to promote its underlying purposes and policies, which are:

---

[172] This "opinion" will not discuss relevant matters which have been treated elsewhere in the book, e.g., the meaning of terms such as "agreement" and "contract" noted in the middle of Doug's memorandum beginning on page 75. The reader is encouraged to review these in connection with the Court's discussion.

> *(1) to simply, clarify and modernize the law governing commercial transactions;*
> *(2) to permit the continued expansion of commercial practices through custom, usage and agreement of the parties;*
> *(3) to make uniform the law among various jurisdictions. Section 1-103(a)(1)(2)(3).*

With the mandate for liberal construction and application to promote the various policies noted above, the Court will proceed to analyze the present situation.

2. Choice of Law

Pursuant to clause number seven of the agreement, the parties hereto have contracted that the laws of the State of Georgia shall govern this agreement. This they were entitled to do by reason of Section 1-301 which states in pertinent part as follows:

> *Except as provided hereinafter in this section, when a transaction bears a reasonable relation to this state and also to another state or nation the parties may agree that the law either of this state or nation shall govern their rights and duties.*

Plaintiff is, as noted, a Georgia corporation. It manufactures the subject boats in Georgia and ships from Georgia. Clearly a reasonable relation to Georgia exists in the instant situation and the law of Georgia, including applicable case law, will apply. In this latter connection it must be pointed out that case law of other jurisdictions may also be considered pursuant to Section 1-103(a)(3) noted earlier. [173]

3. Was There a Modification of the Contract?

As noted, Defendant does not deny the existence of the original contract. Defendant does however, argue that the contract between itself and Crown Boats was modified by action or non action taken by Crown.

Defendant bases its argument to support its modification theory on three provisions of the Uniform Commercial Code. Defendant first calls the Court's attention to Section 2-209(1) and (3) which states that:

> *(1) An agreement modifying a contract within this Article needs no consideration to be binding.*

> *(3) The requirement of the statute of frauds section of this Article Section 2-201 must be satisfied if the contract as modified is within its provisions.*

Finally, the defendant directs the Court to Section 2-201(2), which states:

> *Between the merchants if within a reasonable time a writing in confirmation of the contract and sufficient against the sender is received and the party receiving it has reason to know its contents, it satisfies the requirements of*

---

[173] Case law from all jurisdictions is relevant to interpreting the Uniform Commercial Code in any state. The policy of promoting uniformity of law has been interpreted by many courts to include case law from other jurisdictions.

> *subsection (1) against such party unless written notice of objection to its contents is given within 10 days after it is received.*

The Court understands defendant's argument to be that the failure of the plaintiff to respond to defendant's February 8, 2007 request to sell Royal boats amounted to a modification within Section 2-201(2).

Defendant's argument must fail for several reasons. First, defendant neglected to mention clause numbered eight of the agreement which states:

> *This agreement embodies the full understanding of the parties hereto, and **may not be modified except in writing signed by both parties*** [emphasis the Court's].

This contractual provision must be read in connection with Section 2-209(2) which states in pertinent part:

> *A signed agreement which excludes modification or rescission except by a signed writing cannot be otherwise modified or rescinded, but except as between merchants such a requirement on a form supplied by the merchant must be separately signed by the other party.*

The eighth number clause, when read with Section 2-209(2) leads this Court to the inescapable conclusion that there could be no modification of the instant contract except in conformance with that provision. Clearly, plaintiff signed no such modification and this Court is of the opinion that the mere request by it to sell the Royal boats is not within Section 2-201(2). That section requires, *inter alia,* **a writing in confirmation** [emphasis the Court's].

In this Court's opinion the confirmation of Section 2-201(2) requires more than the letter sent to plaintiff by Stephen's Boats. For example, had the defendant testified to ongoing discussions with plaintiff relating to its proposed sale of Crown Boats, said discussions being favorable to defendant, followed thereafter by a *confirming* letter thereto, defendant's point might have some merit. In the circumstances and testimony before the Court, however, defendant's present modification argument must fail.

4. Is There an Estoppel?

Defendant offers as an alternative affirmative defense the theory that plaintiff is estopped to bring the cause of action based on a breach of paragraph numbered five since plaintiff failed to respond to its letter requesting permission. Plaintiff cites Section 1-103(b) to the Court's attention:

> *Unless displaced by the particular provisions of this Act, the principles of law and equity, including the law merchant and the law relating to capacity to contract, principal and agent, estoppel, fraud, misrepresentation, duress, coercion, mistake, bankruptcy, or other validating or invalidating cause shall supplement its provisions.*

This Court does not dispute the applicability of Section1-103(b) to the instant case. Indeed, as this very important section states, *all* law not displaced by the Code supplements its provisions.

The basic element of estoppel is a detrimental reliance based upon the actions of another. It is a fundamental principle of the doctrine that the duration of the behaviors involved must occur for a time span sufficiently long to justify a reasonable reliance thereon. The Court is of the opinion, however, that waiting three weeks to respond does not constitute conduct amounting to an estoppel.

Furthermore, the Court does not find such a three-week delay as amounting to a lack of good faith under Section 1-201(b)(20) or Section 2-103(1)(b). It must be remembered that defendant's letter of February 8, 2007, was a *request* for permission to sell boats of Crown, not a letter stating it was going to unless it heard from Royal or a letter in confirmation as noted above. Surely taking three weeks to act in such situation is not commercially unreasonable.

5. Is Plaintiff Liable for Failure to Ship Boats?

Defendant has taken the position that even if it breached provision number five of the Distributorship and Sales Agreement, it is nonetheless entitled to damages by reason of plaintiff's refusal to make further shipments under the contract. Defendant Counter Claimant further contends that pursuant to Section 2-715(2) it is entitled to lost profits suffered by reason of such refusal to ship.

Section 2-715 deals with a Buyer's Incidental and Consequential Damages. Consequential damages are defined under Section 2-715(2)(a) which states in full as follows:

(1) *Consequential damages resulting from the seller's breach include:*

(a) *any loss resulting from general or particular requirements and needs of which the seller at the time of contracting had*

*reason to know and which could not
reasonably be prevented by cover or
otherwise;*

. . .

In addition to lost profits, defendant seeks
attorney's fees under Section 1-305 which states that:

*(a) The remedies provided by [The Uniform
Commercial Code] shall be liberally
administered to the end that the aggrieved
party may be put in as good a position as if the
other party had fully performed but neither
consequential or special nor penal damages
may be had except as specifically provided in
[The Uniform Commercial Code] or by other
rule of law.*

The Court is of the opinion that Defendant Counter
Claimant's arguments must fail.

6. Cancellation of the Contract

Section 2-106(4) states that a contract is cancelled
when *either party puts an end to the contract for breach
or by other. .* The section goes on to note that the effect
of such cancellation is in part the same as a
"termination" under 2-106(3), in that *all obligations which
are still executory on both sides are discharged...*
Inasmuch as this Court finds that the defendant
breached the Distributorship and Sales Agreement and
that plaintiff effectively cancelled the contract by letter on
the date the complaint was served, the Court finds no
merit in Defendant Counter Claimant's action for
consequential damages.
As indicated the cancellation discharged executory
obligations by the plaintiff. Since we find that the plaintiff

was not in breach of contract, we find it unnecessary to discuss the claim for attorney's fees under Section 1-305.

Based on the foregoing analysis, we find the plaintiff was entitled to cancel the Distributorship and Sales Agreement and that Defendant Counter Claimant's actions must be dismissed.

An order will be entered accordingly.

Statutory Index

Article 1

Article 2

Article 2A

Article 3

Article 4

Article 4A

Article 5

Article 7

Article 9

Statutory Index
(Bankruptcy)

Statutory Supplement

Article 2

Section 2-305

(1) The parties if they so intend can conclude a contract for sale even though the price is not settled. In such a case the price is a reasonable price at the time for delivery if

(a) nothing is said as to price; or

(b) the price is left to be agreed by the parties and they fail to agree; or

(c) the price is to be fixed in terms of some agreed market or other standard as set or recorded by a third person or agency and is not so set or recorded.

(2) A price to be fixed by the seller or by the buyer means a price for him to fix in good faith.

(3) When a price left to be fixed otherwise than by agreement of the parties fails to be fixed through fault of one party the other may at his option treat the contract as cancelled or himself fix a reasonable price.

(4) Where, however, the parties intend not to be bound unless the price be fixed or agreed and it is not fixed or agreed there is no contract. In such a case the buyer must return any goods already received or if unable so to do must pay their reasonable value at the time of delivery and the seller must return any portion of the price paid on account.

Section 2-307

Unless otherwise agreed all goods called for by a contract for sale must be tendered in a single delivery and payment is due only on such tender but where the circumstances give either party the right to made or demand delivery in lots the price if it can be apportioned may be demanded for each lot.

Section 2-308

Unless otherwise agreed

(a) the place for delivery of goods is the seller's place of business or if the has none his residence; but

(b) in a contact for sale of identified goods which to knowledge of the parties at the time of contracting are in some other place, that place is the place for their delivery; and

(c) documents of title may be delivered through customary banking channels.

Section 2-309

(1) The time for shipment or delivery or any other action under a contract if not provided in this Article or agreed upon shall be a reasonable time.

(2) Where the contact provides for successive performances but is indefinite in duration it is valid for a reasonable time but unless otherwise agreed may be terminated at any time by either party.

(3) Termination of a contact by one party except on the happening of an agreed event requires that reasonable notification be received by the other party and an agreement dispensing with notification is invalid if its operation would be unconscionable.

Article 3

Section 3-104(a)(1)(2)(3)

(a) Except as provided in subsections (c) and (d), "negotiable instrument" means an unconditional promise or order to pay a fixed amount of money, with or without interest or other charges describe din the promise or order, if it:

(1) is payable to dearer or to order at the time it is issued or first comes into possession of a holder;

(2) is payable on demand or at a definite time; and

(3) does not state any other undertaking or instruction by the person promising or ordering payment to do any act in addition to the payment of money, but the promise or under may contain (1) an undertaking or power to give, maintain, or protect collateral to secure payment, (ii) an authorization or power to the holder to confess judgment or realize on or dispose of collateral, or (iii) a waiver of the benefit of any law intended for the advantage or protection of an obligor.

Section 3-303(a)(1)(2)(3)(4)(5)(b)

(a) An instrument is issued or transferred for value if:

(1) the instrument is issued or transferred for a promise of performance, to the extend the promise has been performed;

(2) the transferee acquires a security interest or other lien in the instrument other than a lien obtained by judicial proceeding;

(3) the instrument is issued or transferred as payment of, or as security for, an antecedent claim against any person, whether or not the claim is due;

(4) the instrument is issued or transferred in exchange for a negotiable instrument; or

(5) The instrument is issued or transferred in exchange of the incurring of an irrevocable obligation to a third party by the person taking the instrument.

(b) "Consideration" means any consideration sufficient to support a simple contact. The drawer or maker of an instrument has a defense if the instrument is issued without consideration. If an instrument is issued for a promise of performance, the issuer has a defense to the extend performance of the promise is due and the promise has not been performed. If an instrument is issued for value as stated in subsection (a), the instrument is also issued for consideration.

Section 3-304(a)(1)(2)(3)(b)(1)(2)(3)(c)

(a) An instrument payable on demand becomes overdue at the earliest of the following times:

(1) on the day after the day demand for payment is duly made.

(2) if the instrument is a check, 90 days after its date; or

(3) if the instrument is not a check, when the instrument has been outstanding for a period of time after its dated which is unreasonably long under the circumstances of the particular case in light of the nature of the instrument and usage of the trade.

(b) With respect to an instrument payable at a definite time the following rules apply:

(1) If the principal is payable in installments and a due date has not been accelerated, the instrument becomes overdue upon default under the instrument for nonpayment of an installment, and the instrument remains overdue until the default is cured.

(2) If the principal is not payable in installments and the due date has not been accelerated, the instrument becomes overdue on the day after the due date.

(3) If a due date with respect to principal has been accelerated, the instrument becomes overdue on the day after the accelerated due date.

(c) Unless the due date of principal has been accelerated, an instrument does not become overdue if there is default in payment of interest but no default in payment of principal.

Section 3-305(a)(1)(2)(3)

(a) Except as stated in subsection (b), the right to enforce the obligation of a party to pay an instrument is subject to the following:

(1) a defense of the obligator based on (i) infancy of the obligor to the extent it is a defense to a simple contract, (ii) duress, lack of legal capacity, or illegality of the transaction which, under other law, nullifies, the obligation of the obligor, (iii) fraud that induced the obligor to sign the instrument with neither knowledge nor reasonable opportunity to learn of its character or its essential terms, or (iv) discharge of the obligor in insolvency proceedings;

(2) a defense of the obligor stated in another section of this Article or a defense of the obligator that would be available if the person entitled to enforce the instrument were enforcing a right to payment under a simple contract; and

(3) a claim in recoupment of the obligator against the original payee of the instrument if the claim arose from the transaction that gave rise to the instrument; but the claim of the obligor may be asserted against a transferee of the instrument only to reduce the amount owing on the instrument at the time the action is brought.

Section 3-305(b)

(b) The right of a holder in due course to enforce the obligation of a party to pay the instrument is subject to defenses of the obligor stated in subsection (a)(1), but is not subject to defenses of the obligor stated in subsection (a)(2) or claims in recoupment stated in subsection (a)(3) against a person other than the holder.

Section 3-306

A person taking an instrument, other than a person having rights of a holder in due course, is subject to a claim of a property or possessory right in the instrument or its proceeds, including a claim to rescind a negotiation and to recover the instrument or its proceeds. A person having rights of a holder in due course takes free of the claim to the instrument.

Section 3-417(a)(1)(2)(3)

(a) If an unaccepted draft is presented to the drawee for payment or acceptance and the drawee pays or accepts the draft, (i) the person obtaining payment or acceptance, at the time of the presentment, and (ii) a previous transferor of the draft, at the time of transfer, warrant to the drawee making payment or accepting the draft in good faith that:

(1) the warrantor is, or was, at the time the warrantor transferred the draft, a person entitled to enforce the draft or authorized to obtain payment or acceptance of the draft on behalf of a person entitled to enforce the draft;

(2) the draft has not been altered; and

(3) the warrantor has no knowledge that the signature of the drawer of the draft is unauthorized.

Article 9

Section 9-521

A filing office that accepts written records may not refuse to accept a written initial financing statement in the following form and format except for a reason set forth in Section 9-516(b).

Financing Statement Form

UCC FINANCING STATEMENT
FOLLOW INSTRUCTIONS (front and back) CAREFULLY

A. NAME & PHONE OF CONTACT AT FILER [optional]

B. SEND ACKNOWLEDGMENT TO: (Name and Address)

THE ABOVE SPACE IS FOR FILING OFFICE USE ONLY

1. DEBTOR'S EXACT FULL LEGAL NAME - insert only one debtor name (1a or 1b) - do not abbreviate or combine names

1a. ORGANIZATION'S NAME			
OR 1b. INDIVIDUAL'S LAST NAME	FIRST NAME	MIDDLE NAME	SUFFIX
1c. MAILING ADDRESS	CITY	STATE	POSTAL CODE	COUNTRY

1d. Check only if applicable and check only one	Debtor is a Trust	Debtor is a Trustee acting with respect to property held in trust	Debtor is a Decedent's Estate

2. ADDITIONAL DEBTOR'S EXACT FULL LEGAL NAME - insert only one debtor name (2a or 2b) - do not abbreviate or combine names

2a. ORGANIZATION'S NAME			
OR 2b. INDIVIDUAL'S LAST NAME	FIRST NAME	MIDDLE NAME	SUFFIX
2c. MAILING ADDRESS	CITY	STATE	POSTAL CODE	COUNTRY

2d. Check only if applicable and check only one	Debtor is a Trust	Debtor is a Trustee acting with respect to property held in trust	Debtor is a Decedent's Estate

3. SECURED PARTY'S NAME (or NAME of TOTAL ASSIGNEE of ASSIGNOR S/P) - insert only one secured party name (3a or 3b)

3a. ORGANIZATION'S NAME			
OR 3b. INDIVIDUAL'S LAST NAME	FIRST NAME	MIDDLE NAME	SUFFIX
3c. MAILING ADDRESS	CITY	STATE	POSTAL CODE	COUNTRY

4. This FINANCING STATEMENT covers the following collateral.

5. Check only if applicable and check only one box.		
A Debtor is a TRANSMITTING UTILITY	Filed in connection with a Public-Finance Transaction	Filed in connection with a Non-UCC Filing
Filed in connection with a Manufactured-Home Transaction	Filed in connection with an Agricultural Lien	

6. ALTERNATIVE DESIGNATION [if applicable]:	LESSEE/LESSOR	CONSIGNEE/CONSIGNOR	BAILEE/BAILOR	SELLER/BUYER

7. OPTIONAL FILER REFERENCE DATA

International Association of Commercial Administrators (IACA)
UCC FINANCING STATEMENT (FORM UCC1) (REV. DRAFT 02/28/09)

Section 9-627 (a)(b)1(2)(3)(c)(1)(2)(3)(4)(d)

(a) [Dispositions that are commercially reasonable]. A disposition of collateral is made in a commercially reasonable manner if the disposition is made:

(1) in the usual manner on any recognized market;

(2) at the price current in any recognized market at the time of the disposition; or

(3) otherwise in conformity with reasonable commercial practices among dealers in that type of property that was the subject of the deposition.

(c) [Approved by the court or on behalf of creditors.] A collection, enforcement, disposition, or acceptance is commercially reasonable if it has been approved:

(1) in a judicial proceeding;

(2) by a bona fide creditors' committee;

(3) by a representative of creditors; or

(4) by an assignee for the benefit of creditors.

(d) [Approval under subsection (c) not necessary: absence of approval has no effect.] Approval under subsection (c) need not be obtained, and lack of approval does not mean that that the collection enforcement, disposition, or acceptance is not commercially reasonable.

Subject Matter Index

Article 1

Article 2

Article 2A

Article 3

Article 4A

Article 5

Article 7

Article 9

Bankruptcy Index

CPSIA information can be obtained
at www.ICGtesting.com
Printed in the USA
BVHW010021171022
649326BV00005B/1

9 780615 308357